AT THE BALLET

To The Ballet · *1934*
by IRVING DEAKIN
Ballet Profile · *1935*

AT
THE
BALLET
A Guide to Enjoyment

IRVING DEAKIN

THOMAS NELSON & SONS
Toronto
New York
Edinburgh

All rights reserved under International and
Pan-American conventions.
Published in New York by Thomas Nelson & Sons and simultaneously
in Toronto, Canada, by Thomas Nelson & Sons (Canada) Limited
Copyright 1956 by Irving Deakin
Library of Congress Catalog Card Number: 56-8531
Printed in the United States of America
DESIGNED BY LEO MANSO

To dear friends,

rare and wonderful

human beings

Contents

AT THE BALLET

Ballet Has Arrived!

It was late in 1933 that ballet as an art and entertainment floated into the consciousness of the North American people after a long absence.

Early in 1935, there appeared in the United States and almost simultaneously in Great Britain the first of what was destined to be a long line of books dealing with ballet, although the palpitating author of that first slim volume did not suspect it at the time. The book was called *To the Ballet*. It had a foreword by John van Druten in which the playwright told in his deft prose of his introduction and conversion to ballet. The book itself was, like so many of its successors, a passionate plea to those who knew not ballet to go to it and find it out for themselves.

The deluge of books on various aspects of ballet that has followed may be said to have been initiated by the author of the present volume, since his *To the Ballet* was, so far as North America is concerned, the pioneer work in what was the beginning of our ballet renaissance.

Nearly all of these early books stressed, and rightly so, the enjoyment of ballet. Unfortunately, some of them stressed and still continue to stress the purely visual enjoyment. Many of these books were born of necessity and from a deep conviction that if ballet were to grow in popularity, even to exist and persist, only the most ecstatic enthusiasm would be of help.

Two decades ago there was no audience for ballet. There was, for all general purposes, one ballet company of any standing, an international aggregation, the best of its kind then extant. It was the Monte Carlo Ballet Russe, with Leonide Massine, whose tireless personality and genius made the continuation of ballet possible, as its moving spirit, and W. de Basil, a keen business man with a talent for organization, as its general director.

Today ballet thrives, with large audiences supporting sometimes as many as four simultaneously touring companies in North America, at least three of them permanent American and Canadian organizations. The number of permanent ballet institutions in Great Britain is in excess of those on the Western side of the Atlantic.

As audiences have grown in size, however, there is not much indication that their progress in appreciation, understanding, or discrimination has kept pace with their numbers. There has been, to be sure, some improvement in the quality and standards of professional criticism; but there still exists a rather depressing lack of such standards on the part of the average audience.

Ballet, it should be constantly borne in mind, is a theatrical art. A profound and intimate understanding is not necessary to the enjoyment of it; but some knowledge of it helps. Of all forms of the arts of the theater it is, perhaps, the most difficult to "understand"; yet audiences, bursting into applause at something that seems to them a marvellous acrobatic feat (which is often merely a basic technical procedure) would seem to give the lie to the preceding statement.

In this little volume I shall try to provide something in the way of a practical guide to the layman, as objectively as possible and, obviously, in general terms.

Basically, ballet is, as a theater art, grounded in traditions, hedged about with precedents. This book is not the place for a detailed discussion of them, as such a discussion would not necessarily add to the layman's pleasures. The important thing is to induce a person to see ballet once, whatever his prejudices against it may be. Not long ago, a chance meeting in a café with an engineer led to a pleasant and interesting discussion of nearly everything under the sun, ranging from the price of eggs to the latest atom development. It was at the end of the evening when the engineer made some oblique query as to what was my "line." On learning that my "line" was in some vague manner connected with ballet, he vouchsafed neither he nor his wife had ever been to a ballet performance; that he was sure she wouldn't like it; equally certain he couldn't bear it. I chided him a bit on his preconceived prejudices, italicizing the obvious by suggesting that his scientific mind should be an open one seeking for proof, and wound up by offering him seats at a forthcoming ballet performance, and took my leave. The letter I received from him shortly afterwards told the story: "This is to express a million thanks from both my wife and myself for the tickets to the Ballet. With complete frankness, and to my surprise, it was really most enjoyable and pleasant, and I certainly don't want to miss the next one."

There are those who feel ballet and opera have much in common. They have been to opera and they do not care for it. Therefore, they are certain they would not like ballet. It is true ballet and opera have elements in common. Both embrace music, painting, drama. Theoretically, opera would seem to be as fortunate a blend of the ingredients as ballet. Practically, it does not often work out that way. Voice, which may be heavenly, is all too frequently found in a physique lacking beauty and grace, with a temperament devoid of dramatic ability. A robustly healthy Mimi whom we are asked to believe is at the point of dissolution from aggravated tuberculosis; a lumbering Venus; a roly-poly Madame Butterfly, all serve only to excite mirth and inspire ridicule unless one steadfastly regards the coiffure of the lady at one's side or closes one's eyes. Opera, unlike ballet, is an art more keenly enjoyed through radio transmission or fine recordings than it is in the opera house or theater. There are times when the music is really of poor quality, when the operatic conventions of singing something that would be infinitely less silly if spoken, help destroy illusion.

Many people find it absurd that people should sing everything that they have to say. People do not sing in ordinary life, except in the bathroom. Opera plots are, for the most part, fatuous. Opera singers seldom act; and if they are not ridiculously corpulent (which they are more often than not) they seldom look in the least like the sort of people they are pretending to be. One cannot help feeling that one of the chief motives that leads people to pretend that they enjoy opera is pure snobbery.

Here the layman joins hands with others: with the frequenter of concerts, with the serious musician, with the playgoer, with the man of letters; for the one the opera spoils the play, for the other it ruins the music. But more than anything else, it is avoirdupois that too often is opera's downfall.

What is it, then, that makes ballet superior to opera both as entertainment and as an art form? Why is ballet, to very many people, the most satisfying form of the theater?

For many years, it was one of my duties to review all forms of theatrical manifestations in Europe, Great Britain, and the United States professionally; which is to say I earned my living by doing so. There was scarcely an evening of the week when I was not in a theater, opera house, or concert hall. Today I almost literally have to be dragged to any theatrical performance, be it drama or opera. It is not the case with ballet. Of all theatrical manifestations, I find ballet more satisfying more often than I do any of the others.

With ballet, while there are inferior companies with substandard productions and lighting, my intelligence is never assaulted by routinized stock characterizations nor by dull, stupid, and unnatural dialogue masquerading as conversation.

I should not like to give the impression that everything in all ballet companies and performances is perfect; that in ballet God's always in his Heaven and all's right. That would be palpably ridiculous. Dancers are, despite assertions to the contrary, human. They are subject to human limitations and frailties. Roles may be more difficult than their normal abilities. They have their "off" days, as who does not? However gifted a choreographer, even genius nods, and each recurring work cannot be expected to be an undying masterpiece.

I have mentioned inferior companies. Without mentioning names, which would be invidious in this context, it is impossible here at the outset to overstress the importance of production in ballet, though it is not strictly one of its primary elements. Nevertheless, production is vitally important. It is true that the ballet-goer who simply wants to observe dancing, as he watches the dancers, listens to the music, may be willing to shut his eyes to a ludicrous and incompetent setting, to tasteless costumes, and still be able to enjoy himself. But if ballet appeals only to those interested exclusively in a dancer's technical prowess and the use thereof, it is doomed to failure, for there are not enough of them to keep it going.

The layman, whether directly conscious of it or not, is immediately impressed by a beautiful production and costumes, by lighting that is subtle and satisfying. This may be taken for granted. Only the ballet fanatic extracts much pleasure from a work done in "practice clothes" danced before a drab and colorless curtain or cyclorama. There are ballet companies still content with the inferior in settings and costumes. They badly want a large public. But as the public is more and more exposed not only to the best in ballet production, but to modern theater craft in the domain of the spoken drama, which has made such strides in good taste and ingenuity, it is simply ludicrous to expect that public to look without protest upon some of the atrocities of setting, costuming, lighting, and general decrepitude that characterize the productions of some of the inferior companies.

One is sorry for struggling companies, naturally; but ballet as an art is of far greater importance, and it will never find the support it requires and grow to be loved by the people at large as long as it cannot be relied on for being at least adequately presented in every department.

So, for the layman, it is well to reiterate that it must be emphasized that ballet is an amalgam of various factors springing from seemingly unrelated forms such as composition—both musical and choreographic—painting, sculpture, architecture, acting, and dancing, all embraced within a cocoon called production. There has always been a tendency to concentrate attention on individual dancers, to focus interest on particular and what may be called spectacular dancers, for want of a better term. This follows the pattern of the theater and films, where the "star" is made the focal point. While it would be stupid to relegate Personality and Personalities to the limbo of the unnecessary, it is equally crass to concentrate attention exclusively on them so that one is unable to see the woods because of the tree. The dancer, it should be borne in mind, is but one of the elements in what must be the total fusion of parts, albeit an important one.

This book, therefore, will not be concerned with an assessment of personalities that are to be found in ballet today. There is available for those interested a welter of historical and biographical material (both fact and fiction), together with sentimental reminiscences accentuating the personal in the comprehensive literature of ballet.

Perhaps the best way to attempt to give the layman a key or set of keys to an understanding of ballet sufficient to satisfy some of his queries and thus to increase his enjoyment of ballet both as an art and as an entertainment, will be briefly to consider each of the elements that go to make up ballet, looking at them aesthetically, historically, and, at the same time, pointing out how they may be observed and enjoyed in practice, which is to say, in performance. This latter, by calling attention to some of the ballets that may be found in the repertoires of various ballet companies currently before the public.

The potential ballet-goer, having been told what he has a right to expect at performances in the way of basic elements, and before going into an analysis of those elements, may now without offence be reminded of a few things that can be reasonably expected of him.

One of the most primitive and at the same time offensive bad habits is that of arriving late, a transgression equalled only by that of leaving before the end. It must be admitted that both are complicated by a tragic possibility of misunderstanding. It may well be that a late-comer, who tries desperately to present a brazen front before all the glowerings that assail him on all sides, is actually consumed with shame at making a disturbance and vexed at not being able to explain to everybody how his car was held up in traffic and still further delayed by a policeman who may know all about traffic problems but has no regard whatever for ballet. Those who leave early, too, may possibly have found that the performance is taking longer than they expected and that the last train on which they depend will be missed if the fall of the final curtain is not.

With such cases one may sympathize theoretically; but the fact remains that in practice late coming and early going are among the foremost things to make one hate not only ballet but mankind and all its blundering ways. Quite plainly, it is the duty of all who attend a theatrical or musical function, a duty to art, to other people, and not least to themselves, to be punctual. It is quite possible to make doubly sure about cars, trains, dinner and the other nuisances of civilization in planning an evening at the ballet. Those who do not must be prepared to be looked upon, possibly unjustly, as among the barbarians who do not scruple to disturb a whole audience by turning up late and those who start that exasperating avalanche of early leavers—for there are always plenty of sheeplike people ready to follow the bad example—merely because they cannot be bothered to get into a bit of a crush at the end of the performance.

Another trespass that is much too frequently committed at ballet performances is that of creating a disturbance in the middle of a work by misplaced outbursts of enthusiasm or at least benevolence. It is true that this sort of annoyance used to be more rife that it is nowadays. But there is still far too much of this un-called-for applause at the wrong time.

If the ballet is composed of a string of variations, one after another, there is really no harm in a little demonstration of pleasure in the middle, provided it is sincere and well conducted. But where the music continues and is in itself continuous, any interruption before the end is a lapse of taste, and it is always well to remember that a ballet is not finished when the curtain begins to descend, but only when the music has stopped. You may find to your embarrassment—embarrassment, that is, if you have been clapping too rashly—that though the curtain may have dropped, the music does not stop at all, but leads on to the next scene. Therefore, if you do not wish to look like the abject hero of a *faux pas* in a *New Yorker* cartoon, you will be well advised never to applaud at a ballet until you are quite sure the proper moment has arrived.

I shall have more to say about audience behavior at the ballet later on. Now a choice must be made, in a fairly arbitrary fashion, as to the order in which the elements of ballet shall be treated. Therein lies a problem: that problem is which came first, the chicken or the egg? So interwoven are the elements in the fusion that is ballet that the choice is difficult.

2

On Music and Conductors

An inquiring reporter once queried Dame Ninette de Valois, the indefatigable founder, director, and moving spirit of the Sadler's Wells Ballet, on which of the elements that make up ballet she felt was of primary importance. Unhesitatingly she replied, "Why, music, of course."

The admiration in which I hold this distinguished practitioner of the balletic art is such that I shall let her make the decision for me. No relationship can be more important than that of music to ballet or, if one prefers, that of ballet to music.

The base on which ballet must rest is a musical one. It is music that provides the springboard from which ballet leaps.

Generally speaking, there are three different methods of utilizing music in relation to ballet. First of all, the creation of ballets to music already existing, either familiar or obscure. Secondly, creating a ballet to a specially commissioned score. Thirdly, and the most rare, creating music for a ballet that has already been choreographed, which is to say, arranged.

The first method is most often followed in general practice. It is, perhaps, the easiest. It is certainly the least expensive, since

11

the majority of the musical works so used are in the public domain and thus are not subject to the payment of royalties to the composers. It often has the advantage of a certain amount of popular appeal when the music is familiar. Ballets of enduring popularity have come from this method, and some that may be regarded as masterpieces, and which either remain as standard works in various repertories or are frequently revived.

Since ballet is of the theater, and the theater deals with themes, ballet requires a theme to interpret, if not always a story to tell or a plot to unravel. Movement exclusively is not enough, and if pursued too far can degenerate into mere "dumb-show," something that ballet definitely is not. By the use of existing music, the theme is provided. Music stimulates the imagination of the choreographer, inspires the dancers.

And now that the term "choreographer" has come into this text, a word more and more commonly used in the past couple of decades, let me define it so that no one shall shy away from it as something pretentious or impossibly "long hair." It is a perfectly good English word, springing from the Greek *khoreia,* meaning dancing, and, possibly, *khoros,* meaning a dancing company, together with *graph:* to write, or design. Hence choreographer, a designer of ballet.

There are, to be sure, objections to the first method I have mentioned, and the most vocal come from musicians and musical persons. For example, the composer has one conception of the music, often the choreographer has another. Another objection is that dancers, generally speaking, are insensitive to music; that much of the balletic adaptation of existing music is tastelessly done; that, in too many cases, music written for the piano is orchestrated for ballet and that its essential characteristics are changed. In short, that musical masterpieces are butchered and distorted to make a balletic holiday. The defense takes the position that, in using existing music, it has not been used literally, but applied to a theatrical performance.

The specially commissioned score has numerous advantages. It presupposes collaboration between composer and choreographer,

ideal if the two collaborators are able either to see eye to eye or
to compromise any differences. Some of ballet's most enduring
works are the result of this method. As examples, I shall list a
handful of the most successful and most popular: *Le Lac des
Cygnes* (*Swan Lake*) and *The Sleeping Beauty,* commissioned
from Tchaikowsky by the historically famous Franco-Russian
choreographer, Marius Petipa; *Coppélia,* composed by Léo Delibes
for the Paris Opera; *Petrouchka* and *The Fire Bird,* composed by
Igor Stravinsky for Michel Fokine, a name to be remembered
and honored in ballet; *The Three-Cornered Hat,* by Manuel de
Falla for Leonide Massine. Some more recent examples include
The Rake's Progress, by Gavin Gordon for Ninette de Valois;
Miracle in the Gorbals, by Arthur Bliss for Robert Helpmann,
in the repertoire of the Sadler's Wells Ballet; Paul Hindemith's
Saint Francis, for Leonide Massine, a work unfortunately no
longer extant; *Cakewalk,* for Ruthanna Boris, actually a commissioned work from the American Hershy Kay, who wrought a
homogeneous orchestral work from melodies by Louis Moreau
Gottschalk, in the repertoire of the New York City Ballet. Morton
Gould's *Fall River Legend,* for Agnes de Mille, commissioned by
the Ballet Theatre, is another American example of the commissioned score for ballet. All such works, to be successful, must
be the result of close collaboration between composer and
choreographer.

The third method I have mentioned presumes the dancer is
merely the moving part of a design. This would seem to be a
false presumption. The idea would seem to be to provide an
egocentric choreographer with an opportunity to design a series
of abstract patterns and then let someone improvise some sort
of music. A school of thought negating the importance of music
in ballet, clinging to a theory that all ballet should be entirely
abstract. Surely this would be, to say the least, theatrically ineffective, and it cannot be too often emphasized that ballet is a
theatrical art. A work created along these lines and seen in
America a few seasons ago in the repertoire of the Ballet Theatre
was *A Young Man and Death* (*Le Jeune Homme et La Mort*)

choreographed by Jean Babillée. The work was choreographed to
assorted jazz pieces. It was produced to the accompaniment, of
all things, of Johann Sebastian Bach's tremendous *Passacaglia.*
   Music does not "accompany" ballet. It is not "background"
music, to use a motion-picture, radio, television term. Music is
a fundamental and vastly important part of the whole fabric.
The third method would also seem to spring from a misleading
argument that primitive dancing was without music. Drums,
chants of some sort, inevitably go hand in hand with primitive
dancing. Primitive peoples do not dance in silence.
   Ballet, like music, is not a science but an art; in ballet an
instant of true appreciation and perception is worth an age of
learning and lore. Those moments are likely to come through
some extrasensory emotional impact, and music will invariably
play an important part in their arrival.
   Since rhythm is so essential to ballet, it is music's rhythm that
propels it. Rhythm comes naturally, since all creation moves to
it—the stars, the seasons, all growth; man's heart throbs rhythmi-
cally, his feet march to a lilt. It is the oldest impulse of all.
Ceremonial dancing was and is a great outlet for savage emotions—particularly that of fear. Elaborate drumming exists—
from what distant times we cannot tell—in both savage and cultivated peoples. In India, for example, two rhythms will be
drummed together, with more subtle effects even than those Igor
Stravinsky sought in his ballet, *The Rite of Spring* (*Le Sacre
du Printemps*), a commissioned work by the great founder of
modern ballet, Serge Diaghileff, that serves as a perpetual re-
minder of the ritual significance of dancing, now, unfortunately,
rarely presented. This latter subject is a big one in itself, but
outside our present scope.
   For deeper acquaintance with some of the music of the ballet
the best preparation is, beyond doubt, some kind of hearing at
home. Mechanical and electronic reproduction has made that
not only possible but often perfectly easy. There are always the
phonograph and the radio. Today's high fidelity reproducers and
records can be hardly said to have any defects. They may be

productive of abuses; but the reproduction of the best discs on the best instruments may be said to have come as near living performances as one may desire. The performances on discs will, in nearly every case, be superior to most of those given by travelling ballet orchestras. A list of ballet recordings will be found in the appendix.

In a few cities radio programs concerned exclusively with ballet and its music are to be found with considerable regularity. Both these and phonograph records can be of immense assistance in helping to an understanding of ballet if they are listened to attentively.

I have pointed out that the commissioned score is the best form of all. The composer thus commissioned and, to an extent, subsidized is, of course, faced with several problems, among the chief of which is that standard forms of musical composition seldom can be utilized. This because the dramatic content and the mood are frequently determined by the choreographer, to say nothing of the problems presented by the physical limitations of the dancers. Dancers must keep together; consequently, while the rhythms may be complex, each one of them, at the same time, must be definite.

In well-conducted and well-directed ballet companies the music direction is, as it should be, in the hands of the musical director, who has complete authority over all musical matters. Music specially composed for ballet is not necessarily music that stands up well by itself in the concert hall, since it has been composed primarily for a special purpose. Yet this is by no means always true; take, for example, the concert hall popularity of such works as Stravinsky's *The Firebird* and *Petrouchka*; Tchaikowsky's *Swan Lake* and *The Sleeping Beauty*. The vitally important thing about specially composed ballet music is the impression it makes upon the audience at the time the ballet is being performed. The music heightens the emotional impact of the danced work, and the final test of such music must be the scope with which it helps rather than impedes the mood, atmosphere and imagery. Ideally, the end result should give the paradoxical feeling that one is hearing the dancing and seeing the music.

From the layman's point of view, taste must inevitably play an important part. To hear everything with an open mind, to accept nothing too gushingly and dismiss nothing hastily, is to lay the foundation of true enjoyment and understanding.

By training a wide sympathy, by forming no prejudices, taste will be made comprehensive. For the ballet-goer, like the music-listener, must beware of acquiring too individual an outlook. To become so fastidious as to be able to tolerate only half a dozen choreographers or composers or the products of only one period or one country is to become a bore to others and in the end a nuisance to oneself. On the other hand, a taste that has no individuality at all, and no spice of personality, is too dull and commonplace for words. Only, if you do possess idiosyncrasies of outlook, beware of always indulging your peculiar taste, lest it should grow into mere affectation. It must always remain possible to look and listen with interest even at and to distasteful things. It should be quite impossible to find any work intolerable to watch and listen to the first time, however much one may wince at repeating the experience.

This brings us to an accomplishment even the most amateurish of ballet lovers must acquire if his love is to bring him reward. It is of the most vital importance to be able to hear and see a number of things going on simultaneously. When I say "going on," I mean it literally. There are those in ballet and at the ballet who are concerned only with the visual aspect of the art; the dancer and the dancing; perhaps the costumes, possibly the scenery and the lighting. But they must also pay attention to the music and listen to it to be able to get the most pleasure out of ballet.

As soon as the necessity of attending the ballet with all one's faculties—ears as well as eyes, to say nothing of mind—becomes plain, then ballet will constantly gain in plasticity and life; attendance at the ballet will become more and more of an adventurous delight.

The conductor of the orchestra at a ballet performance, if he be a good one, is an extremely important part of the whole. It is true that, on occasion, the conductor is himself the star performer, which can be extremely annoying. One of ballet's most spectacular occasional conductors is Sir Thomas Beecham, and without the genius of that supreme master of the orchestra, he could be a source of constant irritation. In his association with the Diaghileff Ballet, for which he accepted no fee, he inaugurated the highly admirable custom of having one of the interludes between the separate ballets going to make up the program a purely orchestral one, giving young composers first hearings of their works or else very old and rarely played compositions. Beecham will perform no music he feels to be uncongenial; he conducts conspicuously and with some mannerisms that seem superfluous; he sometimes exaggerates a tempo either on the slow or the fast side; occasionally he over-points music that should be kept quite simple; in short, he has his little perversities which indeed can become fascinating, because after all one knows from the intoxicating beauty of his musical phrasing and shaping that he is passionately in love with ballet as an art, precisely as he is in love with music.

Sir Thomas is the individualist *par excellence*. I have heard orchestral players say that he "mesmerizes" them into excellence. He has something of that effect on the audience too. Who among music and ballet lovers has not waited for his stately walk to the center of the orchestra, noting the cool, almost arrogant, imperturbability of it, and then the elegant, deliberately leisured bow, first to the audience, then to the orchestra?

Before long, the orchestra boils and magic spells are weaving. Sir Thomas cannot be discussed in terms of conventional technique. He makes his own. It reminds me of the fencer's, that sudden lunge of the baton, which has almost a physical effect even though you are behind it in the auditorium. Then that flashing flick of his wrist is to conducting what the flick of his tongue is to public speech.

In a work to which he is devoted the fire of his temperament has a fascinating effect, but the controlling brain is ice-cool. Note how from the Olympian detachment of the moment before the music begins, he catapults himself into the center of the battle. On one or two occasions I have sat with the orchestra facing Beecham. His face, when he is in action, is hypnotically expressive and compelling. All of him seems to be living the music: the tense crouch, the hissing for a *pianissimo,* the urgent sweep of the right arm, the almost balletic miming in a dainty, dance-like movement, and finally the two-fisted assault on the orchestra when the climax is about to be reached. Here is heterodoxy at white heat.

There is nothing new that can be said about this extraordinary man, for we have long known and enjoyed his art, but each fresh appearance he makes still has the quality of a shattering début. His memory, of course, is fantastic, and it is seldom that he has a score. Orchestral players unfamiliar with his methods no doubt find him difficult to follow. Bernard Shore, violist and author, in his book, *The Orchestra Speaks,* says that "he breaks every orthodox rule. No one else in the world could get away with it as he does."

His rehearsals are usually quiet and invariably productive of a few good laughs. His wit always sparkles, and the stories that cluster about his name and fame are legion. Most conductors cannot be imagined in any other role. Beecham, with his brilliance, his wit, his oratorical gifts, would have been an outstanding figure and "character" in several other spheres of human activity.

However, to watch the conductor at ballet performances is dangerous, unless one has trained oneself very carefully to be sure of listening to the music intently at the same time; and, of course, if one watches the conductor, one runs the risk of missing the visual aspects of ballet. But these remarks can be applied even more directly to a symphony concert, and it is not a natural thing to do or an easy thing to achieve. It is perfectly possible, unfortunately, to take the interpretation from the sight of a conductor who has the gift of gesture, instead of from the sound of the music. I remember a performance of Tchaikowsky's Fifth Symphony (once used as the musical base for Leonide Mas-

sine's first "symphonic" ballet, *Les Présages*) many years ago
during which I wished the conductor, no less a figure than the
late Serge Koussevitzky, had been placed behind a screen, for
I felt certain that a stone-deaf man could have seen from his
extremely telling antics exactly what the work was all about. But
as stone-deaf people do not as a rule frequent ballet or concerts,
the danger of Koussevitsky's method (which I found became
much modified later in his career, while the musical effect was
as telling as ever) was greater than its advantages. The music
was splendidly done; the only trouble was that it was not at all
necessary to listen to it, and I am certain that many people in the
audience were so captivated by the conductor's extremely fine
histrionic and choreographic display that they really did not
listen.

What is infinitely worse, of course, is to be engrossed by the
sight of a conductor who merely attitudinizes, without obtaining
any convincing musical effect at all. This happens quite frequently, for orchestral performers, who are very shrewd people,
invariably play badly, as badly as possible as a matter of fact,
for a mountebank. They would rather turn out a pleasant performance off their own bows, so to speak, for a respectable
dullard who merely beats time for them, and perhaps even cannot do that properly. In which case again the audience might
judge badly by merely looking at the conductor, and so it might,
once more, where the permanent conductor in charge of a rigor-
ously governed orchestra—a man like the late Wilhelm Furtwängler, let us say—obtained with a minimum of outward show
a variety of sensational effects that had been carefully drilled into
the players beforehand. It is thus a good rule for ballet-goers and
concert-goers to beware of watching the conductor unless they
are quite sure they can listen intently at the same time.

This musical side of ballet reveals its importance also in the
making of programs. In the ideal ballet company the programs
should be arranged by the artistic director or chief choreographer
in close consultation with the musical director or chief conductor.
They are, individually and jointly, faced with many difficulties in

program-making, about which something may perhaps be said here in a general way, though I may have something further to say on the subject when we consider choreography. Here we shall consider program-making largely from the musical point of view.

How is the ballet-goer, unless he is familiar with all the works, to know a good program from a bad one beforehand, from the mere look of it? Unless, of course, it is an evening of full-length ballet, a work in four or more acts, such as *The Sleeping Beauty,* the complete *Swan Lake,* or one like Prokofieff's *Cinderella.* But most ballet programs are composed of three or four works, one of them, too often, a short *pas de deux* to exhibit the technical virtuosity of a pair of dancers. Broadly speaking, the ballet-goer is likely to find something familiar in one respect or another: a title of which he has heard, music with which he is reasonably familiar, and will make up his mind without difficulty whether it contains something which is, in his opinion, worth seeing and hearing. But it is quite possible to make up an unsatisfactory program scheme with nothing but fine works. A choreographer cannot simply throw together a number of works that happen to be congenial to him. There must be contrast but not confusion. A certain harmony must be arrived at: musical as well as choreographic harmony. Styles should not be mixed too much, except possibly for certain purposes which may have to do with periods, or in cases of programs having some chronological idea. Again a program, like a single ballet, should have a climax, or a series of graded climaxes, the placing of which ought to be very carefully considered. The most significant contribution may be gradually worked up to towards the end of the program, or better still, since people so often discover they have a train to catch or a supper to eat before the end of the performance, in the middle of the program. In the latter case it is well to observe the rule that the descent towards the close should be less steep than the ascent has been at the beginning. To end a ballet program with a purely flashy work seems to me the height of folly, for that is simply asking the most cultivated section of the public to depart early and only the indiscriminately omnivorous to remain to clean up the leavings of the feast, and rapturously to demand more when they know no more is coming.

A good ballet orchestra is composed of the best symphonic players available. In London and in Europe the players have a guaranteed employment, usually on an annual basis, and are a completely homogeneous body. In the United States, where there is little or no possibility of guaranteed annual employment, the players are usually selected by audition from the finest instrumentalists available at the time required for their engagement. Yet there are ballet orchestras in America that number among them, year in and year out, the same first-class first-chair players and many of the same supporting personnel. The closest to the Anglo-European ideal of a permanent orchestra in America, so far as ballet is concerned, is, perhaps, that of the New York City Ballet, the only American ballet company with anything resembling a permanent home.

To those ballet-goers who pay scant attention to the orchestra, it should be pointed out, by a repetition of the statement at the beginning of this chapter, that music is the basis of all ballet. To put it another way, it is the orchestra that is, in a sense, the stage itself, for it quite literally puts a floor under the dancers.

Presiding over the ballet orchestra is the conductor who has an added task not within the responsibility or province of the purely symphonic conductor. In addition to conducting the score, to interpreting it and revealing the composer's true intent, there is the constant necessity of keeping an eye on what is happening on the stage. Dancers being human and not automata, their performances vary, due to any number of reasons. Tempi vary from performance to performance, from both psychological and physiological causes. One night the soloist may be faster, another slower. A faulty floor or a mere miscalculation may cause a dancer to slip and lose a beat or two. Something may occur off-stage to cause an entrance of a dancer or a group of dancers to be late by a second or a fraction thereof. In such cases, the conductor's problems are intensified. Instant reaction is required to restore harmony between sight and sound. The conductor, on the alert, flicks his baton for a split-second warning, and the orchestra players, equally alert, it is to be hoped, respond to these sudden, unexpected and completely unpredictable signals.

The list of distinguished and famous conductors who have come to that distinction and fame through ballet is long. Let us confine ourselves to comparatively recent times. First the Diaghileff conductors: Ernest Ansermet, one of the foremost interpreters of contemporary music, permanent conductor of the orchestra he founded, L' Orchestre de la Suisse Romande, whose records are a household word among those who treasure fine recorded music; Pierre Monteux, for years director of the San Francisco Symphony Orchestra, one time of the Boston Symphony Orchestra, and the dean of conductors in the United States. At various times, Sir Malcolm Sargent and Eugene Goossens, two of Britain's most prominent orchestral leaders; Roger Désormière, an outstanding Parisian musical director. Sir Thomas Beecham, heretofore mentioned, has also conducted contemporary ballet in the United States.

In even more recent music in ballet, one name stands out over all. The late Constant Lambert, the remarkable English composer-author-critic-conductor, who was singlehandedly responsible for the high musical standards of the Sadler's Wells Ballet, and a tower of strength to music of the ballet in our time. Lambert, essentially a composer, gave up much on account of his preoccupation with ballet, and contributed to musical criticism of a high order.

In the United States, ballet has produced two outstanding conductorial figures: Antal Dorati, brilliant musical director of the Minneapolis Symphony Orchestra, whose recordings of music for the ballet are among the most remarkable available, and Efrem Kurtz, one-time conductor of the Kansas City and Houston Symphony orchestras. Other American ballet conductors include Franz Allers, Robert Zeller, and Leon Barzin.

Legends about conductors are many, for their authoritative, supreme position, though fully understood by musicians and the musically-minded, is apt to be misinterpreted by a larger and less discerning world. Let us, for a moment, consider the conductor's role. For the sake of argument it can be assumed that Beethoven is a household word: a world-figure, like Napoleon or Shakespeare, Julius Caesar or even (for the nonce) Sugar Ray Robinson—that lately deposed champion of fisticuffs. But whereas there may be millions of the uninitiated who know the pseudo-title, if not the music, of Beethoven's "Moonlight" Sonata, there are relatively but few acquainted with his symphonies and still fewer able to appreciate any sustained argument concerning the merits or demerits of a conductor's *interpretation* of those symphonies.

For the word "interpretation," as applied to the conductor of an orchestra, conveys to many a meaning so ambiguous as to be almost unintelligible. They find it difficult to appreciate the finer points of an art that, like ballet, in its technique is intimately bound up with some kind of mysterious silence, while, on the contrary, the contributions of the players themselves is one of rich and glowing sounds. And so, to them, the conductor is little more than a "time-beater"; his baton but a modern development of that roll of parchment which did rough and ready service in those days of long ago when orchestral music was practically unknown.

Yet without the silent gestures, the wave of the arm or the quick exchange of glances between conductor and instrumentalist, the art of interpretation would be in a sorry plight. The actual time-beating is nothing more than elementary technique, acquired by instinct or study, incorporated in due course as an integral part of the conductor's equipment, and then reproduced by him quite automatically. And until he has mastered the technique of the baton (a not too happy phrase, I feel) as a directing agency he will never be able to interpret music with any skill or feeling, for every technical shortcoming is noticed at once by the instrumentalists supposedly under his control: a feeling of uncertainty will prevail and thereby prevent anything in the nature of style or the reproduction of the inner spirit of the music.

The conductor, therefore, like the dancer, learns his technique only to forget it—a truism that applies here as much as it does to all human endeavor. His sole object is to concentrate on the artistic side of the performance and to re-create in living sounds what the composer has put inspiredly on paper.

Now it can be stated in Malvolio-like language that some are born conductors, some achieve conducting and others have conductorship thrust upon them. No branch of the art of music is so open to misconception and abuse; charlatanism and insufficiency of knowledge are more in evidence here than anywhere else. Many, indeed, are the orchestral conductors who find themselves directing orchestral forces with which they are all too little acquainted. From textbooks they may have picked up a fair amount of theoretical learning, which, a dangerous thing in itself, carries them but a short distance along the road of practicalities. A passing acquaintance with one or possibly two instruments is hardly adequate for dealing with the thousand and one problems that must be faced during the course of rehearsals, problems cropping up from every corner of the orchestra.

For the work of the conductor falls into two distinct categories: rehearsal and performance. Without the ability to rehearse, the conductor can scarcely hope to give a satisfactory performance, however talented his instrumentalists. The composer, who of necessity must be well acquainted with the peculiarities of all instruments, may write the most intricate passages requiring patient, laborious and detailed rehearsal. If the conductor is unable to communicate to his players any definite ideas of what is required, it is obvious that any meritorious performance is out of the question. In brief, the conductor must be a man of parts, able at all times to explain the music in terms of the instrumentalist he is addressing. It requires but a small stretch of imagination for the reader to realize that the perfect conductor, completely equipped, is about as nonexistent as the phoenix.

Even when a conductor possesses a sound general knowledge of the orchestra—and there are many whose practical experience is quite phenomenal—it does not necessarily follow that his performances will have more than average merit. Other qualities are

Ernest Ansermet
Conductor

Halsman

Frederick Ashton, c.b.e.
Dancer, Choreographer,
Director

Bert Cann

Constant Lambert
Composer, Conductor,
Musical Director

Baron

Antal Dorati
Conductor

NINETTE DE VALOIS
In "Douanes" (1932)

"Anthon

ALICIA MARKOVA   *Constantine*

JEROME ROBBINS *and* NANCY REED
In "Fancy Free"

Alfredo Valente

MARGOT FONTEYN, D.B.E.
Ballerina of
Sadler's Wells Ballet

Houston Roger

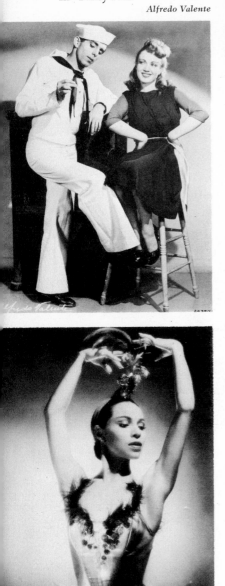

MARIA TALLCHIEF
Classical Ballerina

Alfredo Valente

MICHAEL KIDD *and* NORA KAYE
In "On Stage"

Serge Lido

OLGA PREOBRAJENSKA
Imperial Russian Ballerina Teaching
in her Paris Studio

ADOLPH BOLM *and* IGOR STRAVINSKY

ALEXANDRA DANILOVA
and
LEONIDE MASSINE

Maurice Goldberg

VASLAV NIJINSKY

Underwood & Underwood

MICHEL FOKINE

Maurice Goldberg

needed. Magnetism, personality, strong telepathic powers and other marked characteristics are required to set the spirit of the music afire. And this flame of inspiration can only be rekindled through the conductor whose mind must soar with the composer. Thus only can the beauty of the music be matched by the beauty of its interpretation. For without the inspiration of the conductor the greatest masterpiece is no better than a heap of dead notes, the composer's temple of sound but a ruin.

It follows that the conductor can indulge in many extravagances of style far removed from the original intentions of the composer. By the undiscerning and by the lover of the sensational such extravagances are termed "individual readings" (a term one hears too often from radio commentators) for which the conductor is far too often lauded when his treasonable betrayal of the composer should earn universal condemnation. Unfortunately, such readings are becoming all too fashionable nowadays, the cult of the bizarre having produced that successor to the old-time *prima ballerina,* the "virtuoso" conductor.

But the earnest conductor, he who reveres his art, desires no more than the re-creation of the composer in all the expressed detail of the score. He will be sparing of gesture, but such as are needed will carry a full significance. Not a single one will occur that is not born of the music itself, for his last thought will be to place himself between the composer and the audience. He will use his right arm, with or without the baton, merely to indicate the time of the music; and, where additional stress or strength is required, will occasionally introduce the left arm as an extra rhythmical pointer.

But, generally, the left arm and hand will function independently of the right. "Let not thy left arm know what thy right arm doeth" might well be the motto of many a conductor unskilled in technique. There is nothing so ungainly, so meaningless in interpretation, so irritatingly windmill-like in its movements as the left arm and hand (unconvincingly loose-wristed) of a conductor incessantly reproducing what is being indicated on the right. Such actions but flog the music, bringing to it a sense of monotony, both aural and visual, that renders true interpretation impossible. (Arthur Nikish, the great German conductor, is said to have tied a pupil's left arm behind his back for a whole term of lessons—a most convincing preventative.) The left arm and hand should be the phrase and expression makers: delicately poised "instruments" prompted into action by the conductor's inner feeling for the music and withdrawn when not required. By such means as are here described the heart of the music is sought and found, and, under the spell of inspiration, there is established between conductor and orchestra some altogether inexplicable form of telepathy that galvanizes everything into life.

He is no time-beater. His knowledge must cover a wider field than that of any other musicians, while his art, viewed as a whole, undoubtedly rises superior to all other forms of musical expression.

It may, therefore, be seen without too much trouble, that the role of the orchestra conductor in ballet is not only even more arduous than that of the purely orchestral conductor, but one of vital importance to the performance as a whole. It is, moreover, a role that often is not accorded its due importance and recognition.

As for the music itself, there is one other point to be considered, one that arises from a question often raised and put to me: "Why can't the music for modern ballets be more beautiful?"

In the manner of the New England Yankee, I reply with a question: "Need music be beautiful?"

It is usually assumed that music aims, at least, at being beautiful—if we use the term in its most comprehensive sense, so that it will include all degrees and qualities of beauty from austere sublimity to tinkling prettiness. On this footing the defenders of the contemporary idiom, which to innumerable lovers of the art appears ugly in many of its aspects, point out that it is only its strangeness that makes it seem so.

They remind us of the shock which the syncopations of Monteverde, the vigorous profundity of Beethoven, and the unending melody and chromatic harmony of Wagner caused to some of their more conservative contemporaries. This being the case, it is not difficult to deduce from them the assumption that the most uncompromising works of Schönberg, Von Webern, and Bartók will one day be thought lovely, and that their beauty is only obscured from us today by the unfamiliarity of their idioms.

That the art of music has undergone, and is constantly undergoing, during this century a more profound change than any through which it passed in the last three hundred years is generally recognized. But reflection has aroused in me the notion that the direction in which it is moving is misunderstood by many of its own champions. The music of Berg, Bartók, and Schönberg (since *Pierrot Lunaire*) is not beautiful by any ordinary standards, and, I venture to think, never will be thought so by the majority of lovers of the art. Otherwise, they would have discovered beauty in it by this time, now that the strangeness of its means of expression has worn off. This does not necessarily mean that atonality, or even polytonality, will necessarily survive the test of time—at least as practised by all those who employ them—but that we must seek some kind of merit other than beauty in the works which resort to them.

Different civilizations have had different standards of the worth of music. Judging from Plato, it would seem that the ancient Athenians assessed it according to its moral effect. Western civilization for a few hundred years, culminating about the middle of the nineteenth century, had assumed that its merit depends upon its aesthetic beauty. Yet beauty is not the only test for all the arts. Need it be for music?

You do not condemn a satirical poem for not being beautiful; you do not expect it to be so, but you do demand that it be witty and pointed. If beauty were the only test, where would be the satires of Horace and Pope? If an artist paints a brilliant portrait of a very ugly person, as many of the greatest of them have done, we can hardly describe the result as beautiful (unless the clothing is), but we may still admire the picture. When Dante describes the terrors of Hell, or Shakespeare the horrors of villainy, we praise these works to the skies, but "beautiful" is not quite

the right word to use. Countless musical compositions—not all
of them recent in date—are amusing or clever, but cannot properly be described as possessing beauty.

I suggest that music can be admirable even if it is not beautiful,
and also that once Berlioz and Wagner had started on the path
of elaborate character drawing, it was bound, sooner or later, to
embrace ugliness as well as beauty. You surely cannot describe
the motive of Alberich's curse as being beautiful: it would have
been singularly inappropriate if it had been.

A good deal of water has flowed under the Brooklyn Bridge
since Richard Strauss first startled New York with the din of
battle in *Ein Heldenleben*. It was meant to be ugly, just as war
is ugly, and it remains so to this day and is all the more effective
for being so. It is now about forty-three years since the *Rite of
Spring* from Stravinsky's youthful fertile imagination first aroused
a storm of opposition. Its strident dissonances are just as exhilarating today as they were then. Of course they aren't beautiful.
Why should they be? Nature is not always beautiful, and it is
the function of some music, at least, as well as of dramatic acting,
"to hold the mirror up to nature."

Some parts of the *Rite of Spring*, however, seem beautiful to
us now, though they did not at its first appearance. The reason
for this is simply that we have become accustomed to their idiom,
as has happened with the works of other innovators in the past.

The only unpardonable sin which an artist can commit is to
be dull and lifeless. A lot of ugly contemporary music is unutter-
ably boring and pedantic. We need not worry; it will die a natural
death. There is no reason why present and future composers
should not write beautiful music in a modern idiom, as Vaughan
Williams, Sibelius, and Benjamin Britten have done; but there
is also no reason why they should, so long as they are interesting.
Nevertheless, the greatest music will always be that which is
recognized as being beautiful either by its contemporaries or by
later generations.

3

A Brief History of Ballet

B y this time, someone who has come this far may have lifted an eyebrow to inquire to himself, "Isn't ballet concerned with dancers?"

Of course, ballet is concerned with dancers; the point is that ballet is not merely a matter of a little "fancy dancing." But the dancer is of sufficient importance to come high up on the list of elements that make up ballet. Important though the dancer is, without those other elements there would not be ballet, but merely dance recitals.

As the curtain rises, let us say, on a "classical" ballet, one is conscious, first of all, of dancers, plural, doing a variety of things. They seem quite unreal. They may be ghosts of departed virgins (as in *Giselle*) or human beings changed by a magician into swans (as in *Swan Lake*) or fairies (as in *The Nutcracker*) or both fairies and countesses (as in *The Sleeping Beauty*). The first impression is that that is what they are rather than what they actually are: people (usually young) trained as dancers, performing a sequence of steps and movements. One is also conscious they are performing these steps and movements, creating this magic to music, creating it in a wood, or in a palace, or in some never-never land, which is scenery; that they are wearing costumes, which help the general effect of emphasizing color and form against the painted background which is the scenery, costumes and scenery being often referred to as the *décor*.

Later, these dancers, at first so seemingly disembodied, will take on personality as individuals, and one will become conscious of their style, their physique, their ability both as dancers and actors.

What the layman is seeing is the dancer in the finished product. It has not just happened. The training has been going on for years and years. It must always go on. It is continuous.

The training of the individual dancer in ballet is as continuous as is the history of ballet itself. For an understanding of the position of the dancer and his training a brief glance at the history of ballet cannot be other than helpful. The history of dance is a long one and for purposes of this guide, for the mythical man in the street, it will be confined to those highlights that shed their glow on the finished product of ballet in mid-twentieth century.

The balletic annotator may be regarded as the counsel for the defense; but his job is, as I conceive it, to present the facts and let the jury arrive at the verdict. So, to the facts:

Any account of the history of dancing would be an account of the most primitive and universal human activities. It is a fixed law of the material structure of the human being that every impression conveyed to the brain through the senses tends to incite a movement in some part of the body. Dancing in its simplest and most primitive form is the end-product of joy, grief, pleasure or pain, excitement or anger. With the attainment of rhythm and measure it becomes a more calming vent for emotion and, at the same time, a more corporate means of expression, something which, so to speak, can be done together.

Historically and philosophically, dancing is found almost everywhere to play a chief part in the religious rites of primitive peoples. It continued to do so in the civilizations of Egypt,

Greece, and Rome, and does so still in Africa, Asia, and in the American Indian and related civilizations.

As a social enjoyment, often closely connected with courtship and the manifestation of sexual attraction, it has taken shape in the popular dances of different nations, while, in antiquity, war-dances, serving both as a drill to develop the muscles and as a stimulus to the instinct of pugnacity, were widespread.

In this brief historical survey we must confine ourselves to dancing as a branch of art in the West. Therefore Greece would be our starting-point, and we find the testimony of Greek litera-ture, sculpture, vase paintings, all corroborating the common agreement of the educators and philosophers that dancing was of inestimable value.

From Greece to Rome—a step forward toward mimetic dancing in the Roman adaptation of the Greek theater called pantomime, where the Roman actor performed in dumb show—dancing ac-quired an enormous popularity. However, the art was decadent from its start, and its lasciviousness eventually deteriorating into gladiatorism with real executions and other horrific exhibitions brought upon it the execration of the growing power of Chris-tianity.

Through the Middle Ages there is vagueness, as there is in the history of most forms of art and entertainment during that clouded period. The Church frowned upon all forms of panto-mime and dancing. But the Fathers were unable to extirpate dance either from the lives of the downtrodden masses or from the diversions of those in high places. What is more, there is a good deal of evidence that dancing penetrated into the very services of the Church.

Dancing again came into its own during the Renaissance, an age of grand spectacles, particularly in courts and houses of the nobility. Masques and dancing displays were associated with every festivity. Ballets formed interludes in operas, plays, and even took place as independent pantomimic spectacles, usually in the form of allegories. The basic impulse came from Italy and spread to France.

It was Catherine de' Medici who stimulated the taste in France for Italian modes and manners, and it was in 1581 that she had created the famous *Ballet comique de la Reine*. During the reign of Henry of Navarre some eighty-odd court ballets are said to have been produced. Under Louis XIII, Cardinal Richelieu produced a ballet; Louis XIV appeared in many ballets himself.

From the court ballet passed to the opera, to be developed musically by composers such as Lully and Rameau. At first there were no professional women dancers (*ballerine*), but only male dancers wearing masks. It was the composer, Jean Baptiste Lully, who finally contrived to break down this rule, and trained female dancers. But there was still much to be done before the ballet could be considered free from the heavy, turgid fashions of the court of Louis *le Grand*. Heavy leather masks were still worn for some of the characters, while the high heels, the towering wigs, the full skirts of both men and women, decked out in plumes and helmets, imprisoned and bogged down all rapid steps and movements, and actually made them impossible of execution.

The history of ballet in the eighteenth century is that of the breaking of these fetters. It was an age of great dancers, to nearly each of whom tradition has attributed some step forward. The first famous ballet dancers are the Mlles. Sallé and Camargo. The former is credited with the sheer audacity to appear in London with only a simple muslin robe in the Greek style. To the latter is attributed the creation and use of the *entrechat quatre* (the high springing step, a commonplace in ballet today, in which the feet are crossed several times while in the air). In order to accomplish this movement and to provide for freer motion altogether, Camargo invented a sort of tights.

All this was but a prelude to the real reform, the impulse for which came from a ballet-master, Noverre, who, in 1760, published his famous *Letters on the Dance,* the aim of which was to do away with the artificiality of conventional costume, to simplify the steps of ballet, and to make the expression of feeling and the telling of a tale more important than the mere display of sheer virtuosity, and, in general, to inculcate the Rousseau ideal of a return to naturalism and the virtues of classicism. This, to be sure, took time and infinite patience.

The *pirouette,* the spin round on one foot or on point of toe, a step that presupposes freedom from the trappings of the Louis XIV school, is first associated with the name of Mlle. Heinel. The abandonment of the obfuscating mask is attributed to one Pierre Gardel, who made this a condition of his replacing the dancer, Gaetan Vestris, when the latter was suddenly taken ill and unable to play a leading role. The most distinguished and famous of the successors to Noverre were Pierre Gardel, just mentioned; his brother Maximilian; and Jean Dauberval; along with the two famous male dancers, Gaetan Vestris and his son Auguste, the latter known as "the god of the dance."

With the nineteenth century we find ourselves in a period embracing both romanticism and realism. The reforms Noverre had started were completed by the French Revolution.

The Republic and the Empire were based on models of Classicism, and the Empire, particularly in architecture, furniture and costume, was adept at copying Grecian modes. Paying scant, if any, attention to climatic conditions, women began to appear in gauze draperies, sandals, low-necked dresses, and other adaptations of ancient costume. At last the dancer was liberated from the confining strictures of conventional dress; what is sometimes referred to as the grand age of ballet was at hand.

The interpreter of this "grand age" was Carlo Blasis, whose book, *Code of Terpsichore,* was published in London in 1828, when he was twenty-five and was working at His Majesty's Theatre. The book is a manual of dancing and pantomime based entirely on the classical ideal.

The strictly classical epoch passed into the era of Romanticism without any serious change of basic principles. We come to a name which may be said to be the greatest single name in the history of ballet—Marie Taglioni. Born in Sweden in 1804, of an Italian father and Swedish mother, her debut was made in Paris at the age of twenty-three. She may be said to have founded, single-handed, a new aesthetic of dancing by a highly personal blend of ethereal charm and classic simplicity.

Since the history of ballet is in part a history of costume, it should be noted that the modern classical ballet costume was seen in its first stage in the costumes of Taglioni. Generally speaking, the type is Grecian: sandals, diaphanous skirt, low-necked body, hair in form of a wreath. Camargo's tights (known as *caleçon*) have been developed into the *maillot* (an improved type of tights, so-called after a costume designer at the Paris Opéra named Maillot). Moreover, the skirt has been slightly shortened, although in this period it was not too far above the ankles; but it did flare out from the waist, in order both to free the dancer's legs and to exhibit them. The most important point of all, however, as anyone may see for himself who cares to examine the prints of Taglioni, is that she is usually shown poised on the *pointe,* which is to say on the extreme tip of the toe, an attitude possible only to one who wears a shoe or sandal with a specially stiffened toe.

Whether Taglioni was the first actually to introduce the *pointes,* one does not know. But we do know it was not a characteristic in drawings and prints before her time. This innovation had two distinct results on ballet: it endowed the dancer with greater levitation, greater freedom, the ability to turn more rapidly, and the appearance of floating, something that appealed greatly to the Romantic age, filled as it was with a passion for sylphs and disembodied spirits. The other result is that it considerably lowered the status of the male dancer, and turned out to be the foundation of a cult of pure technique that was the touchstone of ballet as time went on. In other words, this new-found freedom of costume turned the dancer into a sort of aesthetic gymnast.

Only three other names of this period need concern us here. All of them, in a sense, were rivals of Taglioni. They were Carlotta Grisi, for whom Théophile Gautier wrote the ballet *Giselle,* still a regularly performed classic of classical ballet; Fanny Ellsler, a hot-blooded woman of reckless temperament, who triumphantly toured the United States, more of a character dancer than a ballerina; and Lucille Grahn.

The climax of the Romantic Ballet may be said to have been the famous *pas de quatre* danced by the four of them at His Majesty's Theatre, London, in 1845, and which, in a reconstruction, may be seen in its quaint period charm today in the repertoire of the Ballet Theatre.

A comment on fame and glory: Taglioni died in extreme old age and poverty in 1884.

As in life itself, the one thing that persists in ballet is change. From the dancer's point of view, the prevailing tendency to transform a classical discipline into a technical virtuosity went on apace. Although the fundamental aesthetic of ballet dancing has always clung to its Greek roots, it has hardened and stylized so that its origin is concealed from the casual observer. In other words, it established a strict technique of its own. Physical strength and studied dexterity in executing different and exceedingly complicated motions of the feet and legs are one of the results. So that these could be the more easily seen, enjoyed and judged, the flowing skirt was reduced to a mere wisp known as the *tutu*.

This concentration on and elaboration of technique almost as an end in itself changed the character of ballets, reflecting at the same time the shift in literature from the Romantic to the Realistic school. Stage-craft, mechanics began to play their parts increasingly. From this period stem two French ballets, both observable today: *Coppélia* and *Sylvia*, both with score by Léo Delibes.

Ballet needed new blood, fresh ideas. Towards the end of the first decade of the twentieth century an astonishing revival was apparent in a striking departure from the lifeless formalism into which ballet had degenerated. This fresh, new impulse came from Russia.

To explain how this was possible it will be necessary to employ what in film parlance is known as a "flash-back."

When the autocratic Peter the Great introduced Western culture into Russia, one of the results was the inculcation of a passion for dancing. It was in 1735 that the Empress Anne introduced the ballet and a school. Her first idea was to train military cadets as ballet dancers, but it did not take them long to discover that ballet-dancing is a life's job. Accordingly, the school was opened to boys and girls of the poorer classes, receiving maintenance and general education in return for their services. Such was the origin of the Russian Imperial School of Ballet which persists today in unbroken line.

Such was the enthusiasm for ballet and the intense concentration of artistic efforts facilitated by the Imperial School that, despite its isolation from the West, Russian ballet became an instrument of the highest artistic potentiality. Ballet was transformed into the most exciting form of theatrical art.

A few names, all of which loom large in the making of contemporary ballet, are necessary to the understanding of how ballet got to be what it is.

Remember Marius Petipa, who died in 1910, a Frenchman who went to Russia in 1847, became the head of ballet in the country in 1862, remained the dictator who maintained its vitality, though on strictly conventional lines, throughout the entire second half of the nineteenth century.

Enrico Cecchetti, who seconded Petipa in 1888, was a brilliant Italian dancer, mime, and teacher, who died in 1928, and whose career may be said to form a link between the old conservative school and the new.

Now two names, historically linked together, from whose alliance is properly dated the foundation of the new school of ballet, its renaissance: the dancer, Michel Fokine, and the cultured, talented amateur, patron of the arts of music, painting, and ballet, Serge Diaghileff. The former died in New York in 1942; and the latter in Venice in 1929. The alliance of these two men resulted in the formation of a ballet company that gave its first season in Paris in 1909. That season was history-making, taking Western Europe literally by storm. The revelation of a new form of ballet revival to fresh, new audiences (which did not realize that this company was a secession from the Russian Imperial Ballet) resulted in the title of "Le Ballet Russe." Hence the phrase "Russian Ballet" has clung tenaciously to ballet for years and has worked a sometimes undeserved magic at the box-office. Inferior ballet companies, clinging with equal tenacity to and overtly conscious of the value of the term, have offered damaged goods, sleazy productions, scantily rehearsed works, hesitant and insufficiently trained dancers, with far greater success than was warranted. The term "Russian Ballet" or "Ballet Russe," valid in 1909, had little or no validity in mid-century.

This is not the place to discuss *pro* or *con* the merits of the assertion that Michel Fokine was influenced in his ideals by the American non-balletic dancer, Isadora Duncan, whose creed was a return to basic Greek principles. The result seems to have been apparent that Fokine's ideal was not so much one of a Neo-Greek mode as it was to restore ballet to its own first principles before its technique had become so solidified and rigidified that no change was possible. It might almost be said to have been a return to the Taglioni spirit. Example: the ballet *Les Sylphides,* a "moonlit reverie," in the repertoire of nearly every ballet company extant, yet not too often well done, a veritable classic of modern, romantic ballet, done to assorted preludes, nocturnes, and mazurkas of Chopin, and danced in skirts copied from the epoch of Taglioni.

It must, at this juncture, be pointed out that the reforms of the Diaghileff ballet were by no means confined to dancing and the dancer. There was a distinct reform in music, in raising the standard of ballet music, a standard that, with a few Tchaikowskian exceptions, had reached a nadir of banality. The Diaghileff method of musical reform embraced two of the methods discussed in an earlier chapter: one was by the adaptation of existing works by eminent composers. The mention of a few will suffice: Chopin in *Les Sylphides,* Schumann in *Carnaval,* Rimsky-Korsakov in *Schéhérazade,* all of which may be seen today in more or less authentic reproductions. His other method was to commission young composers to write directly for ballet. The list of these is long. Two striking examples of the period with which we are presently concerned: Stravinsky's *The Firebird* and *Petrouchka*.

The third great reform was the veritable revolution Diaghileff wrought in scenery and costume. Through the collaboration of the famous Léon Bakst, Alexandre Benois, and their artistic colleagues, a tremendous broom was used to sweep away all the heavy, ponderous, realistic scenery of the Realistic Age. It may be said that Diaghileff and his collaborators marked the transition from the Realistic to the Impressionistic Age.

The impact of the Diaghileff Ballet, not only on ballet, but on costume, on the decoration of our homes, even on Western culture cannot be over-estimated. However, it is well to bear in mind that ballet did not stop there. From its base, out of its roots, the growth and development were continuous.

The Diaghileff Ballet made two tours of America in 1917 and 1918. Its principal ballerina was Tamara Karsavina, who did not, however, accompany the company to America, and who now lives in London, a powerful, gracious and revered force in the dance of today. Among the men Adolph Bolm as character mimetic dancer and the veteran Cecchetti as pantomimist and teacher of the ballet in charge of daily classes were both prominent.

However, the most important figure in the Diaghileff movement, after Fokine, was the principal male dancer, Vaslav Nijinsky, a young Pole endowed with a physical agility resembling Vestris, who was vulgarly said to float at will in the air and who possessed an intense dramatic talent in pantomime. Nijinsky became a legend even in his lifetime.

His career was short in time-span, yet he may be said to have initiated a new phase in the history of dancing through his quite remarkable personality. Again we have the dancer exerting a profound influence on his art and its direction. The purely "classical" ideal of ballet had never been an object of veneration for Nijinsky. His taste was affected by the barbaric dances of the Slavic warriors and peasantry and also by Oriental ideals, as was demonstrated by his remarkable performance in the Fokine ballet *Schéhérazade.* Strength and significance in dancing were to him more important than mere grace, and he had a close affinity with Cubist and Post-Impressionistic art. He sought to create a new style of dancing roughly based on the same aesthetic principles. *The Afternoon of a Faun,* a sort of living plastic frieze, flat and Cubistic in design, and the mysterious *Rite of Spring* were his chief attempts to express his ideas.

Nijinsky's early breakdown in mental health cut short an astounding career and put an end to any further development of his ideas. Nijinsky died in London in 1950, at the age of sixty. The legendary name lives on with the legend. Books have been written about him. A film based on his life has been threatened time and again.

One of the last creative dancing figures to emerge from the Diaghileff Ballet was Leonide Massine, whose genius and tireless personality, as I have said, made possible the continued growth of ballet into what we now know.

Passing mention should be made, for the record, of some important Russian dancers, unconnected on the whole with the Diaghileff enterprise, or if at all, only briefly so, though contemporary with it. Among them Anna Pavlova has a place of her own, unassailed, in the history of ballet. Her technique, though highly polished, was always subordinated to the poetical inspiration. She had such grace in the use of *pointes* that it vindicated them from the common charge of the period that dancing on the *pointes* was "unnatural." Over all was an inexhaustible fund of great and, at the same time, delicate and highly personal charm. For years the only ballet personality known to America, for a generation Anna Pavlova became the visible symbol of ballet itself. She died in Holland in 1931, still dancing at the age of fifty. One ventures to believe that although her creative qualities were limited, by sheer force of her lasting personality her name will live long in the history of ballet.

Other names of the period that may at one time or another float before the layman's eyes are Lydia Lopokova, an engaging soubrette dancer of the Diaghileff epoch and company; and three great dancers of the strictly traditional school: Ekaterina Gheltzer, perhaps the most highly regarded among technical connoisseurs; the last Tsar's brilliant favorite, Mathilde Kchessinska; and Olga Preobrajenska—the latter two still teaching the important basic classical tradition in Paris.

The last two decades of contemporary ballet are so much of the present that they require only the chronological refresher of dated mention. Following the death of Diaghileff in 1929, there was a depressing lull in both ballet performances and development. In 1932, Colonel W. de Basil and the French René Blum founded their Ballet Russe de Monte Carlo. In 1933, Leonide Massine commenced the creation of his first "symphonic" ballets, charting a new course. The autumn of 1934 saw the formation by George Balanchine, a late Diaghileff discovery out of Soviet Russia, of the first of his series of American ballet companies that has today culminated in the organization known as the New York City Ballet. 1934 saw the formation out of a private ballet society of England's Sadler's Wells Ballet, at the hands of Ninette de Valois and Constant Lambert (emerging to this title from that of the Vic-Wells Ballet), in London, destined to become one of the most powerful forces in contemporary ballet. Another striking development was the formation of Ballet Theatre in New York in 1940, a ballet company inaugurated on a scale of grandeur hitherto unknown outside those countries blessed with governmental subsidy.

Although, as I have pointed out, "Ballet Russe" or "Russian Ballet" had been the predominating influence of the earlier part of the present century, following the deaths of Pavlova and Diaghileff (within a couple of years of each other) English and American ballet had their first great opportunities. The seeds had been planted· by the Russian sower and also nurtured and cultivated.

)4(

The Training of the Dancer

From the foregoing account, it should be apparent that English ballet was born some time between the death of Diaghileff and the arrival in London of the de Basil Ballet Russe de Monte Carlo. Which is to say, between 1929 and 1933. It should be equally apparent that, dates notwithstanding, the audience contact in America with traditional ballet is far more recent than in England. These facts are important in that our concerns are now chiefly with English and American ballet. The American emphasis historically had been on personalities (as exemplified particularly by Anna Pavlova) rather than on ballet itself. Personalities ruled. Even ballet in opera, a somewhat special form, to be sure, was handicapped at the Metropolitan Opera House, New York, by a hide-bound, old-fashioned directorate.

So far as ballet itself was concerned, it was confined to acts on a vaudeville bill, so-called "presentation" numbers in motion-picture palaces in the heyday of the silent film. The result was that the word "ballet" conveyed only legs, more legs, high kicks, and a "kick" for the tired business man. In view of this, the

41

progress in the last two decades has been little short of astounding.

Ballet is traditional; but it must, at all times, express the spirit of its time as well. Some of the works of the past would incite a contemporary audience to laughter, precisely as the antics of a few present-day dancers, still living in the past, do with their almost grotesque exaggerations.

Meanwhile, the reiterated performances, the tours of numerous companies across the length and breadth of the American continent, the exchange of companies across the Atlantic so that ballet is no longer exclusively an import but a cultural export as well, has swelled audiences beyond anything heretofore dreamed. Ballet has invaded and transformed the dancing in the musical comedy theater, largely through the introduction of ballet techniques into theater dance at the hands of the American Agnes de Mille, first in *Oklahoma!* in 1943. It is a considerable ingredient in present-day motion pictures. And, although still far from satisfactory, television is making increasing use of dance in its programing. The dance is more and more coming into its own, so far as opportunity for performance is concerned; yet, if the mythical man in the street has a son or daughter contemplating a dancing career, in addition to genuine talent and sound training, a high spirit of adventure and dedication to an ideal, father's loosened purse-strings are necessary, for the security offered by the dancing profession is conspicuous by absence.

We return to the dancer whom the layman saw as the curtain rose. She was doing a number of things and, in addition to the dancer, the layman's eye was confronted by a number of other things while his ear was occupied by music.

Let us stick to the dancer for a bit longer. She was doing, among other things, steps. The entire history of dancing shows that steps in themselves are only of relative importance. Steps and all other matters must be taught. The study is long and arduous. Great teachers are essential. It is impossible to be a great teacher of dancing without first being an experienced, possibly even a great, dancer. This does not necessarily mean every great dancer is a correspondingly great teacher. But it will be seen that the link of tradition in dancing is this unbroken practical handing on of sound teaching like the baton in a relay race.

The dancer the layman sees has started studying in early childhood—one hopes not before seven and preferably somewhere around nine years old. She has been taught and corrected, and has studied and practiced daily. Her health has been guarded. Her good looks prove this. The dancer's health is reflected in her appearance. She is slender; yet her stomach is, thank you very much, in tip-top shape. She has not dieted to keep slim. It has not been a simple matter. Meals have been at the most irregular times (an occupational hazard); the diet, badly chosen ofttimes. Owing to circumstances of travel and hours the diet has sometimes been lacking in necessary elements; but she has had the good fortune to avoid that arch-enemy of the dancer, auto-intoxication, which, more than anything else, puts on weight and in the least likely place for the dancer, the legs.

During her first couple of years, the dancer who has attracted the layman's attention has made various movements over and over again, although, so far as she herself is concerned, these movements have never appeared to have much if any relation to one another. Her concentration has been upon her feet. Later she discovered for herself that her feet moved without her concentration exclusively upon them, and that certain corresponding positions of the arms and body helped. Later there was added the realization that the music was speaking to her, conveying something. The daily classes have continued now for, let us say, at least seven years. Being one of the luckier ones, she has succeeded in becoming a member of the company, a performance of which the layman is attending. But, having joined the company, having at last become a professional, she continues studying. Each day, as long as she continues to dance, she takes a lesson, subjects herself to criticism, in order to eradicate faults. She will continue to do so if eventually she becomes one of the world's leading dancers.

Before she was accepted into the company, she was thought-fully and extensively auditioned. These auditions have determined to the satisfaction of the auditioners that the dancer is technically efficient. It has yet to be seen if she is more than that. If she is not, she will not go far. The important thing is not steps but what she has to give to an audience. Steps are not enough. Ballet is full of efficient dancers, many of whom are lacking in sensitivity and perception and feeling. It is the difference between the dancer and the artist. An artist must be able to move people. In order to move people one must oneself be moved.

As our layman becomes more accustomed to ballet, which is to say, after he has seen a number of performances, he will begin to single out some dancers over others. The chances are he will not be able to explain why. He feels it. Quite apart from the in-definable something called "personality," there is some quality about her dancing, her movement that will attract.

There is, to be sure, always "personality," which is more easily recognizable than either technical ability or artistry. I cannot at-tempt to define "personality," but I do know it must never be compounded of deliberately drawing attention to oneself. The outstanding dancer *must* have it; but therein, too, lurks danger. An excess of personality on top of a strongly developed technique can result not in an artist but in an unconscious clown, a two-legged imitation of a caparisoned circus-horse.

There are a few virtuoso dancers, possessors of an all-conquer-ing technique, who do nevertheless place themselves at the service of the ballet, often wrongheadedly, but never without passionate sincerity. From such artists it is possible to accept all sorts of things which are alike repugnant in the virtuoso dancer pure and simple—if purity and simplicity are not too fantastically inappropriate terms—and in the earnest dancer of less ability, smaller mentality, and weaker conviction.

The personality-virtuoso is one of ballet's curses. The dancer who thinks only of personal display is an enemy to the fine things she does not even pretend to serve, but arrogantly takes to exist for her own glorification. She will dance in bad ballets shamelessly, not from economic necessity but from choice, so long as doing so gives her an opportunity to exhibit her technical attainments and, if she has any say in the matter, will choose a good work only if by accident it lends itself to the same end. The one thing that redeems the out-and-out personality-virtuoso is, to put it paradoxically, that she is doomed to perdition. She has her day, vanishes, and does not take long to fall into oblivion.

Fortunately the dancer who is a virtuoso, personality flaunting and nothing else, is comparatively rare today. Those who are have "names" and are celebrities. There is no need for the layman to fall into the inverted snobbery that insists on discrediting any artist who has made a resounding name. Even while fame is being exploited to the full, it is still possible to give a valuable performance, and indeed one may often see model performances from artists who have attained to widespread popularity, performances their reputations would naturally lead one to expect. These artists are at least worth trying. But if they are found supercilious in their attitude towards ballet, they had better be dropped at once.

As for the evils of this sort of personality-virtuoso, star-system product, it must be said quite brutally that they have sprung very largely from the public's attitude. The low sport of star-adoration and celebrity-hunting is responsible for some of the most appalling things that go on in the ballet world.

Unfortunately it is the kind of chase that has the peculiarity of being enjoyed as much by the hunted as by the hunters, which means that nobody, not even the tiny minority of humanitarians this wicked world contains, ever cries out vigorously against it. Critics, it is true, occasionally do so, being the only real victims of this monstrous traffic; but as in sheer self-defence they have to cultivate a blend of humor and resigned cynicism, their protests are apt to be somewhat ineffectual. The rest of mankind is divided into the indifferent and the overly enthusiastic. The latter, though very much in the minority, make up a public quite large enough to fill up the theater for at least a single performance where a dancer (I shall not use the word "artist") who has somehow achieved celebrity and is leading a company may be booked to appear.

Those who want to cultivate ballet sincerely for its own sake had better be warned to approach the personality-virtuoso warily, all, that is, save a very few, and even those with a mind and an eye unprejudiced by their reputation. It is always a good plan to judge for oneself.

Every dancer is ambitious. Her greatest ambition is not necessarily to make money. Being human, she very possibly wishes one day to marry. She may even have some thoughts about a sometime family. But if she has one ambition greater than another, it is eventually to become a *prima ballerina,* which is to say the first dancer in a company. This is something not entirely dependent upon her talent, however fine that talent may be. As there are categories of singers: sopranos, mezzo-sopranos, contraltos, there are various types of dancers. And, like the singer, the first of the differentiations in type is a physical one. The dancer's ambition is to become a classical *ballerina,* to dance such roles as the Swan Queen, Princess Aurora, Giselle, the so-called "white ballets." Now, quite apart from talent and technique, for these roles a precise type of physique is absolutely essential. She must not be too tall, her legs must be perfect in formation as the gods and the dancer's ancestors can have made them. The reason for this is that the short classical "tutu" is a short skirt and the legs will be in constant view.

There are also psychological differences between the categories. The true classical *ballerina* may be the possessor of an enormous temperament, but any display of temperament in a classical role can only result in a vulgarization of the part. Therefore, the true classical *ballerina* must have mastered the art of self-discipline.

That is, perhaps, with these physical and psychological problems, one of the reasons why there are so few dancers suited to be *ballerinas.* The striking advantage of the true *ballerina* is that with her self-discipline and self-control it is possible for her to exhibit a tremendous range and thus she is able to overlap all the categories with the greatest of ease. Three examples, two historical and one contemporary, will suffice: Karsavina, the *prima ballerina* of the Diaghileff Ballet, was as noted for her classical dancing as she was for her character dancing; Pavlova was practically limitless in her range; and today Margot Fonteyn, the phenomenal artist of the Sadler's Wells Ballet, is equally at home in every type of work.

In addition to classical and character dancing, there is a third category called *demi-caractère* (semi-character), perhaps the closest approach to the classical, combining as it does classical technique with the creation of a role, but dancing on *pointes*. Whereas in straight character dancing are included both national dances and purely mimed parts.

All this time in considering the dancer we have been discussing the species only in the feminine. With the coming of the Diaghileff-Fokine revolution, the male dancer, who was threatening to become an extinct species existing merely to lift and carry the female dancer, was restored to honor and distinction. Anything that has been said in these pages about the *danseuse* applies equally well to the *danseur*. But there are things to add.

The layman, unaccustomed to ballet, might feel superficially that the male dancer exists only for lifting purposes still. This would not be correct. A good male dancer enriches the work in which he appears by his sheer physical contrast to the woman dancer. The layman may come to a performance with a prejudice against the male dancer because of the ridiculously false legend that all male dancers are effeminate.

It must be admitted that the majority of male dancers to be seen today are effeminate. But just as quickly I must point out that the effeminate male dancer is without exception a bad dancer and should not be dancing. From this it may be accurately deduced that the majority of male dancers to be seen today are bad dancers. The effeminacy of the male dancer damages the entire structure of ballet and the sooner he is eliminated and extirpated from ballet the better it will be for ballet.

On the other hand, it would be well to bear in mind the fact that grace and virility are by no means incompatible. It is possible for the male classical dancer even in a black velvet jacket, white tights, and wearing long, flowing hair to be as masculine as the male character dancer if he is not by nature himself effeminate and if he has the intelligence to understand his function. And that function is to provide the love-interest, the sexual note, if you will, to be the intermediary between the *ballerina* and the audience, to be the chivalrous cavalier.

A knowledge of the technique of the dance is by no means essential to the layman's appreciation of ballet as an entertainment, which it is in addition to being an art. Moreover, knowledge of that technique is not to be acquired from reading a book. It can only be learned from being taught and practised. On the other hand, some of the terms recur so frequently that some of them have come into almost common usage. For that reason, there is included at the end of the volume a glossary of the basic terms with some simple illustrative sketches.

A general acquaintance with the dancer's individual steps can add in various ways to the spectator's enjoyment. So far as the dancer is concerned, technique must be taken for granted. It is a known quantity, distinctly measurable. But technique is not the performance of isolated steps or movements. The difference between the dancer and the artist is that the latter never thinks in terms of individual steps but rather works in the conception of one progressing, dissolving into another.

In watching the ballet, which is to watch all that goes to make it up, try to absorb as much of all the elements that are contributing to the fusion, or as many as you can. Of this fusion, as I have said, the dancer is playing a part, a most important part. And as ballet has progressed, a quality the present-day ballet dancer must have is something which in the history of ballet in the past has not been a conspicuous attribute. That quality is intelligence. Gone are the days, at least in superior companies, when the assertion, "a dancer's brains are in her feet," could hold true. As a matter of fact, where good dancers are concerned, it probably never was. In the few state-supported schools (Moscow, Leningrad, Paris, and London are examples) the dancer receives a sound education as distinguished from technical dance and physical training. In addition to general education, the allied arts of music and painting come in for analysis and elucidation at the hands of trained teachers. In the United States, regrettably the dancer does not have these advantages, and is compelled to form her own background. That background must comprise considerably more than steps.

One more attribute of the dancer that will swim into the layman's awareness after familiarizing himself with ballet will be something called style. I wish it were possible for me to define "style" so that the layman would know for what to look. But "style" is not for words to define. It is the dancer's supreme virtue, and the layman will quickly feel it when it is present, will be conscious of its lack when it is absent. It is, perhaps, the greatest single joy and satisfaction to be obtained from watching dancing.

The preservation of mathematical precision in a series of definitely prescribed movements; the execution of those movements with the flowing sweep of perfect relaxation; the movement through the air like a leaf wafted by a gentle breeze and the alighting with the leaf's gentle airiness; the ennoblement of the violence of the savage with the dignity of a demigod; the combination of the seductiveness of woman with the fragile elusiveness of a spirit—all these things are *not* style, but they are the kind of things style, and style alone, makes possible. They are the well-nigh magic results that proceed from the perfect coordination of many forms, both aesthetic and mechanical.

Michel Fokine, who did more than any single individual in modern times to free the dancer and ballet, believed that a ballet should be as logical a dramatic entertainment as a play; that dancers should in this sense be regarded as actors, and that all the dancing should have a specific and definite relation to the plot or the dramatic action. If the layman will bear this admonition in mind, he will soon be able not only to attain a deeper understanding of ballet, of the function of the dancer, but also to form both taste and judgment.

That this principle may be the more firmly fixed in the mind, let me quote the now famous letter to the *Times* (London), written in 1910, in which Fokine stated the following principles:

"To invent in each case a new form of movement, corresponding to the subject and character of the music, instead of merely giving combinations of ready-made steps.

"Dancing and gesture have no meaning unless they serve as an expression of dramatic action.

"To admit the use of conventional gesture only when it is required by the style of the ballet, and in all other cases to replace the gestures of the hands by movements of the whole body. Man could and should bé expressive from head to foot.

"The group is not merely an ornament. The new ballet advances from the expressiveness of the face or the hands to that of the whole body, and from that of the individual body to groups of bodies and the expressiveness of the combined dancing of a crowd.

"The alliance of dancing on equal terms with the other arts. The new ballet does not demand 'ballet music' from the composer, nor 'tutus' and pink satin slippers from the designer; it gives complete liberty to their creative powers."

Nearly half a century later, these principles as enunciated by Fokine at the beginning of the Romantic Revolution in ballet are the touchstone of ballet dancing, which has become more broadly in its progression theatrical dancing.

The dancer who is able to embrace these principles, who as a member of a ballet company is no selfish prima donna but one of a group of sincere artists perfectly willing to submit to anything that will make a performance good as a whole, is the dancer with a future—in short, an artist.

Now it may well be our layman has been brought to ballet by the fact he has a young daughter already embarked on ballet lessons (a son, I regret to say, is more unlikely). This daughter may envisage a career as a ballet dancer. Father may with reason wonder what her chances of security and a livelihood may be like from this concentrated life.

We must assume she has talent, ability, devotion, even dedication to her chosen career. We will take the foregoing for granted exactly as we will take for granted that she has thoroughly learned her craft.

Having mastered her craft, she has passed her auditions, has had, in short, the "break" that has resulted in her securing a place in a performing ballet company. Her stint has been allotted her, and she will be repeating that stint at least seven or eight times a week, in one city, in many cities. There will be a great deal of traveling, a great deal of rehearsal; there will be daily classes. She has chosen her career. Her heart, her mind, her very soul are in it. She loves it.

Now let us look for a moment at her economics. One day she may have to be entirely on her own, and we are assuming that papa has not been able or, better still, has not been such an idiot as to "buy" her her job by paying some questionable promoter a fee. (Such cases, fortunately, are rare but they do exist.) She will have to live. She will have to pay for her living; pay taxes; buy clothes, food, perhaps run up doctor's bills. We hope she will not have to contribute to the support of her family, but one never knows; that, too, is possible. There will be extended periods of unemployment. Will she be able to save enough during her working periods to see her through until she finds another berth?

There are, of course, every worker's usual expenses and liabilities. Our young dancer will have had and still will have the unusual expenses of an artist, expenses with which the average worker is not burdened. The long years of study in order to attain what is now her professional status have been financed by father. Yet father must bear in mind that, although she has an engagement today, her opportunities are going to be limited; the competition is bitter. On top of it all, she will have another additional worry, one of which the average professional woman is not so keenly conscious. That is the calendar: the swiftly revolving minute-hand of the clock: the inexorable advance of the years. Each recurring birthday, though father and mother may celebrate

it gaily, must, to their dancing son or daughter, have an increasingly sober connotation. There is no profession in which the
legal phrase, "time is of the essence," is of greater moment. In
short, a dancer's professional life is relatively brief.

Let us see, then, what she (or he) will find. From what I
have already said, it will be no surprise to learn that the income,
taken on an annual basis, will be both fluctuating and limited.
In the entire picture of ballet there is only a single individual
here and there possessed of the superlative skill and personality
who is able to command high wages. To most dancers, many of
whom are admired and applauded by a wide public, a balanced
budget is a fantastic dream.

Why? There are a number of factors contributing to it, none
of which is more forceful than the fact that the opportunities for
employment, regular or casual, are extremely limited. Suppose,
for example, this great, prosperous country had only three reasonably respectable hospitals, or an equal number of competently
equipped laboratories, can you imagine how many young people
would spend years training themselves to be doctors, surgeons, or
physicists? That figure "three" constitutes the number of major
ballet companies in the United States, i.e., companies based here.
And that is three more than there were a quarter of a century
ago. Despite this fact, the country from coast to coast is literally
filled with ballet schools of one sort or another, their classrooms
are crowded, and the quality of the product they turn out is not
only good but is steadily improving.

What are her opportunities for work, aside from these three
ballet companies? There has been, it is true, a hothouse development of the mass media in recent years. By "mass media" I mean
television and films. These have opened up some new jobs for
dancers; a few for choreographers. But we are discussing our
layman's dancing daughter, who has been trained for the
theater. The film and television opportunities for the theater-
trained person are not nearly as numerous as one might suppose.
The skill and standards most highly regarded in the theater are
not those of the studio. Films and television, moreover, raise their

own crop very often in other gardens. All of this forces the theater-trained dancer to look for employment in her own field. Since the supply is infinitely greater than the demand, the layman's daughter's bargaining position (unless, of course, she be a genius) is not strong.

Let us regard the picture more closely. There are, as mentioned, three active American ballet companies: Ballet Theatre, the Ballet Russe de Monte Carlo, and the New York City Ballet. Canada has two professional companies: the Canadian National Ballet, with its headquarters in Toronto, and the Royal Winnipeg Ballet, based in the city whose name it bears; but these do not enter into our economic considerations, since we assume our layman's daughter is American.

The three United States ballet companies offer on an average twenty-odd weeks of employment annually. To these weeks may be added a few weeks of pre-season rehearsals, but for this slogging pre-season work the dancers receive a lower salary. So, it will be seen that the average work-year is, if it be a good one, something less than six months.

So far as actual income is concerned (and this, it must be remembered, is on a weekly basis), the dancer's plight is considerably less than it was only a few short years ago. The dancers are, like all workers in the theater, unionized. AGMA, the dancers' union—the American Guild of Musical Artists, to give its full name—has in less than a decade succeeded in doubling the dancer's minimum wage. As recently as 1946, the American ballet companies were paying *corps de ballet* dancers $45 a week. This, thanks to AGMA, in 1955 is $92. There are weeks when dancers are obliged to rehearse at the same time as they are performing, or when rehearsal periods exceed the maximum number of hours permitted by the Union, when overtime pay raises the weekly income.

However, ballet companies simply could not exist in America without long touring periods. Hotel rooms, taxis, restaurant food, laundry, tips, all are expensive, and dancers cannot rightly be expected to live in "flea-bags."

If your daughter is unusually fortunate and remarkably successful, she may, with luck, look forward to earning as much as $4,000 a year. As an antidote to any optimism this figure may have engendered in the soul of the economically concerned father, let me quickly point out that at least eighty per cent of the dancing members of AGMA receive less than $2,000 a year.

It is only fair to point out from the employers' side that ballet is usually a deficit operation. While the Union makes every effort to improve the financial status and the working conditions of the dancer, it is nevertheless tightly squeezed on two sides: by the financial difficulties of those who operate the ballet companies on the one hand, and the strictly limited number of weeks of employment on the other.

I have mentioned the inexorability of time in the dancer's life. Our layman's daughter will have studied and practised from childhood on the long road that eventually will turn talent into a skill. She has arrived. Now she must face it. She must expect to retire (unless, of course, she marries and retires early from professional life) at an age when workers in other professional fields can scarcely be said to be more than well launched.

Without mentioning names, one could note that, even with famous *ballerinas,* there is one here and there who may seem to be immune to the years. There are male dancers who turn up using their other talents in choreography, in teaching, in directing, or have some other skills which they are able to turn to advantage once their performing years are over. But for nearly all dancers time is short and something not to be evaded.

In certain permanent organizations in America, some solution to this problem has been found by AGMA. At the Metropolitan Opera House in New York, for example, a dancer, after fifteen years of consecutive service, is eligible for retirement when he or she has reached the age of thirty-five. That is about all that can be said on the credit side.

I realize this must be an exceedingly gloomy picture to the layman father of our ballet student. Easily and understandably he might say to his devoted wife, "Not for Dorothy, my dear." But

I can assure our layman that this utterance will not stop Dorothy from continuing her dancing career if she is all the things we believe her to be.

I do not pretend to know all the answers, although one is obvious: increase the opportunities for employment. There are a number of methods by which this could be done. Larger audiences can and must be created to support the performances; seasons could and should be lengthened in order to extend the tenure of employment; new companies should be formed. All these require money and lots of it. In the United States the burden of this financing is on, and most of it comes from, private sources, contributions (never sufficient) and, in rarer case, from municipalities (usually meagre). The situation is not likely to be improved until our reluctant congressional solons see to it that the arts in America are not kept among the underprivileged, left squatting without the gate, hat in lap, mumbling, "Alms, alms . . . Alms for the love of Beauty!"

In the 1954 Congress a number of so-called "aid" bills were introduced in the House of Representatives, the general idea of which was to permit the Federal Government to take an active part in the encouragement of the fine arts, including music and drama, through financial aid and by direct assistance to locally organized musical groups. The proposed legislation was reported negatively, but the bills, it is to be presumed, will be re-submitted and the fight is bound to continue.

The congressional opposition was, it is sad to record, against *any* governmental aid for the arts. The best of the bills thus far introduced aimed to furnish scholarships and graduate fellowships in the arts; another feature was to build in the nation's capital a theater and an opera house to be known as the National Opera House, since America is the only civilized country without such a building; and further, this bill aimed to appropriate not more than $20,000,000 annually for grants in aid.

Another bill, likewise murdered in committee and thus unable to come to a vote in the Congress at large, was one designed to appoint a twelve-man board of trustees (the appointments to be

made by the President of the United States) to work for "the
stimulation and encouragement of the *performing* arts and the
public interest, and to stimulate and encourage the presentation
throughout the United States and the armed forces overseas of
productions that have artistic and historical significance." (The
italics here and hereinafter are mine.) Further the bill called for
the provision of financial assistance *"to deserving groups throughout the country."*

Aid for art and the artist has always been necessary. Down the
corridors of history we find the artist has always been obliged to
search for a patron. Out of the long list of great patrons, let us
take only three in as many separated periods of history: Lorenzo
the Magnificent, Andrew Carnegie, Otto H. Kahn. A fourth and
very contemporary: the British Arts Council. The situation
calling for the patron has been established by social and economic
forces over which art and artist have no control whatsoever.

Those most violently and virulently opposed to governmental
subsidy of the arts point to the fact that the so-called "commercial" theater survives without benefit of subsidy. But the "commercial" theater is financed by risk capital for profit. Moreover,
existing principally for profit, it is but an infinitesimal segment
of the theater as an art and the art of the theater.

It is a truism that symphony orchestras, ballet, opera simply
cannot and never will be able to pay for themselves. They could
not do this if every seat at every performance in the largest
auditoriums in the country was sold and the standing-room
crowded to suffocation. It is true the world over. There is a deficit
at New York's Metropolitan Opera House and at that temple of
musical art, Carnegie Hall. London's Royal Opera House, Covent
Garden, home of opera and the Sadler's Wells Ballet. The Paris
Opera, Milan's famed La Scala, Moscow's Bolshoi Theatre, Leningrad's Kirov or Maryinsky Theatre, or the State theaters of
Scandinavia, the municipal theaters of Germany and Italy: all
are, of necessity, deficit operations.

The reason is simple. Historically the lavish productions of
opera and ballet, as was pointed out in the historical section, were

originally devised for the entertainment of the courts and their ruling princes. Balanced budgets had no place in the development of them or the development of any other arts. Today, the courts have crumbled into dust, the princes long since departed. This being the case, the question arises: are ballet, opera, and symphony orchestras to crumble and depart with them?

If your answer to this question is in the affirmative, then you must admit that our scale of cultural life is cheaper, meaner, more impoverished than that of the departed princes. In making this admission, set against it the complacency and noisy emphasis with which we boast of our superior standard of living.

The day of the generous Maecenas of the arts is also departed, as taxation and a changing world limited his means and eliminated his ability to play the Maecenas role. Certain Foundations are able and willing on occasion to make certain contributions. But these are not enough. The federal purse would seem to be the answer.

No finer example of the success of tapping the national purse for the support of the arts exists than in England where the British Arts Council makes possible two ballet companies: the Sadler's Wells Ballet, at Covent Garden, and the Sadler's Wells Theatre Ballet, at the Sadler's Wells Theatre; opera at both these houses; the varied dramatic repertory of the Old Vic; the stirring festivals at Edinburgh and Stratford-on-Avon; the financing of any number of companies that tour the English provinces, Scotland, Ireland, and yet others that tour the British Empire and visit foreign countries both sides of the Iron Curtain. Their sponsored tours of the American continent add immeasurably to the pleasure of the American theatergoer.

Under the British system, there can be no interference of any sort once the money is allotted. It is within possibility that in the United States, filled as it is with political spectres and a tendency towards a political bureaucracy, there might under a similar system be an attempt to interfere and to enforce an official taste (which would be frightful) and even, who knows, a censorship and possible attempts at patronage in the form of some congressman's darling or a constituent's daughter (unqualified as a *ballerina*). There are difficulties and problems, to be sure. But these are things that have to be thought out and worked through.

The federal government recognizes that the nation as a whole needs schools, needs roads. Recognizing these needs, it must also recognize that the nation as a whole needs organizations and institutions for the expression of its artistic and creative impulses. In the effort to arouse Congress into action, one supporter of the bills pointed out that "in the press of many parts of Asia and Europe you find that Americans are often described as gum-chewing, insensitive, materialistic barbarians." Others noted that the Soviet Union has made a fair name for itself in many places abroad by subsidizing the arts.

One can only hope that eventually the federal government will be able to formulate and put into effect a national program which recognizes that the arts are as important to this nation as are super-highways, national parks, and the post office.

Until that happy day arrives our layman's daughter and her colleagues will lack that security they deserve. But both father and daughter should realize that while the dancer's position is precarious, it is by no means as precarious as it was had daughter been born a couple of decades earlier, when ballet was just obtaining a foothold on this continent. It took a great depression to secure any federal recognition of the arts, for every recession affects the theater and its allied arts before almost any other department of our lives. Yet there are abundant evidences that audiences have come to accept ballet as an important art, just as there is evidence that the talent now studying ballet in the thousands of schools has a better chance for employment than ever before.

The layman father concerned about his daughter's career and her future should first be convinced she has a genuine vocation for the dance, not merely a youthful infatuation with its glamor. The figures I have given also indicate the advisability of having some private means to back her up during her lean periods. In all this I hope I have not given the impression the young dancer is today being exploited. Exploitation there has been and it can be taken for granted that irresponsible managements will still try to exploit in the future. However, AGMA has seen to it that she can no longer be exploited, and any such attempts are bound to fail.

However, exploitation or no exploitation, for the dancer who for one reason or another is unable to rise above a place in the *corps de ballet,* it would be less than fair not to point out that, without the private means I have mentioned, the life can be one of great insecurity, endless hard work, coupled with both artistic and personal frustration. I have also pointed out, but should like to underline, the fact that her training is not only long but expensive. Her actual training day is in itself a long one, and only rarely is she able to continue her general education.

During this long training period there will be a plethora of purely physical trials and tribulations—bunions and corns, water on the knee and strained tendons, dropped arches and ingrown toenails—these are but a few of them. The spiritual trials and tribulations may be even harder to bear, for there will be times when to herself she will be making no apparent progress, will be able to observe no improvement whatsoever in her work, and the despair of ever becoming proficient will be heartbreaking.

But all this is likely to be as nothing compared to the heartaches that arise after she has become a member of a company. Her life then will be fantastically hard. Every morning there is a class, and perhaps a rehearsal in addition; in the afternoon another rehearsal or a matinee performance. Since much of her time will be spent on tour, when she returns to her hotel room she will have to spend her time washing and darning underclothes and tights, reinforcing her *pointe* shoes with darning wool. Weekends, the average worker's period of rest, means for the dancer either two performances—matinee and night—on both Saturday and Sunday; or Sunday may be a day spent traveling, which is certainly no rest. However gay and seemingly tireless the exterior, in my experience with ballet I have never known a dancer who was not always tired.

Though the dancer's material hardships are hard enough to bear, they are as nothing compared with the depression induced by the more intangible kinds of frustration. I have mentioned the dancer's endless struggle to keep up and, if possible, improve her technique. This goes on unrelentingly throughout her career, no matter how high she may rise in the caste of ballet or how important an artist she may become. She will at all times be living a life apart and, truth to tell, a limited one, with boundaries that can be and are restricting; for dancers live in a sort of bleak vacuum. It is an inbred existence, for their only contacts are with other dancers; their conversation is the small talk, the unimportant talk, the shop talk of the ballet. Dancers make few friends outside their profession and rarely have any private life.

Managements and directors have an unhappy way of making decisions affecting dancers, their livelihood, their future, without extending them the courtesy of consultation or the opportunity to offer an opinion. Frequently dancers have interesting and often valuable ideas about improving the quality of the performance. To whom can they talk? No one.

It would be the course of wisdom for our layman to take his pleasure at the ballet from his reasonably comfortable seat in front of the curtain in the auditorium. The motion-picture idea of back-stage life is somewhat rosy-hued. The atmosphere back stage at ballet, it is true, varies vastly, depending upon the company; but in the majority of cases it is heavy, murky, stifling.

Once more, to identify companies would be invidious, but from a wide familiarity with ballet companies I can say that there are companies I know where the back-stage atmosphere is permeated with a miasma of fear; companies where suspicion lurks tiger-like in every heart, suspicion of the management, suspicion of every other dancer, suspicion of the stage-manager, the stage-hand, knowing full well that any unguarded phrase, exclamation, or sentence is certain to be repeated in other quarters, embroidered upon, and that sad and serious repercussions are bound to follow.

There is another company within my knowledge where complete cynicism sits enthroned; a company where the dancers are so used to seeing all their hopes of giving decent performances thwarted that they habitually conceal their real feelings beneath a leering mask of horseplay and sophisticated leg-pulling.

Yet another company exists in a state of almost continuous depression induced not only by the management's penny-pinching and downright dishonesty, but by the fact that year after year they are doomed to go the unending round of the country, coast to coast, grinding out the same old, tired ballets, knowing them to be badly performed, abominably staged. The net result, so far as the dancers are concerned, is apathy.

Against all this, for the layman's enthusiastic daughter, there is always latent in her breast the possibility of a satisfactory reward. The lodestar for which she searches in her heart is the chance to come on the stage as something other than an impersonal member of the anomalous and nearly anonymous *corps de ballet;* in other words, in a role which gives her a real opportunity, and with it a chance to exert a spell which is enchanting alike to her and to the audience. It is this hope, springing eternal, that keeps the dancer going through the weeks, months, perhaps years of heartbreak and drudgery.

Now there is also a managerial point of view and a managerial side to this picture. Not to present this side fairly, even if briefly, would be manifestly unfair. Until that fortunate day when American companies are permitted the benefits of federal subsidy, the managerial budget—impossible to balance—must be considered. These budgets must necessarily vary considerably, depending upon any number of things, among them the size of the company, the nature and type of its productions, its standards, its bookings, the extent of its seasons.

Quite apart from the dancers' salaries, there is the orchestra. A touring orchestra of sufficient size can run from $8,000 to $9,000 weekly, exclusive of conductors' salaries. Extra rehearsals can substantially increase this figure. There is the stage crew, including wardrobe. The union requires a minimum of three of the former and two of the latter. A large ballet company carries from eight to ten, and sometimes as many as twenty-five to thirty additional men have to be engaged locally for each performance; a company manager and advance manager, together with the costs of publicity, advertising, printing of posters and folders, have to be added.

Some of this latter expense may be shared by the theater manager who engages the company. This local engagement is sometimes on the basis of a guaranteed sum to the ballet manager or impresario, sometimes on a shared percentage of the gross takings. But whatever the arrangements, the manager's expenses are really enormous. Various arrangements are made between impresarios who handle some of the costs and ballet managements. One of the biggest items is transportation and this can be, and often is, gargantuan. Some idea of its size may be gathered when you realize the best of the companies on their tours go from coast to coast, with considerably more than one hundred people to be transported, in a special Pullman train with as many as seven sleeping-cars, six to seven large baggage cars for scenery, properties, electrical equipment, musical instruments, costumes, together with a dining-car and a lounge-car. The hauling of all the equipment from the train to the theater and back to the train each day is another expensive item.

Then the management has its salary account, its general running expenses, royalties for musical material, renewal of scenery and costumes from wear and tear and the ravages of the "road." The biggest cost of all, perhaps, is that of the production of new ballets. Impresarios and public expect at least three additions to the repertory annually. In the United States a new production may cost from $15,000 to $50,000. In this connection it must be remembered that, save in the case of a full-evening work (e.g., *Swan Lake, The Sleeping Beauty*) rarely if ever produced by an American company, a new ballet accounts for only one-third of the evening, for there must be at least two other works on the program. If the new work is not successful, it may be a complete and utter loss. If it happens to tickle the public's fancy and catch the general favor, it will require regular performances over several years to be able to pay its way, earn back its costs.

The picture is not a bright one and serves to point up the necessity for subsidy. I do not mean to suggest that some persons do not make money out of ballet; but it is seldom, if ever, the ballet management. There is always the battle of performing as long and as much as possible in order to keep the company of dancers intact; for, if the company "rests" or is without bookings for any extended length of time, the dancers disperse, find such jobs as they can, and others have to be recruited. No company can long exist artistically with a constantly changing personnel.

I have said that some people make money out of ballet. No one amasses a fortune and the risk is considerable. However, impresarios and agents prosper when the going is good. On the other hand, any money that may possibly be made by the ballet management must be immediately re-invested in new productions.

All of this affects the artistic picture; explains many of the shortcomings to be seen in present-day ballet production; explains perhaps, but does not excuse, the "corner-cutting" practiced by some ballet managements. If it does nothing else, it points up the vitality of ballet as an art in that it has been able to survive the hurly-burly of the long journey from the luxury courts of the princes to the raggle-taggle shuffling over the continents of the world in gypsy caravans. It also points up once again the necessity for subsidy.

)5(

The Technique of the Dancer

Much of our layman's pleasure at the ballet, however much the other elements contribute to his enjoyment, is bound to be derived from the dancers. It is through the dancers, very likely, he will have been introduced to ballet, and it is to be hoped that through watching them that it will be but the first step to friendship, perhaps love.

If only a grain of pleasure has been found in the first meeting, it will be well to cultivate the acquaintance assiduously. It could be that with repeated acquaintance one can be fairly bitten by love of it. After that it will keep its hold of itself. Indeed, it may become necessary to beware of adoring it too exclusively. In such an attachment, as in that to any other ideal, it is possible, dangerously possible, to become priggish. Ballet audiences are not without their prigs. If taste threatens to transcend an attitude of correctness and unconcern, it will then be time to remember that to pride oneself upon an exceptionally select and exclusive taste is itself a lapse from taste.

We come to something the layman's dancing daughter should be able to demonstrate far better than any writer is able to explain. Enjoyment of ballet performances is quite possible without a knowledge of its dancing technique. Nevertheless, appreciation on the part of the layman can be heightened by even an elementary grasp of its rudimentary base. More than that, a book of this kind cannot attempt.

The first shock to the layman who has been conscious of some steps is to be told that there are more than fourteen hundred of them. It may be slightly comforting to realize that all of them are based on and spring from one or another of the basic five positions shown at the end of this volume. They will strike you at first as being unnatural. The first protest of the non-ballet person is that ballet is unnatural. It is. But it is harmonious, whereas the "natural" movement often is not. The purpose of ballet technique is to give the outward appearance of lightness, ease, and consummate grace. The layman's dancing daughter will quickly inform him that she has had to learn how to walk, run, and jump all over again, quite differently from what she had learned in the nursery. The layman, if his life insurance premiums are fully paid up, might prove this to himself, in case he harbors any doubts, by trying a little leap into the air—just a little leap—from the fifth position noted in the back of this book, and landing in precisely the same position as that from which he leapt.

Examine these five positions for a moment, if you will. You will note that the feet are always "open." For "open," read "turned outward." This "turn-out" is the keystone of ballet technique and, once learned, it is not nearly as cumbersome as it appears to be. There are, as a matter of fact, prizefighters who have adopted such a stance. One of the most important things this "turn-out" does is to stabilize the dancer's equilibrium. This stabilization is accomplished through the distribution of the weight of the body equally on each foot, and, perhaps the most important for both dancer and fighter, enables them to dart to right or to left without that infinitesimal and otherwise unavoidable hesitation required for the shifting of weight.

Look now, if you will, at the fifth position. At first glance, it is the strangest of all of them. Yet, despite its strangeness, it is the one most often used both at the start of a movement or series of movements and at their conclusion. It is, in effect, almost a sort of punctuation. The advantages of these "turned-out" feet to the dancer are numerous. Among them is increase of the ability to move sideways and still be full-face to the audience. Another is the elimination of the danger of the ankles knocking together while performing the *entrechat,* which by this time our layman knows is that vertical leap in which the legs are quickly crossed and uncrossed, as quickly and as often as possible. Still another advantage in the fifth position is the virtue it has of serving as a pivot in making *pirouettes* (rapid turns) and in leaps.

Our layman is courting disaster if he too enthusiastically attempts the "turn-out" of the feet, for perfection in this is rarely attained until after years of twisting the pelvic joint quite out of shape. This is something which, if you will take the trouble to observe dancers closely, you will find has actually altered the dancer's figure.

A few of the most frequently used technical terms of ballet-dancing are in order. The layman is bound to be hearing a great deal of them at the ballet.

Having assimilated the five positions, let us then briefly consider the most frequently used of the technical steps and movements in classical ballet. These steps and movements are relatively the same for the girl dancer as for the boy, although the leaps of the male dancer are bound to have more breadth and greater vigor than those of his partner.

Perhaps one of the most common of all leaps is the *jeté.* Now there are *petit jetés* and *grand jetés,* signifying exactly what we expect. The word derives from the French *jeter:* to throw. The dancer literally throws himself forward, with, at the height of the *jeté,* the legs wide apart like an open scissors.

Another step, frequently used, is the *cabriole* (literally in French: a goat's leap). As a *pas* (step) it is a high-flying leap, and is executed much more often by the male dancer than by his female counterpart. It starts from what is known as the *plié* position (see illustration). From this position, the dancer takes a step forward, executes the *cabriole* rapidly, then lands on his left leg, which is bent as he lands, in order to cushion the shock of the fall. In an unbroken series of *cabrioles*, the dancer will take two further steps forward; then, flexing his left leg like a taut spring, will launch his right leg into the air and bring his left leg up beside it. It is at this point in the *cabriole* that legs and body should form an obtuse angle, which, if he remembers his geometry, the layman will know is greater than one and less than two right angles.

The *entrechat* has by this time become familiar, with its crossing and recrossing of the legs several times during the leap, with the arms held out sideways, finishing or landing in the *plié* position. The number of *entrechats*, depending of course on the number of crossings and recrossings, varies and is labeled accordingly: *entrechat quatre, cinq, six, sept, huit,* etc.

Coupled with the *entrechat*, related to it, and likewise used choreographically to express striking and violent emotions are the *sissones*. In simple terms, a *sissone* is a straight leap into the air, starting, of course, with the *plié*, going up with the right leg raised sideways, and with the arms above the head.

Another frequently used *pas* is the *brisé*. There are three types of *brisés*: the *brisé volé*, executed by throwing the right leg out to the side, as the left leg flickers towards it and touches it; it is then stretched out to the front, while the weight of the body is permitted to fall on the right leg. This latter movement is called the *brisé dessus*, and it is completed by the *brisé dessous*, which is actually the same movement in reverse, ending with the weight of the body falling on to the left leg. When they are executed cleanly and precisely, *brisés volés* give the impression of a fluttering bird.

Perhaps the *pirouette* is the movement most familiar to the layman. The word carries the association and connotation of grace and lightness. It is, of course, the movement in which the dancer literally turns herself into a top. A common (sometimes all too common) ballet movement, it is by no means one of the easiest when well done. In executing it, the dancer spins on one leg, while the other is either bent or raised. In order to retain her balance, the head and body must be held absolutely perpendicular. If you will watch carefully, you will note that at the beginning of the *pirouette* the dancer will extend her arms outward. This is to help her gain momentum for the spin. As the speed increases she draws the arms inwards, only to extend them again to assist in her balance.

These are but a few of the more common *pas* or steps leading into movements, which form the vocabulary of the classical dance, sometimes called the *danse d'école*.

Quite apart from the classroom training in these steps and movements until, like a musician's scales, they become a matter of second nature to the dancer, the uses to which they are put in ballet is a matter for the choreographer and what he has in his mind; for the same step or movement can be utilized to express widely varying emotions. For example, a turn in mid-air can express violently contrasted emotional states, ranging from hatred, despair, rage, to happiness, joy, glee. Take, for example, a scene calling for a battle. The dancers are not furnished with lethal weapons. Rather is it the joint task of the choreographer and the dancers with whom he is working to create the balletic-theatrical illusion of a battle by the use of the technique of ballet, utilizing the leaps, the *cabrioles* and *entrechats* we have mentioned.

Later we shall consider the story element in ballet, but in connection with the technique of the dancer it should be obvious that the plot element in ballet is limited to a certain extent by the technique itself. It is for that reason that the conventional classical ballet follows a fairly conventional formula.

The rising curtain will reveal the stage filled with the *corps de ballet*. The choreographer, realizing the necessity for setting the stage, is manoeuvering to build up the proper atmosphere for introducing the leading figures of the work and to commence the business of performing purely narrative dancing.

In the strictly classical ballets (*Giselle, Swan Lake, The Sleeping Beauty*), there are the *corps de ballet* dances; there are *varia-*

tions—and for *"variations,"* read "solos"—*pas de deux* (duets), *pas de trois* (trios), *pas de quatres* (quartets), etc., which serve in the ballet to mark a pause and perform much the same purpose as do the arias and concerted numbers in opera; namely, they emphasize and underline, italicize as it were, emotions and sentiments. The strictly classical ballet can deal admirably with spectacle and emotion; it is more difficult for it to be successful in transmitting themes or ideas. For that reason there has come into being with the development of ballet the freer and, in a sense, more expressive theater ballet.

Classical ballet—and to many people this is the only form, being a synonym for ballet—is an ideal form for expressing deep emotions, usually violent; for it is frequently a spectacle in which one emotional climax on another's heels doth tread.

If our layman's daughter has a speaking acquaintance with a dancer of position, a soloist, let us say, or even a ballerina, it might be of interest to know the reply, should daughter inquire of her friend how much and how many of these emotions she feels when dancing a great classical role. Does the Swan Queen suffer pangs of despair and remorse at being separated from her princely lover? The chances are that, if she is honest, the ballerina will reply that she simply does not have time to feel. The things the ballerina does so beautifully, so elegantly, so feelingly—when she executes a thrilling *arabesque,* leaning far forward, with one lovely leg straightened and stretched out behind her in the very picture of longing, melancholy, tenderness—it is very likely that her mind is acutely concerned with something quite different. It is quite likely that she is thinking less of steps and position, less of the emotions of the part, than she is of being able to follow the music. She is trying to remember not to lower her head (which would suggest to the audience that she was looking for a dropped pin). She is also trying to remember not to lift her head too high (which would suggest to the audience that she was feeling utterly superior to them). She is remembering not to clench her fingers, something that could serve only to reveal tension and would serve also to break the line of the *arabesque.* She is trying to remember a hundred and one other little things.

It is only through the as nearly as possible perfect execution of the vocabulary of the classical dance that the dancer can expect to move the audience.

It cannot be too much stressed that *all* dancers—beginners, members of the *corps de ballet,* soloists, ballerinas—all must go through long daily sessions of training, periods of mental concentration and physical exercise which take so much out of them that there are times when the lesson, however much the dancers are dedicated to the dance, can become an almost intolerable form of torture.

Save when a ballet company is on tour, when, in most cases, lessons have to be given on the draughty stage at those times when it is not occupied by the staff in putting up or taking down and changing scenery, or in the conduct of a light rehearsal, lessons are given in a room as large as is available. Along the sides of the room runs a wooden rail or *barre.* The other walls have full-length mirrors fixed in them.

The dancers and the ballerinas—now all pupils, all equal—are assembled. One is struck by the general good looks of the girls; a certain handsomeness about the men; one is also conscious of a general level of height. None is too tall. Rarely is there to be found a ballerina more than five feet four inches. Many of them, however tall they may seem from one's seat in the orchestra stalls, are considerably less. One is impressed by the fact they are all seemingly well-built. They have spent long and arduous hours learning how to stand still, how to hold their heads, how to hold their arms. The result is an air of general, overall elegance. In the development of ballet, the stocky girl with bulging calves and muscular thighs has disappeared (largely as the result of a different type of training) and one is now likely to find that the dancers' arms and legs are longer than the average. This latter is particularly true of American dancers, and it may be due also in some degree to orange juice in childhood.

The spectator will have been given a chair against the wall, possibly in a corner near the piano, so as not to obstruct the view the dancers have of themselves in the mirror. The pupils, having been poured into their oldest tights, the room is permeated with the pungent odor of stale sweat, as they begin the lesson. They take their places at the *barre d'appui*, the railing support that is attached to three sides of the room. Grasping the *barre* with one hand, the free arm is outstretched like a wing, turning one foot in one direction, the other opposite . . . and the class is on. The piano, frequently out of tune, crashes out a lively melody for the limbering-up exercises. . . .

They commence with the five positions, those basic five positions that are the foundation of ballet movement. Herein lies the rock-bed base of all dancing, helping to keep the body upright during everything that follows. The first position is used mainly as an exercise for balance; the second position is used merely at the beginning and at the end of a few movements; the third position is often used at the end of a leap; the fourth is actually a transition position, and is utilized in certain types of *jetés* and in *pirouettes;* while the fifth is the most commonly used of all of them.

There are, it should be remembered, corresponding positions of the arms, and these, when performed correctly, add beauty to each step. They also assist the dancer in gaining momentum and in retaining balance. In a "preparation" for a *pirouette,* for example, six positions of the arms are used, and they may be used with any of the foot-positions. Sometimes two arm-positions are combined; for example, before executing the *pirouette* I have mentioned, by a dancer holding one arm in the first position (as noted in the appendix) and the other arm in the second position.

The class continues. Every pupil is equally serious as he and she bend down, straighten up, throw their legs in front of them and behind, trace wide circles on the floor with the very tips of their toes, arch their backs, wave their arms in undulating ripples, grab firm hold of a leg and raise it vertically in the air, and stand up on one toe with one leg tucked under like nothing so much in the world as a heron.

This limbering-up is an obligatory part of every daily ballet lesson. The dancer bends her body backwards and forwards alternately in what are called *cambrés* (from the French verb, *camber:* to arch, to bend, to curve). The describing of circles on the floor with each foot in turn, develops the stomach muscles, at the same time making the hips supple. Also at the *barre* is done the *developpé* in which one leg is raised with the knee bent; this is a step the dancer is likely often to use in a *pas de deux*. If the raised leg is extended behind the body, it is called a *developpé en arrière,* which, in simple language, is an *arabesque* executed with one hand on the *barre*. Lastly come the *battements* —raising and lowering of the outstretched leg—excellent practice for the hips and the sense of balance.

Approximately fifteen minutes are spent in these exercises. By that time the class is warmed up, and there comes a brief pause at the end of the exercises at the *barre*. But our layman will note that not one of them sits down during this break. It is not permitted. To be seated would be to soften the muscles and compel the dancers to return to the *barre* again for more stretching. Rather do they wipe their dripping faces and necks, while they lean against the wall, crossing and uncrossing their pointed feet the while, like flashing rapiers.

A hand-clap from the teacher, ballet-master, whoever is in charge. A sharp "In the center, please!" and they are now in the middle of the room, ready for the next part of the lesson, which consists of the arm movements and the various steps as called out by the teacher. At the end of the break that has just finished, the girls changed their soft shoes for their *pointes*.

These *pointes* are now a commonplace of ballet. They were anything but that when they were introduced into the romantic ballet in the early nineteenth century. The men, of course, do not wear *pointes,* and while their partners work at *pirouettes* and other turns, they concentrate on their more masculine leaps.

The barrage of correction and criticism is unceasing:

"Those arms! Those arms! Stop flapping your arms!" (As I have pointed out, there is an arm movement corresponding to every leg movement; but, while it is human to synchronize arms and legs, it is necessary oftentimes for the dancer to move his head and arms a shade behind his legs.)

"Gloria, drop your instep!" (When a dancer executes an *entrechat*, she must remember to keep her knees out and, as she crosses and uncrosses her legs in mid-air, she must also remember to keep her feet pointing downwards.)

"Raise that leg higher!" (Every movement must be executed full-out.)

"Don't raise that leg so high!" (Ballet is not a matter of music-show high-kicking.)

In America and France, to a lesser degree perhaps in Great Britain, ballet companies and ballet teachers are a polyglot lot, with a distinct hangover still of Russian teachers and ballet-masters. As a result, the room may from time to time reverberate to a drumfire of epithets as impressive to our layman as they are incomprehensible. From out of the mixed Russian and incomprehensible English there may emerge a few words that are understandable, such as *cabriole* or *entrechat* or *pirouette*. These words bob to the surface and are intelligible because the technical language of ballet has remained French; and the dancers of any country—Italy, France, Russia, Scandinavia, England, America —can make themselves understood in ballet by the use of the balletic language common denominator.

The criticism in class is often merciless and, since in class a dancer, whatever the rank, is always a pupil, the dancers accept this criticism without flinching and with a "thank you." And our layman will observe that as they work, their eyes never leave the mirror. This is not because of what the psychologists in their jargon might call a "Narcissus Complex," but because only by steadily regarding themselves in the mirror will they know how they look to their audiences.

The lesson drives on, continues without break or respite. A dancer may bend down for an instant to adjust a shoe-ribbon; a man may pause for a second or two to hitch up his tights, mop his brow with a towel that has been draped over the *barre*. But in another instant both are back in the midst of it. Then, when it seems the breaking-point has long since passed, the dancers drenched with sweat, the air in the room unbearable with its heavy sweat-scented atmosphere, one and all seemingly tottering at the very end of the rope, the lesson comes to an end. Two hours of dancing are the equivalent of a full day's work of ditch-digging.

When a dancer flies across the floor of the room in, let us say, three long strides and then leaps to the ceiling where he appears to hang suspended indefinitely before he descends, when a soloist or ballerina spins on her *pointes* 'and executes a perfect series of *fouettés,* pirouetting on one leg as she folds and unfolds the other, using the leg not unlike a propeller, then our layman will begin to understand, perhaps, why ballet is a lyrical art. One tawdry little tune clanking out of the untuned piano suddenly takes on the aspect of noble music. As he watches, our layman will discover that each gesture is so precise and well done that it seems inevitable and could not be otherwise.

The company's leading ballerina in her oldest tights, a bandanna wound round her head, moves to the center and does what everyone else has been doing. Suddenly she is transformed into a goddess who seems to fly rather than walk. At the cost of a thousand tricks of the trade, a thousand groaning, aching muscles, and a thousand pairs of shoes, worn, blackened, and burnt out by her effort, she has become the very incarnation of beauty.

Has it all been worth it? To the ballerina it has. And now I must return to a fact I mentioned earlier. Our ballerina who has transformed herself, who has become before our eyes in this dingy room the incarnation of beauty, will not remain this for long. Her hard, grinding career is terribly short. The greatest of them dance under a cloud, condemned in advance to early oblivion. Exceptions only prove the rule.

How young should a child commence the study of ballet? Not until the small feet bones are thoroughly "set." A child can, in most cases, begin her first lessons at eight years of age. By the time she is twelve, her entire body is "set"; that is to say, her muscles are already those of a dancer; by eighteen she has solved the problems of ballet's basic technique and is ready to combine technique with expression. From eighteen to thirty she is in her prime. She has her own individual style, it is to be hoped. She is in possession of her own conception of beauty. So far as vigor and precision are concerned, she has reached her peak.

Then comes that indeterminate period, from thirty to forty, during which she will still be able to remain in perfect physical condition and even, by dint of hard and unremitting work, polish her technique. Indubitably, she is certainly more of a master of her art than she was at eighteen. But sooner rather than later her muscles will begin to betray her. With a few widely isolated exceptions, the ballerina past forty is old, even though she may still be a vibrantly beautiful and genuinely attractive woman. Her muscles may still be supple, but each day they give way bit by bit, more and more.

What is her future? There is always the possibility of teaching, although the dancer who looks forward to a teaching career is rare indeed. It is not a happy future unless one is temperamentally suited to pedagogy.

But—and this is one of the greatest justifications of classical ballet—no dancer and no ballerina I have ever known would ever abandon his or her life of hard labor, even though they know during every minute they dance that their careers as artists performing in public can be nothing more, at best, than the dazzling flight of a shooting star.

)6(

Choreography and Choreographers

We have considered the dancer, the composer, the conductor. What is it all three combine to interpret? It is, of course, the choreography: the design of the ballet. Dancing is not ballet. The dancer does the bidding of the choreographer, that creator I attempted to define earlier.

Under the guidance of the choreographer (who must never be confused with the ballet-master, who drills and polishes technique), the dancer passes from steps to the fulfillment of a specific artistic function: becomes an element in a design, a note in a complicated and involved score.

Earlier I pointed out that the choreographer's basic function is to design and arrange the dances and the dancers in terms both of movement and drama. The word "choreographer" is often rather loosely used. Any reasonably competent dancer can arrange a dance or a group of dances, drawing upon the knowledge gained along the balletic classroom road. Such has become the common usage of the word "choreographer" that we find it applied to those who set the simplest and most banal sort of "routines" for vaudeville acts, cabarets, cheap revues, and even school graduating exercises.

In a sense, the choreographer is a sculptor, whose concern is with the single figure in its relation to the group. He is also a painter in that he is concerned with foreground, background, and all the space in between. But, on the other hand, unlike sculptor and painter, the choreographer is not dealing with static plaster or stone or bronze groups. It is the choreographer's task, not only to assemble and arrange groups, but to move them from grouping to grouping, to make the movement significant. Ballet can never be static. It is in arranging *movement* that the greatest skill is required. In addition to skill, great knowledge is essential. Even more than that, the greatest quality required in a choreographer is imagination.

It may be helpful to consider the choreographer's task in a series of progressions. This will involve the use of a few technical ballet terms, most of which speak for themselves, but all of which will be found in the glossary at the back of this volume. First, there is the *pas seul,* a dancer dancing alone; second, the *pas de deux,* with two dancers performing different steps and movements. We are now entering the field of choreographic movement, for a *pas de deux* can be a miniature ballet, to be found on many ballet programs. This can be extended and developed almost indefinitely: *pas de trois, pas de quatre, pas de cinq, pas de six,* etc.

Thus, the final stage in choreography is reached with the assembling of all these various *pas* and mass movements into that vast and complex dramatic structure that is a ballet. In order to do this, first of all the choreographer must have a theme. In the exploitation of the theme on which he finally decides he must determine upon a set of characters who react to each other.

How is this theme chosen? It may be suggested by almost anything under the sun. It could be a musical composition; it could come from an episode in a play or a novel; it could come from a poem, a short story, a painting, a legend. There are choreographers who find their themes in a choreographic problem, in terms of movement alone.

In the days of the Russian Imperial Ballet, it was by no means uncommon for a professional writer to work out a literary libretto or scenario in collaboration with the choreographer, in much the same manner as screen and television writers today devise scripts in collaboration with directors. This practice has more and more been discontinued until today the method is practically in the discard. One of the most potent reasons for this is that writers today usually lack the special kind of knowledge required for the creation of ballet scenarios and, I am sorry to say, as ballet today is constituted, they have no way of acquiring that familiarity with the subject that can only come from experience. On the other hand, in today's ballet practice, it is not unusual for a ballet theme to be a composite product of choreographers, directors, managers, composers, and even designers of scenery and costumes.

The choreographer's next step in the creation of a ballet goes back to a question put earlier: whether the music is to be chosen from existing music or is to be an original commissioned score. If the determination is on existing music, it is more than likely that the structure of the ballet will to some extent be dictated by the music's form. Should the music chosen, for example, be a complete symphony (such as the Tchaikowsky, *Les Présages*; Brahms, *Choreartium*; Berlioz, *Fantastic Symphony*, by Leonide Massine), or a symphonic poem (Franck, *Symphonic Variations*, by Frederick Ashton), the music will dictate the complete structure of the balletic work.

If the musical work selected is to be a commissioned composition, there devolves upon the choreographer the necessity for breaking down the overall movement of the ballet he has in mind into separate scenes, which are later joined or linked together, forming a definite pattern of development, together with contrasts. As rehearsals proceed, it may be found necessary to toss out some incidents, even together with some characters, found to be superfluous, or which may not suit the style of the work as he has envisioned it, or which may not be capable of interpretation by the dancers with whom he is working, because of the latter's talents and training. He may have to replace the discarded incidents and characters with others more suitable.

Then comes the work to which I referred earlier, the necessity for the choreographer to work out each scene in terms of dancers for one, two, or more groups of various sizes, soloists with groups, always seeing the whole, with an awareness of the general development, being meticulous to be sure to provide proper contrasts. Working with and setting the general plan on dancers, the choreographer is now in a position to make his requirements clear to the commissioned composer, and as the music is written the choreographer is able to continue with his creation.

By this time the rehearsals are in full swing, with the choreographer inventing the rhythmic dance patterns to convey the ideas, the individuality of the characters, their emotions, their actions. We have seen that classically trained dancers have learned a wide variety of steps in the classroom. Carefully and judiciously the choreographer will select and use these steps in *enchaînements* (the linking of one step and movement with another), using them in appropriate combinations to indicate different moods, conflicting emotions. The classical vocabulary having its limitations, frequently the choreographer is obliged to go afield from the purely classical technique and vocabulary and invent new combinations of steps and movements, giving expression to a new field, the field of the "free" dance, and sometimes using adaptations of the mood, spirit and style of the folk dance.

In addition, the choreographer must bear in mind the relation of all the movements to the geometry of the stage. I have mentioned the choreographer as both a sculptor and a painter, with attributes of each; but the choreographer's plastic sense, unlike that of the painter and the sculptor, must extend in time as well as in space. His musical sensitivity and sensibility should equal that of the orchestra conductor.

If the choreographer is gifted with a pedagogic talent, so much the better. It is essential that the choreographer be a knowledge-ful theater man, sensitive to and aware of theater techniques, especially stage lighting. He should be, or at one time have been, a dancer, for unless he is able to dance, how can he demon-strate how he wants the various roles danced?

Obviously, it is essential that the choreographer worth the price of his ballet shoes be a man of varied talents. And, of course, we have not even mentioned the important matter of taste and its importance.

It should also be fairly obvious to our layman that so-called "classical" ballet is not, by any means, the whole of dancing. I have tried to avoid the use of hard and fast definitions since they have a way of limiting through their very preciseness. But as close as I should care to come to a definition of ballet would be to say that it is a scientific development of popular dancing, in much the same manner that "classical" music is a scientific development of "popular" music, and by "popular" music I do not mean jazz but rather folk music. There are, of course, many different styles of dancing; but they are not within the province of this book. Suffice it to say that the technique of classical ballet, when it is properly understood, is capable of every type of movement.

The layman with an alert eye will observe back bends, astonish-ing leaps and falls, jazz movements (the Jerome Robbins ballet, *Fancy Free,* is a remarkably fine ballet utilizing a good deal of the jazz idiom); movements that are both "turned in" and "turned out," Spanish rhythms involving heel-and-toe movements; Rus-sian cossack dances; the hoe-down of the American Western plains (Agnes de Mille's *Rodeo*). The point is that there are really no limitations to the choreographic scope of ballet or to its infinite variety.

The choreographic art can and does wander far afield. In the dramatic theater ballet has had an historical place. Molière, in producing and staging his own plays, very often included elaborate ballets. Opera and ballet have been linked in collabora-tion for centuries, although in American opera houses ballet has until very recently been treated as a sort of Cinderella sister and still has a long way to go before it exists other than as merely an interlude in which the corpulent singers may regain their breath. Throughout Europe the State Operas and Opera Houses include the State Ballets. In Great Britain, at the Royal Opera House, Covent Garden, the Sadler's Wells Ballet plays to larger audiences than does the opera. So important and vital has ballet been to opera that composers (Wagner being but a single example), who failed to include one in the operatic score, were forced to write one and insert it between the acts, if necessary.

With the recrudescence of ballet interest in America, ballet as an art and entertainment had its roots exclusively embedded in an international form and was exclusively international. It was the style and form loosely called Russian Ballet. As time went on, something in the way of an indigenous native style developed, with its roots still firmly rooted in the classical tradition, but with something added that was essentially different. As ballet developed and public interest in it grew, ballet in one form or another began to find other outlets and spread into fields other than the theater, thus drifting into the consciousness of those who had no ideas about ballet and were, as a rule, uninterested in ballet.

The musical comedy and revue theater had had its too familiar and completely routinised chorus-line. There was a great deal of dancing but of a strictly formalized pattern. The change came as the result of a single musical comedy, *Oklahoma!*, for which, as the direct result of her ballet, *Rodeo*, Agnes de Mille was engaged by Rodgers and Hammerstein in 1943 to stage the dances in what turned out to be a new type of musical comedy dance. It signaled the entry of the genuine choreographer into the musical comedy field. Its success is a matter of theatrical history, an experiment that came off. The attempt was to create a new theatrical style in which dialogue, dancing, and singing become integral parts of the whole, each element used to carry on the dramatic story. In *Oklahoma!* the action did not stop while singers sang and dancers danced.

The road thus opened by *Oklahoma!* led to many other musical pieces providing opportunities for the choreographer, who supplanted the "dance director." To mention a few; *Carousel* (Agnes de Mille); *Brigadoon* (Agnes de Mille); *High Button Shoes* (Jerome Robbins); *Finian's Rainbow* (Michael Kidd, a former Ballet Theatre dancer and choreographer); *Annie Get Your Gun* (Helen Tamiris, a non-balletic choreographer).

Much later, in the field of opera, the Metropolitan Opera House in New York, after a long period of balletic doldrums, began to take more than a perfunctory interest in ballet. Antony Tudor, the distinguished British choreographer, whose contributions to the repertory of Ballet Theatre are among that organization's most significant works, was engaged as opera choreographer for a season. Lack of opportunity resulted, however, in very little in the way of accomplishment. More recently, another former Ballet Theatre dancer, Zachary Solov, was engaged and given greater opportunities. A special ballet was ordered and created, a departure from Metropolitan Opera previous policy. *Vittorio,* to unfamiliar music by Verdi, its grandiose style certainly more operatic than balletic, was not a success, but the step was in the right direction. In addition, the Metropolitan engaged one of the world's great *ballerinas,* Alicia Markova, to appear as guest star in *Die Fledermaus,* and, more notably and appropriately, in a successful revival of Gluck's *Orpheus and Eurydice.* Subsequently, *Soirée* to the music of Benjamin Britten was less pretentious and more generally successful.

The spoken drama naturally provides less opportunity for ballet, but a recent (1954) notable, if controversial, example of ballet in drama was the London Old Vic's production of *A Midsummer Night's Dream,* with a great deal of emphasis on ballet, two dancers in the leading roles of Titania and Oberon, a large corps de ballet, the full Mendelssohn score, and extended ballet sequences, headed by Moira Shearer and Robert Helpmann, and choreographed by Helpmann and Frederick Ashton.

Many people unfamiliar with ballet have had their introductions to the art through the medium of the film. Here is one of the most potent media for ballet, and although there have been numerous films in which there has been a great deal of ballet of one sort or another, the surface, so to speak, has barely been scratched. There have been interesting experiments in dance movement in some of the Disney cartoons. Fred Astaire and Gene Kelly, remarkable dancers both, have made interesting contributions. George Balanchine choreographed a number of Hollywood films of not much artistic value. Two ballets from the repertory of the American Ballet Russe de Monte Carlo have been filmed, almost literally: Leonide Massine's *Gaité Parisienne* and *Capriccio Espagnol*. Filmed literally, save that they were tricked out with all sorts of motion picture "slick production values," they, as a result, succeeded in dissipating any feeling of ballet by the too frequent use of the "close up." It is a dancer's body that tells the story of a ballet, not a grotesque enlargement of his heavily made-up features.

Perhaps the motion picture that did most to awaken film audiences to an interest in ballet and choreography was the extraordinarily ambitious *Red Shoes*. In *Red Shoes* the choreographer was given as free a rein as possible in collaboration with the film director. There was a main ballet nearly twenty minutes in length, together with snippets of other familiar ballets, including *The Fantastic Toy-Shop, Coppélia, Les Sylphides,* and *Swan Lake,* and there were shots of ballet classroom training, but all too short. Despite its immense popularity, *Red Shoes* really did more harm than good to ballet. It is true it made the beautiful Sadler's Wells *ballerina,* Moira Shearer, into a household name; but so far as the film is concerned, a fine idea got lost somewhere before the film reached the public. A graphic illustration of the reaction to it may be found in a review of the film by Richard Whittington, in the London *News Chronicle,* from which the following excerpt will point up what I have in mind. The critic summed up the film as "an ambitious attempt at a great film subject—the tragedy of Diaghileff and Nijinsky—that falters into Technicolor magnificence. At first the film partakes of the authentic fantasy of backstage ballet; then the interpolated specially devised ballet occupies the screen for twenty minutes and clears it for a hackneyed plot to wind its way to a sticky end." The critic further describes the ballet as an "escape into the realms of Disney and the Hollywood dream sequence. Far from gaining by such license it becomes blurred by Technicolor, overpowered by *décor* and confused by its own fantasy. The Red Shoes ballet is an essay in complicated camera trickery for its own sake, assisted by some no more than adequate music and dancing."

In *Tonight We Sing,* the cinematic treatment of the life of S. Hurok, the impresario whose interest in ballet has been so influential in America, there was far too little use of ballet. A sequence purporting to re-create the magic of Pavlova's *The Dying Swan* did little enough for the balletic art.

Another ambitious British film, although principally dealing with an opera, *The Tales of Hoffmann,* utilized ballet and ballet talents to a considerable extent in the telling of the tales. The choreography was by Frederick Ashton. A distinguished pair of choreographer-dancers appeared in leading roles: Leonide Massine and Robert Helpmann. Two *ballerinas,* one English and one Franco-Russian, Moira Shearer and Ludmilla Tcherina, were leading figures on the distaff side. Over all presided the brilliant baton of Sir Thomas Beecham. A new technique in production was also tried: the complete score, orchestral and vocal, was recorded on film in advance. The picture then was made, beat for beat, note for note, to the reiterated play-back of the recorded music. To be sure, the final product was not without its short-comings, but it will remain a signpost on the route to the future.

There has existed in the vaults of Hollywood for some time, but never shown to the public, a film exclusively danced. It is *Invitation to the Dance,* a Gene Kelly creation; filmed for the greater part in Britain and France, it does not contain a single spoken word. It deals with movement, with dance in all its phases. An expensive production, it has been placed on the shelf by its makers, for reasons best known to themselves. I have not seen it; but an official of the producing company has told me he doubts it ever will be generally released. Eventually, he added, it may be shown in the so-called art cinemas in an effort to recoup some of the company's investment. Why? In the opinion of the official, the film marks too great a departure from the cinematic norm. It is too experimental. How they are able to determine the lack of public interest without permitting the public to decide for themselves, is one of those mysteries that make Hollywood the enigma it is.

Ballet has been used, of course, in many films. The French choreographer, Roland Petit, has choreographed sequences for popular films, among them the film biography of Hans Christian Andersen, the ballet being loosely based on Andersen's *The Little Mermaid,* with the greatly talented Danny Kaye. The British Arts Council has financed ballet documentary films. But the fact remains that our mammoth film producing companies lag woefully in realizing the possibilities of the motion picture as the means for an independent art. Balletic motion pictures have no language barriers; no necessity for "dubbed-in" translations or multi-lingual captioning. One day, it is to be hoped, a film magnate with a high heart and an open mind, together with an open purse, will appear over the horizon, and then there will be film ballets that will become a major branch of theatrical art.

However, even before that day arrives, there is an extremely practical use for film in ballet. There have been throughout the history of ballet attempts at some satisfactory system of notation for writing down the steps, movements, *enchaînements,* groupings of individual ballets. None devised has been entirely satisfactory. So choreography has for the greater part been a matter of memory, the handing on from generation to generation of what one or another dancer remembers. Memory being by no means infallible, even when a ballet is still in the repertory, it will often bear little resemblance to the intent of the original choreographer. A motion picture film of the work as the choreographer designed it and as it was originally danced under his direction is, obviously, extremely valuable. There can be no question that all important ballets should be filmed for this reason alone. So far as I know, only the leading choreographer, Leonide Massine, has taken the precaution to protect his works in this manner. Moreover, since choreographic copyright law is vague, the film affords some copyright protection.

Now we come to that most recent medium of mass entertainment, television.

The adaptability of television to ballet and vice versa is little short of remarkable. But, although dancers and, for the most part, lesser choreographic talents have found employment now and then in the medium, the balletic story on television is even sadder thus far than it has been on the motion picture screen.

Here is no case of lack of funds with which to experiment. Television in the United States from its inception was handed over to the same people who control radio, the same networks, the same stations, the same "sponsors." It is being used to the same ends that radio, with the exception of a few public-minded stations, is used. As a consequence, handled as it is by the broadcasters, the chances for experiment in television are slim.

One of television's chief objections to ballet is the hoary claim that it is the business of the people who run it to give the viewer what he wants. It seldom occurs to the myopic minds who control the medium and the advertising that pays for it that it might be an excellent idea to give the viewer a chance to want other things as well.

There are a few television programs worth a minute of one's time. The Ford Foundation *Omnibus* is one. There is presently going on a sort of half-hearted attempt to set up so-called "educational" television stations. At the moment, only one non-commercial station of which I know is making a serious, single-purposed attempt to cater to an adult audience. The rest provide an endless string of banalities for an audience with the intelligence of seven-year-olds. The station I have in mind is in Boston, where one might reasonably expect to find it. It is the only television station of which I know that has, in its planning and policy, an important place for the dance as an important and regular feature of its programing.

Television has shown a few isolated ballet programs. None

that I have seen has succeeded in revealing ballet at anything like its fullest and best, and none was fair either to television or to ballet. At various times television has shown snippets of *Les Patineurs,* a charming ballet based on a skating theme, by Frederick Ashton; a *pas de deux,* torn from the context of Ashton's *Homage to the Queen;* a twenty-minute program of unrelated snippets by the Sadler's Wells Theatre Ballet company; a one-hour telecast of the classic *Giselle,* in two acts. Strangely enough, the most successful telecast of ballet to swim before my eyes took place more than a decade ago when the Columbia Broadcasting Company televised the American ballet, *Billy the Kid,* with the Aaron Copland score and the choreography of Eugene Loring.

Late in 1955 the National Broadcasting Company used ninety minutes including annoying "commercials" for a "live" televising of a truncated *The Sleeping Beauty* by the Sadler's Wells Ballet. According to the "ratings," it was a tremendous success from the number of viewers of it. Artistically it had much to commend it. However, so timid was the approach of the televisers that it was felt necessary to surround the ballet with a banal tale involving trying children and an equally annoying motion-picture star "name." This handicap, to the surprise of no one except the television executives, the ballet overcame. Even in their pre-telecast announcements, the televisers avoided any emphasis on ballet and almost any mention of it. After its nation-wide success, ballet then was permitted to take precedence over hokum.

However, the limitations of the television tube and camera were obvious. The most successful scenes, television-wise, were those involving small groups of dancers. Large choreographic movements became a crowded blur. Is it not possible that the solution may be some sort of ballet expressly commissioned and designed for the limitations of the medium rather than an attempt to transfer the theater into the living room?

One day, in televising ballet, those in charge may learn that a dancer dances with his entire body, and they will not insist on moving the camera up for a close-up of head and bust; they will appreciate that the choreographer deals with patterns and will photograph this patterning rather than constantly singling out individuals and portions of individuals moving outside the context of the work itself.

The hope and future of all ballet, whatever the medium for its revelation and dissemination to the public, whether it be in its true theater home, or on film, or over television, lies with the choreographer. He must deal with the masterpieces, but at the same time he must constantly be looking forward with imagination. The choreographer must still create and it is our duty to find him an audience.

Coppelia.

Sainthill
Sadler's Wells Production
Swanilda 1st Ac

Costume Plate for "Coppelia"
Loudon Sainthill (1951)

Costume for "BILLY THE KID"
Jared French

ont *Curtain of* "THE FIREBIRD"
Mark Chagall

Photographed for The
Museum of Modern Art
by Sunami

Drop *Curtain for* "ROMEO AND JULIET"
Eugene Berman

Photographed for The
Museum of Modern Art

Backdrop of "EL CAFE DE CHINITAS"
Salvador Dali

Setting for "CUCKOLD'S FAIR"
Joan Junyer

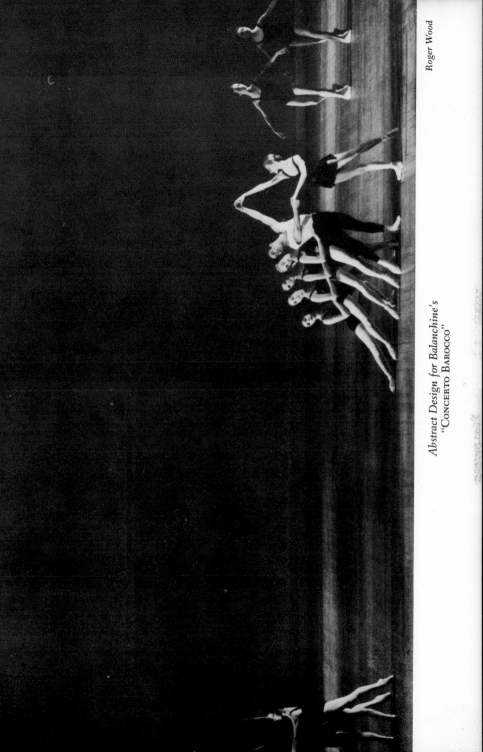

Abstract Design for Balanchine's "CONCERTO BAROCCO"

AGNES DE MILLE'S *Three Virgins and a Devil*
L. TO R. Eugene Loring, Agnes de Mille, Anabelle Lyons, Lucia Chase

Alfredo Valente

FOKINE'S *Les Sylphides*
Danced Before Thousands in a Sao Paulo Bull Ring

New York City Ballet in *Symphonie Concertante*
Abstract Ballet by Balanchine, Setting by Morcom

Le Blang

SADLER'S WELLS PRODUCTION OF *The Sleeping Beauty*
Margot Fonteyn and Michael Somes in Center

Décor

The combination of scenery and costumes in ballet is usually referred to as décor, a French word that has become Anglicized.

We have seen how it was necessary to get rid of the machinery, the stiffly brocaded dresses, the high-heeled shoes, the heavy wigs, the impeding masks, in costume. At the same time there was going forward the reform in music, coincidental with a reform in scenic investiture (as well as in costume) by abandoning the ornate and fussy Baroque constructions, which reveled in acres of arches and pillars and columns. The trend was in the direction of a naturalistic illusion.

It was a long row to hoe, however, since there was little or no collaboration between painters and choreographers, a state of things obviously necessary. Historically, another setback occurred in what is sometimes referred to as the "great" period of ballet in Russia, when ballet retrograded from the attempt at naturalistic illusion to a period of profuse architecture with costumes of sumptuous artificiality rather than of admirable simplicity. One of the most frequently recurring features of the enormous settings of this period of ballet development was the almost inevitable fountain, up stage center, or just off center. Often this was an extremely ornate affair and was piped with real running water.

The importance of scenery and costume to ballet is something that should not need to be stressed for the layman. That the general public will not go to "see" ballet, as that public would certainly put it, unless the ballets are beautifully staged, may be taken for granted.

That is, of course, true in the dramatic theater; and décor in ballet has always been rather closely attached to design in the theater of the spoken drama. Towards the end of the nineteenth century and early in the twentieth, a new form in theater design revolutionized the stage designs of Europe with the clean-breezed experiments of Gordon Craig, Appia, and others. Whatever their differences in approach, they had one common meeting-ground, namely, simplicity and the attempt to create the proper atmosphere. It was in the first decade of the present century in Russia that these influences began to be felt in ballet. A group of painters, through the influence of Serge Diaghileff (at that time in the executive department of the Imperial Theatres), were given opportunities to apply their ideas as painters to designing scenery and costumes. When Diaghileff left the Imperial Theatres and launched himself on a new course of presenting ballets for Western Europe, he commissioned these artists to do both scenic decorations and costumes. From this innovation in ballet came the names of distinguished painters whose influence on the entire structure and future of ballet was enormous. At least four of them must be noted.

Alexandre Benois may be said to have killed the traditional spectacular realism with his fine, delicate, and quite aristocratic refinement and his no less remarkable sense of period. One of his outstanding designs, realizations of which may be seen in ballet today, are those for *Petrouchka.*

Perhaps the most striking and arresting of the group was the extraordinarily versatile Léon Bakst, able to work in every school and style. One of the great world figures of stage design, as well as in easel painting, a genuine revolutionist, he should not be remembered by ballet-goers of the last half of the twentieth century exclusively for the richly erotic Orientalism of his setting and costumes for *Schéhérazade*. Bakst was a painter who succeeded in mastering the entire art of scenic design, having applied himself to the study of all the great designers who had preceded him. He was concerned with the *entire* stage picture. Backcloths were linked with floorcloths and groundcloths. Never, however, would he permit his scenic and costume creations, however opulent and colorful, to deteriorate into mere naturalism or realism, for he ever worked in that realm of fantasy that is so appropriate to ballet.

A third and much more austere painter was the Asiatic-Mongolian Nicholas Roerich, a primitive interested in the art of early Russia, whose masterpiece was the slumbrous barbarian camp of the Scythian nomads that is even today's evocative setting for the Fokine ballet, *Prince Igor*.

A married couple, Michel Larionov and Nathalie Gontcharova, completed the quintet of Russian painters gathered by Diaghileff. Both husband and wife, profoundly influenced by the peasant art of Russia, concentrated on the use of violent color contrasts, even carrying contrast too far until one risked not being able to see the choreography because of the brilliance of the scenery and costumes.

After Diaghileff took his Ballet away from Russia and made its permanent home in Western Europe, the opportunities for design were given to the most forward-looking painters of the time, chief among them being Georges Braque, Max Ernst, Henri Matisse, André Derain, Pablo Picasso. As ballet in America and Great Britain developed we have had in the United States the emergence of such painters in ballet as the Japanese Isamu Noguchi, the Russo-American Eugene Berman, the Spanish-American Joan Junyer, the native American Raoul Pène Du Bois, Irene Sharaff, the widely international Salvador Dali, the greatly talented and deeply lamented French Christian Bérard, the distinctly American Oliver Smith, and the Russo-American Boris Aronson.

Ballet Theatre's painters and designers have been notable. They include among others the British sisters who prefer to be known simply as Motley; the late Nicholas De Molas; the chic Marcel Vertès; the brilliantly controversial Marc Chagall; the traditional Russians: Nicholas Remisoff and Serge Soudeikine; the stylish British Cecil Beaton; the legitimate theater's American Lucinda Ballard and Jo Mielziner; and, among yet others, such diverse easel-painters as Chicago's Raymond Breinin and Moscow's exiled Mstislav Doboujinsky.

The New York City Ballet, through its various incarnations as Ballet Caravan, American Ballet, and Ballet Society, has, whenever their means have permitted, used distinguished contemporary painters and designers importantly. These include many mentioned before and in addition Stewart Chaney, Pavel Tchelitchew, Corrado Cagli, Kurt Seligman, Esteban Francés, David Ffolkes, Jean Lurçat, and, often working costume magic, Barbara Karinska.

The growth and development of British ballet has equally kept pace with the opportunities offered painters and designers in other countries, and has perhaps used them even more effectively as collaborators. As a matter of fact, design in ballet in England has been a noteworthy feature from the first. Having been exposed, for the most part, to the Diaghileff experiments, the English artists were already professionals in stage design. The early 1931-1935 designers for ballet included among others Duncan Grant, John Armstrong, Edmund Dulac, John Banting, Edward Burra and Vanessa Bell, Nadia Benois, Hugh Stevenson, William Chappell, Sophie Fedorovitch, Doris Zinkeisen, and, notably, Oliver Messel and Rex Whistler. Whistler had a rare talent for re-creating period atmosphere with contemporary material. Messel is a highly experienced designer with a magnificent knowledge of theatrical problems and their solution. Messel's best known balletic work is, of course, the truly remarkable settings and costumes for the Sadler's Wells production of *The Sleeping Beauty*.

Other distinguished designers for ballet in Britain include such

significant painters as Michael Ayrton; the American poster designer, E. McKnight Kauffer, Leslie Hurry, Roger Furse, Chiang
Yee, Graham Sutherland, Osbert Lancaster, and, by no means
least, John Piper.

These lists of noted painters compose, I believe, a representa-
tive cross-section of the important painters and designers who are
making distinguished and important contributions to ballet in our
time.

There are certain features of design that are requisites for the
artist-painter in the theater, in the preparation of scaled-up easel
paintings. These features, with balletic variations, are those common to all design for the theater. First, there must be kept pre-
eminently in mind the necessity for keeping the artists from
being swallowed up by the setting, for the setting must never
be an end in itself. A distinguished Anglo-American stage pro-
ducer and director once asserted to me that a setting, *any* setting,
was of value only for the first five minutes after the curtain had
risen and that it should be so essentially right that within five
minutes the audience would take it for granted and, to all intents
and purposes, would forget it.

This opinion is, as may be suspected, an over-simplification.
The setting and lighting must never obtrude, but must always
maintain and sustain the atmosphere and mood; setting, costumes
and lighting must not only do this but, at the same time, must
reflect the theme of the ballet in its own medium, as does the
choreographer's contribution. The three-walled realism of the
legitimate theater's setting for a drawing-room comedy, for example, must at all costs be avoided, if for no other reason than
the vast difference in subject matter and atmosphere of the drawing-room comedy and the freer imaginative qualities of ballet.

In costume design the balletic problem is intensified, for in
ballet the human body, its movements, and the varying qualities
of textile materials have to be taken into consideration. Yet, once
again, the painter-designer is compelled to reflect in his costume
designs not only the character being portrayed by the person who
is to wear the finished costume, but the atmosphere and period

of the ballet as well. At the same time the costume must be so designed as to give the greatest possible freedom to the wearer for the proper and reasonably easy performance of the movements the choreographer has devised. Unlike the designer of costumes for the dramatic theater, the designer of costumes for ballet always has to bear in mind that, whatever the period or style with which he is dealing, the dancer's legs should be revealed as much as possible, for it is through the lines delineated by the legs that is found the foremost means of expression.

Above all it is necessary that the painter, together with the dressmaker (and the latter is vastly important to the finished job, for there is good dressmaking and something less than good), must work not only in close collaboration but in close harmony with the choreographer; for each setting and every costume not only must aid in establishing atmosphere and style, but must, at all times, parallel the movement.

)8(

Must Ballet Tell a Story?

There is also a literary side to ballet. A school of thought, neither the most contemporary nor the most enlightened, places great stress on the "story" element in ballet. "What is it about?" they demand. "What is its story?"

I shall attempt to point out why this attitude is wrong. Yet the "story" idea as the basis for a ballet is one that stubbornly persists, and directors, managers, impresarios, choreographers, still receive manuscripts and literary ideas of every imaginable sort from well-intentioned persons. All of these have to be returned to the senders. Ballets usually grow from the inside out; rarely do they spring from extraneous ideas.

It was not always thus. The older ballets were heavy with story, the very earliest concerning themselves with mythology, the stage stalking with mythological figures, heavily weighted with gods and goddesses. The emergence of early romanticism brought heavily plotted tales in the Hoffmann manner, *Giselle* and *Coppélia* being outstanding examples. The latter is a Hoffmann tale dealing with the doll that comes to life; the former, by

Théophile Gautier, out of Heinrich Heine, has as its basic theme
the romantic but ever-so-cold Willis.

The gradual tendency from these literary sources was towards
the more purely fairy-tale, witness *Swan Lake* and *The Sleeping
Beauty*.

During the pre-Diaghileff days of ballet in Russia, there was
a firm insistence on plot and story, not always of the fairy-tale
variety. *La Esmeralda,* based on Victor Hugo's heavily plotted
The Hunchback of Notre Dame, was a pillar of the repertory of
the Imperial Theatres. A recent British revival of it served to
point up its dullness, and when it was imported to the North
American continent the overall effect, in the second half of the
twentieth century, was such as to excite the risibilities of the audience. The long four-act work was quickly truncated to one act
only, devoid of plot implications and concerning itself with dancing of considerable variety.

This ballet and a substantial number of others are representa-
tive of the period of ballet decadence that characterized the last
half of the nineteenth century. Many of them bore pretentiously
"literary" names; a few will suffice as examples: *The Hunch-
Backed Horse, The Daughter of Pharaoh, Cinderella, King
Candule, The Talisman, La Bayadère, The Vestal* (the last a
frequently recurring idea).

The change in values in ballet, literary as in most others, came
with Diaghileff and Fokine. The literary element became either
much slighter, or, founded on character, became more concentrated and more intensely dramatic, depending upon the theme.
The basic story of *Petrouchka* is perhaps the most conspicuous
example of the Diaghileff revolution in story and scenario.

Later, after a period of utilizing Russian legends (*The Firebird*), came Leonide Massine, concentrating for a time on the
grotesque, with such enduring works as *Pulcinella, The Three-
Cornered Hat, The Good-Humored Ladies, The Fantastic Toy-
Shop*.

More recently, the tendency has been towards less and less
"literature," and again one goes back to the Diaghileff revolution,

for, according to his system, modern ballet is not based on a written libretto or scenario or story, in the sense that a "story" dictates the form of the ballet. The point is that it is more often than not based on the vaguest sort of idea that springs from anywhere, anyone. The idea, once dropped on fertile ground, develops, stirs, takes on form in the collaboration of composers, conductors, painters, choreographers.

It is true that many ballets (and, one may say, most opera) have been shackled with bad librettos. Diaghileff knew this. As an example of a method used, first in the early Diaghileff period, and one of a later date, I can think of no finer illustrations than the *Rite of Spring, Petrouchka,* and *Apollo:* three balletic masterpieces by Igor Stravinsky. It will be simpler to tell the story of the conception of these three works in the composer's own words, from his biographical work, *Chronicle of My Life**: "One day, when I was finishing the last pages of *The Firebird* in St. Petersburg, I had a fleeting vision which came to me as a complete surprise . . . I saw in my imagination a solemn pagan rite: sage elders, seated in a circle, watched a young girl dance herself to death. They were sacrificing her to propitiate the god of spring. Such was the theme of the *Rite of Spring*. I must confess that this vision made a deep impression on me, and I at once described it to my friend Nicholas Roerich, he being a painter who had specialized in pagan subjects. He welcomed my inspiration with enthusiasm, and became my collaborator in this creation. In Paris I told Diaghileff about it, and he was at once carried away by the idea, though its realisation was delayed. . . .

"Before tackling the *Rite of Spring,* which would be a long and difficult task, I wanted to refresh myself by composing an orchestral piece in which the piano would play the most important part—a sort of *Konzertstück*. In composing the music, I had in my mind a distinct picture of a puppet, suddenly endowed with life, exasperating the patience of the orchestra with diabolical cascades of *arpeggi*. The orchestra in turn retaliates

---

* *Chronicle of My Life.* Igor Stravinsky. London: Victor Gollancz Ltd. 1936.

with menacing trumpet-blasts. The outcome is a terrific noise
which reaches its climax and ends in the sorrowful and querulous
collapse of the poor puppet. Having finished this bizarre piece, I
struggled for hours, while walking beside Lake Geneva, to find a
title which would express in a word the character of my music
and consequently the personality of this creature.

"One day I leapt for joy. I had indeed found my title—
Petrouchka, immortal and unhappy hero of every fair in all countries. Soon afterwards Diaghileff came to visit me at Clarens,
where I was staying. He was much astonished when, instead of
the sketches for the *Rite of Spring*, I played him the piece which
I had just composed and which later became the second scene of
Petrouchka. He was so much pleased with it that he would not
leave it alone and began persuading me to develop the theme of
the puppet's sufferings and make it into a whole ballet . . . We
worked out together the general lines of the subject and the plot
in accordance with ideas which I suggested. We settled the scene
of the action: the fair, with its crowd, its booths, the little
traditional theater, the character of the magician, with all his
tricks; and the coming to life of the dolls—and their love tragedy,
which ends with Petrouchka's death. I began at once to compose
the first scene of the ballet. . . .

"I was terribly anxious about the fate of *Petrouchka*, which
had at all costs to be ready for Paris in the spring . . ." There
was an interval of illness. Stravinsky continues: "Fortunately I
recovered my strength sufficiently to enable me to finish my work
in the ten weeks which remained before the beginning of the
season."

Stravinsky went to Rome where the Diaghileff Ballet was giving performances. "There," he continues, "*Petrouchka* was rehearsed, and there I finished the last pages." The company proceeded from Rome to Paris, where *Petrouchka* was to have its
first performance. "At the dress rehearsal at the Châtelet, to which
the Press and the élite of the artistic world had been invited, I
remember that *Petrouchka* produced an immediate effect on
everyone in the audience with the exception of a few hypercritics.

One of them—it is true it was a literary critic—actually went up to Diaghileff and said: 'And it was to hear this that you invited us!' 'Exactly,' replied Diaghileff. It is only fair to add that later on the celebrated critic, to judge by his praise, seemed to have forgotten this sally. . . .

"And now for the *Rite of Spring*. . . .

"As I have already said, when I conceived the idea, immediately after *The Firebird*, I became so much absorbed in the composition of *Petrouchka* that I had no chance even to sketch preliminary outlines. After the Paris season, I returned to Oustiloug, our estate in Russia, to devote myself entirely to the *Rite of Spring*.

"Although I had conceived the subject of the *Rite of Spring* without any plot, some plan had to be designed for the sacrificial action. For this it was necessary that I should see Roerich . . . I joined him, and we settled the visual embodiment of the *Rite* and the definite sequence of its different episodes . . . In composing the *Rite* I had imagined the spectacular part of the performance as a series of rhythmic mass movements of the greatest simplicity which would have an instantaneous effect on the audience, with no superfluous details or complications such as would suggest effort. The only solo was to be the sacrificial dance. The music of that dance, clear and well-defined, demanded a corresponding choreography—simple and easy to understand. . . ."

Thus the "literary" background in two great ballets. As for the third, many years later, let Stravinsky again tell the story: ". . . I was asked by the Washington Congressional Library to compose a ballet for a festival of contemporary music, which was to include the production of several works specially written for the occasion. The generous American patron, Mrs. Elizabeth Sprague Coolidge, had undertaken to defray the expense of these artistic productions. I had a free hand as to subject and was only limited as to length, which was not to exceed half an hour by reason of the number of musicians to be heard in the available time. This proposal suited me admirably, for, as I was more or less free just then, it enabled me to carry out an idea, which had long tempted me, to compose a ballet founded on movements or episodes in Greek mythology plastically interpreted by dancing of the so-called classical school.

"I chose as theme Apollo Musagetes, that is to say as master of the Muses, inspiring each of them with her own art. I reduced their number to three, selecting from among them Calliope, Polyhymnia, and Terpsichore as being the most characteristic representatives of choreographic art. Calliope, receiving the stylus and tablets from Apollo, personifies poetry and its rhythm; Polyhymnia, finger on lips, represents mime. As Cassidorus tells us: 'Those speaking fingers, that eloquent silence, those narrations in gesture, are said to have been invented by the Muse Polyhymnia, wishing to prove that man could express his will without recourse to words.' Finally, Terpsichore, combining in herself both the rhythm of poetry and the eloquence of gesture, reveals dancing to the world, and thus among the Muses takes the place of honor beside the Musagetes.

"After a series of allegorical dances, which were to be treated in the traditional classical style of ballet (*Pas d'action, Pas de deux, Variations, Coda*), Apollo, in an apotheosis, leads the Muses, with Terpsichore at their head, to Parnassus, where they are to live ever afterwards. I prepared this allegory with a prologue representing the birth of Apollo. According to the legend, 'Leto was with child, and, feeling the moment of birth at hand, threw her arms about a palm-tree and knelt on the tender green turf, and the earth smiled beneath her, and the child sprang forth to the light . . . Goddesses washed him with limpid water,· gave him for swaddling clothes a white veil of fine tissue, and bound it with a golden girdle.'

"When, in my admiration of the beauty of line in classical dancing, I dreamed of a ballet of this kind, I had specially in my thoughts what is known as the 'white ballet,' in which to my mind the very essence of this art reveals itself in all its purity. I found that the absence of many colored effects and all the superfluities produced a wonderful freshness. This inspired me to write music of an analogous character. It seemed to me that diatonic composition was the most appropriate for this purpose, and the austerity of its style determined what my instrumental *ensemble* must be. I at once set aside the ordinary orchestra because of its heterogeneity, with its groups of string, wood, brass, and percussion instruments. I also discarded *ensembles* of wood and brass, the effects of which have really been too much exploited of late, and I chose strings."

Apollon Musagète was first presented in Washington on 27 April, 1928, with Adolph Bolm's choreography. As Stravinsky was not in the country at the time, he is unable to say anything about it. But he did conduct the first performance in Paris with the Diaghileff Ballet on June 12, the same year, at the Théâtre Sarah Bernhardt. Stravinsky has this to say about it: "As a stage performance I got more satisfaction from this than from *Les Noces,* which was the latest thing Diaghileff had had from me. Georges Balanchine, as ballet-master, had arranged the dances exactly as I had wished—that is to say, in accordance with the classical school. From that point of view it was a complete success, and it was the first attempt to revive academic dancing in a work actually composed for that purpose. Balanchine . . . had designed for the choreography of *Apollo* groups, movements, and lines of great dignity and plastic elegance as inspired by the beauty of the classical forms. As a thorough musician—he had studied at the St. Petersburg Conservatoire—he had had no difficulty in grasping the smallest details of my music, and his beautiful choreography clearly expressed my meaning."

The composer was impressed with the quality of the participating dancers. "But," he says, "my satisfaction was less complete in the matter of costume and *décor,* in which I did not see eye to eye with Diaghileff. As I have already said, I had pictured it to myself as danced in short white .ballet-skirts in a severely conventionalised theatrical landscape devoid of all fantastic embellishment such as would have been out of keeping with my primary conception. But Diaghileff, afraid of the extreme simplicity of my idea, and always on the look-out for something new, wished to enhance the spectacular side, and entrusted scenery and costumes to a provincial painter, little known to the Paris public—André Bauchant, who, in his remote village, indulged in a *genre* of painting somewhat in the style of Douanier Rousseau. What he produced was interesting, but, as I had expected, in no way suited to my ideas.

"My work was very well received, and its success was greater than I had expected seeing that the music of *Apollo* lacked those elements which evoke the enthusiasm of the public at a first hearing.

"Directly after the Paris performance of *Apollo* I went to conduct it at its first London appearance. As always in England, where the Russian Ballet enjoys established and unwavering popularity, the piece had a great success, but it would be impossible to say in what degree this was due to music, author, dancers, choreography, subject, or scenery."

The foregoing gives an insight into the varying "literary" methods employed in the making of these balletic masterpieces. A pair of others will serve to point the methods. Let us for a moment go back to the very beginnings of the Diaghileff revolution, since the Diaghileff revolution paved the way for the new approach. It was in St. Petersburg in 1909. Diaghileff had had a triumphant opera-ballet season in Paris, the first in Western Europe. He had returned to Russia, often referred to as the Conqueror of Paris, and was formulating plans for a yet bigger invasion of the West.

On his return to St. Petersburg, Diaghileff called his group of collaborators together. Serge Grigorieff, the faithful *régisseur* or stage director for the Diaghileff Ballet throughout its existence, in his record, *The Diaghilev Ballet: 1909-1929* (Constable, London, 1953), says: "As soon as we were all seated round the table with the inevitable *samovar*, Diaghilev produced his large black exercise book and began thus: 'Before we start planning a second Paris season, I should like to impress on you that after the prodigious success we scored this summer, we must be especially careful in framing our new policy. The ballets we choose for next year must on no account be less interesting than this year's.

But here we are faced with a problem. We could not possibly show Paris any of the ballets now given at the Maryinsky (the Imperial Theatre of St. Petersburg), or for that matter in Moscow. So, after thinking it over, I have come to the conclusion that we must invent new ones; and I shall begin by inviting my old professor of harmony, A. K. Liadov, to compose the music for a ballet on the Russian fairy tale of the Firebird.'

"We approved this suggestion," Grigorieff continues. "Nouvel (Walter Nouvel, an invaluable Russian adviser of Diaghileff), however, pointed out that Liadov composed very slowly and that it was doubtful whether the score would be ready in time. 'At any rate I propose to see him and find out,' said Diaghilev. 'And for a second ballet I thought of Rimsky-Korsakov's symphonic poem *Schéhérazade.*' Here he paused a moment and then continued, 'My only doubt is over the third movement, which is unsuitable for dancing and anyhow not very interesting.' We all liked the idea of *Schéhérazade,* though some of the committee were shocked at the suggested cutting of any part of a work by Rimsky. Diaghilev, however, was quite definite about it; and after he and Nouvel had played the music through on the piano, in an arrangement for four hands, Fokine had to admit that he was right. This accounted, then, for two ballets. But there still remained two to choose; and Diaghilev asked us all to think our hardest. During a momentary lull in the conversation Benois (Alexandre Benois, distinguished painter and collaborator) observed in his quiet voice that it might be a good move to show *Giselle* in Paris. We might, he thought, make much of its being a French classical ballet with attractive music by Adam. For 'we must remember,' he said, 'that the Russian school of ballet dancing grew out of the French, and so in taking *Giselle* to Paris, we should be paying a tribute to France.' General Bezobrazov (His Excellency General Bezobrazov, a Privy Counsellor and one of the greatest connoisseurs of ballet in St. Petersburg) shared Benois' opinion, and so did Svetlov (Valérien Svetlov, one of ballet's most distinguished and knowledgeable critics).

"But Diaghilev made a face and said, 'Shoura (Benois) is quite right, of course. But *Giselle* is too well known in Paris, and would not be likely to interest the public. I'm quite prepared to consider it, though. We'll decide at the next meeting. . . .' "

Grigorieff continues: "Fokine had always wanted to compose a ballet based on a Russian fairy tale. *The Firebird* gave him the opportunity, and he at once began working out a scenario in detail. I obtained several collections of Russian fairy tales; and between us we evolved a story, by piecing together the more interesting parts of several versions. This took us about a fortnight; and we were ready for the next meeting at Diaghilev's flat. The scenario was approved; but Diaghilev reported (as Nouvel had foreseen) Liadov, whom Diaghilev had approached about the music, had said that it would take him a year to write it. Diaghilev had therefore decided, he said, to order the score from a young composer named Igor Stravinsky, whose piece called *Fireworks* he had heard at a concert at the Academy of Music, and whom he considered very talented. 'The composition made a great impression on me,' said Diaghilev. 'It is new and original, with a tonal quality that should impress the public. I have commissioned him to write the score for the *Firebird*, and he is extremely enthusiastic about it.' At this an ominous silence fell on the committee, who had heard of Stravinsky, if at all, only as a promising beginner. But Diaghilev was not to be deterred, and asked Fokine to arrange a meeting with Stravinsky as soon as possible to discuss the story.

"The question of the *Firebird* being thus disposed of, we passed on to *Schéhérazade*. The theme that had inspired Rimsky's symphonic poem was not really suitable as a ballet plot. Benois tried improvising an altered version, and we all joined in with various suggestions. I remember Bakst's (Léon Bakst, revolutionary painter and brilliant colorist) jumping on to a chair, gesticulating, and showing how the Shah's retainers should cut everyone to pieces, 'everyone, his wives and above all their Negro lovers!' But despite our contributions, the plot as eventually used was the invention of Benois—and not of Bakst. Yet Diaghilev used to attribute it to

Bakst—why I do not know; and this led to a later quarrel between him and Benois."

From this something will be gathered of the wide variety of methods and contributions which went into the "literary" element of the early Diaghileff ballets and a picture of how they came into being. Accounts vary as to how the definitive and accepted "stories" were reached; but I think enough has been said to show that it was at all times a close collaboration between composer, painter, and choreographer.

Actually, these new works were, in a sense, mimetic dramas that drew raw story material from legends that ran from the savage and dark to the dreamlike and lyrical. The best of them survive today in standard repertory. A few examples will suffice: *Cleopatra,* heavily plotted tale of love and caprice, dealing with a queen of fabled Egypt who had too much time on her hands, has gone the way of lumbering ballets, and deservedly so. *Prince Igor* is very much with us and, when well done, is still a thrilling work laid against a background of the ever-threatening Mongol horde, encamped outside the eastern gate of Europe. *Schéhérazade,* for all its Oriental passion, is undeniably dated. The more delicate and lyric works are still part of modern ballet's vertebrae: *Les Sylphides* and *Carnaval* as examples. The latter brings to life and unites, in the slightest of plots, a group of *Commedia dell' Arte* characters such as Pierrot, Harlequin, Columbine, Pantalon, and Papillon. *Les Sylphides* is a plotless reverie in the field of pure beauty, of tissue unsubstantial as the rainbow. These two classical studies in romanticism are, perhaps, of all ballets the most difficult to revive and, in present-day companies, often, one regrets to say, receive performances bordering on the execrable. One of the chief reasons for this is that they immediately reveal the artistic possibilities of a company in a manner that the work of no contemporary choreographer possibly can. No matter how well drilled the *corps de ballet,* that is not the point, for, as Diaghileff once remarked, "There should be no *corps de ballet* in *Les Sylphides,* but an ensemble of finished dancers." *Carnaval* suffers still more today. It is an extremely delicate work, depending largely upon characterization and style, qualities not too often found in our present-day ballet companies.

The scope of this volume does not permit of a detailed history of all the gradations that have taken place in the last two decades. Suffice it to point out that the "literary" element has come to play an even less important part. There would be little point in dwelling on the "Symphonic" ballets of Leonide Massine here, epoch-making though they were, for they are not performed today, largely for economic reasons advanced by the holder of the performing rights.   .

The story-telling function of ballet requires in its performance a good deal of pantomime. Contemporary audiences, at least in the Western Hemisphere, unaccustomed to and inexperienced with the fine art of pantomime, are impatient with it. Moreover, particularly in the United States, there is very little training in and consequently equally little knowledge of pantomime on the part of the average dancer. Contemporary audiences are therefore principally interested in dancing, and that is what they go to see. For that reason, there has been less emphasis on the story, more on the dance rhythm. A good deal of this has been the result of the choreographic works of George Balanchine, who has been an active and vital part of the American balletic scene for more than twenty years. Today he is the artistic head and moving spirit of the New York City Ballet.

It may be due to training more than to any other single thing, but the Balanchine tendency (and for "Balanchine" one could almost read "American") has been largely in the direction of more and more ballets with less and less story, until they have become pretty much "storyless." This "storyless" ballet has become almost an "American" type ballet.

Mention should be made of the highly successful and tremendously interesting choreographic experiments (important and lasting works when properly performed) of Antony Tudor. Tudor, an English dancer and choreographer, has been resident in the United States since 1939, and his works have been choreographed or revived and re-staged largely for Ballet Theatre. There are many people who are unable to find little meaning in ballet dancing *per se* and yet find meaning in the ballet figures in Tudor's ballets, such as *Romeo and Juliet, Pillar of Fire,* and *Lilac Garden.* All of these tell stories, and the author of the first is, of course, that prime poetical story-teller and plot-weaver of the theater, Shakespeare. Tudor in his choreography has been able to tell a story in terms of bodily movements, in tensions and relaxations that are in themselves expressive, without resorting to ordinary, accepted pantomime. Yet his works are quite definitely pantomimic ballets.

It is interesting to compare this story-telling approach used by Tudor with the earlier Diaghileff-Fokine approach. One of Tudor's most striking works is *Pillar of Fire.* We have mentioned Fokine's *Schéhérazade* more than once. Both are "story" ballets. Each has a tale to tell and in each the tale is a straightforward one, with a beginning, a middle, and an end. Each has a big orgy in the course of its telling. *Pillar of Fire* is a slow dissection of the subject. *Schéhérazade,* in the Fokine method, is overt and brash.

The "storyless" ballet usually deals with a suite or succession of dances, while the pantomimic ballet, whether the approach is subtle or forthright, is bound to concern itself with various types of stylized movements. In some dance ballets—for example, *Coppélia*—there is another sort of approach and it may be that our layman will find it has a somewhat different type of appeal. *Coppélia* is, of course, based on that tale of Hoffmann's dealing with the doll who presumably comes to life. There is a very definite story, and a considerable portion of it must necessarily be told in terms of and through the medium of pantomime. But, despite its story-weight, it is the dancing that predominates and holds a good deal of the chief interest.

An example of the freedom of subject matter and of how far the ballet story has moved from the fairy tale, the myth, the legend and from gods and goddesses, is *Fancy Free,* a ballet that may be called a "typical American work." The creation of the

American Jerome Robbins, it is danced to a crackling commissioned score by the American conductor and composer, Leonard Bernstein. Here is a story of today: about three girls and three gobs. The girls are charmers. The setting is low-life. The three sailors are on shore leave. True to the Service, once ashore they head for a bar. Outside the bar, they pick up a girl who happens to be passing by. Comes a second girl. They pick her up. Three sailors: two girls. And that's not good. The three sailors show off for the girls. They fight. Result of fight: they lose the two girls. Then, too late, a third girl shows up. The three sailors think it over; decide the game's not worth the candle, i.e., she's not worth fighting about. If the work were being done with words, one might say there is a tag-line and a vaudeville sketch black-out.

The "story" is told balletically with sharp references to the dance-hall steps of the day. It is told with economy and wit. I mention the work particularly for Robbins worked out a highly detailed scenario for *Fancy Free*. So detailed is it, as a matter of fact, that one is struck by the unusualness of it, since ballet stories are hardly ever worked out so articulately in literary language.

One more example of Jerome Robbins' choreography, this one a "serious" story, will suffice to point out the variety possible in ballet as it grows and develops. The work I have in mind is *The Age of Anxiety*. Here Robbins again joined forces with the composer Leonard Bernstein, taking his inspiration from the latter's Second Symphony. The Symphony in turn took its inspiration from W. H. Auden's poem, which gives the ballet its title. The ballet follows the general pattern of the poem as it is outlined in the music, although there is no attempt to translate specific words with specific gestures. Thus we have the "story," which is the poem, coming into ballet through the music. It is a complicated theme, dealing with four unhappy, sensitive people who meet by chance, each deeply disturbed by those things that concern and disturb sensitive folk in our own contemporary life—the uncertainties of our time. Driven by the ever-present spectre of frustration and insecurity, they discuss, with that mixture of stupidity and cloudy wisdom that is the hallmark of the semi-intoxicated state, the seven ages of man and the seven stages of escape into other worlds and other selves. They mourn the collapse of their dreams of salvation through the intervention of an all-powerful Protector. With frenetic energy they grasp blindly and feverishly at an empty, hollow gaiety which is as far removed from joy as it possibly can be, until at the end, in the realization of their own insufficiency, they succeed in the attainment of a certain mutual reassurance which, if not complete peace, is peace of a sort.

*   *   *

In this necessarily condensed discussion of the "literary" element in ballet, and of the gradual changes that have taken place, we have dealt with relative beginnings and endings: the "classics" of the first Diaghileff era—*Schéhérazade, Prince Igor, Carnaval, Petrouchka, Firebird, Les Sylphides;* some of the middle Diaghileff works—*Apollo* in particular; and some of the more recent works out of American ballet. It would be well, for the better understanding of this gradual change, to mention a few of the interim works of one of the finest choreographers and balletic minds of the century: Leonide Massine.

Leonide Massine, the Diaghileff choreographic successor to Michel Fokine, has been called by Merle Armitage, American ballet connoisseur and propagandist, "the purest extension into this day of the Diaghileff tradition and attitude." Massine's contribution to the ballet education of the United States has been immense. In the whole history of ballet it is difficult to think of a creator of more brilliance and fecundity. In addition to his choreographic talents, Massine combines in himself a superb dancer (primarily character) and an extraordinary stage personality.

Of all his works, perhaps the most noteworthy is *The Three-Cornered Hat,* originally created by him for the Diaghileff Ballet in 1919. Today it can be found in the repertory of the Sadler's Wells Ballet. No longer is it presented by the Ballet Russe de Monte Carlo, which is as well; for the dilapidated wreck of a great work that this company shoved across the country was an offence to Massine and an insult to the public.

Massine's "Symphonic" ballets, a major contribution to the development of ballet, no longer can be seen; for that reason I shall not discuss them in this context.

To return to the "story" element, let me cite a few examples of Massine's later works. In 1934 Massine staged in Philadelphia and New York, and later across the country and in Europe, his first "American" work. It was *Union Pacific*, with a score by the Russian-American Nicolas Nabokoff, settings and costumes by the American Albert Johnson and Irene Sharaff. The "story" was by one of America's most distinguished literary figures, the poet Archibald MacLeish. As an example of how great literary figures can in their writing be utterly wrong for ballet, let me set down the MacLeish scenario as printed in the ballet program:

"The first trans-continental American railroad was completed in 1869. It was built in two sections by rival groups of capitalists, one section from the East toward the West with Irish workmen, the other from the West toward the East with Chinese. As the road was pushed across the plains and the sierras, the workmen were followed by itinerant saloons, of which the most famous was the Big Tent, and by trainloads of camp-followers. Fighting between Irishmen and Chinese was common as the two roads drew near each other and the final stages of construction became a competitive race ending at Promontory Point, in the State of Utah, where, in an elaborate ceremony, a spike of gold was driven into a tie of laurel to join the rails.

"Surveyors and workmen are building the two converging sections of the railroad, Irishmen building from the East, Chinese from the West. As the Chinese work they are approached by a girl from the Big Tent called the Lady-Gay. The work is interrupted. The surveyor becomes amorous of the girl. The scene shifts to the Big Tent where Mexicans, gamblers, Irish workmen and girls are gathered at the bar. A

Mormon missionary enters. The barkeeper entertains his guests. While they dance, the Lady-Gay enters with her surveyor, followed by some of the Chinese gang. The Irish surveyor approaches her. She prefers her original companion and they dance. Irishmen and Chinese threaten each other. A general fight is imminent. Suddenly the scene shifts back to the roadbed of the line. The hostility of the Big Tent has become a rivalry in work. The two gangs, driving the rails before them, approach each other while cheering crowds of women and Indians and Mexicans look on. The last rail is about to be laid. Pompously and solemnly the capitalists enter. The golden spike is driven into the tie of laurel. The telegraph instrument beside the tracks ticks out the word *D-O-N-E*. And while the nation celebrates with cannon and bells in San Francisco and Omaha and Chicago and with the hymn of 'Old Hundred' played upon Trinity chimes in New York, the capitalists and workmen and girls and Indians pose before the camera at Promontory Point."

Massine's second attempt at an American work had an interesting idea, namely, to translate the spirit of the *New Yorker* magazine into ballet. It was not successful. Perhaps the reason for its lack of success may best be found once again by setting down the program note:

"*The New Yorker* (Book: Rea Irvin' and Leonide Massine. Music: George Gershwin, orchestrated by David Raskin. Settings and Costumes: Carl Kent, after Rea Irvin and Nathalie Crothers).

"A dioramic view of New York's café society in three scenes presenting a nocturnal adventure of the animated drawings made famous by Peter Arno, Helen E. Hokinson, William Steig, Otto Soglow and other artists' creations whose habitat are the pages of the *New Yorker* magazine—To Central Park's Plaza come Arno's Colonel, Dowager and Timid Man; Hokinson's Clubwomen; boys and girls; each intent on hotspotting. Venal headwaiters, baby-faced debutantes, keyhole columnists,

Steig's 'small fry,' gullible gangsters, Thurber's introverts, Soglow's Little King, all these with gentle madness people the parade of New York after dark.—The thread of the story is incidental to the portrayal of characters whose lives begin when the city goes to bed."

But it was approximately during this period that Massine created one of the most outstanding balletic works of the century, a genuine masterpiece. The ballet's "story" source and treatment are equally interesting. Originally, in Europe where it was first produced, entitled *Noblissima Visione,* in the United States it was known as *Saint Francis.* Massine called it "a choreographic legend"; his "story" inspiration was "The Little Flowers of St. Francis." Of it Massine has said, "It translates the moving medieval simplicity and mentality of its strange world into the highly formalized language of ballet." In the ballet the life of St. Francis was treated as a story in the form of a simple narrative in five scenes. However, that became something more than mere episodes in the unfolding of the legend, and took on symbolic form, masterfully fulfilling the choreographer's intention.

It is cause for regret that our layman is not likely to have opportunity to familiarize himself with the best work of this remarkable choreographer and ballet personality. Though still at the peak of his creative powers, few openings are accorded him in the United States today and his creations are, for the greater part, confined to Europe. As for revivals or even continuing performances of his works with American companies, it is increasingly apparent that Massine is the only person capable of supervising the former, and the stage managers and ballet masters who attempt half-heartedly to keep such works of his as remain in the repertory in some kind of shape, fail miserably, both from lack of knowledge in themselves and also from the fact that the current crop of dancers have no feeling for the Massine type of movement and are unaware of his philosophy of the dance.

Before leaving Massine, it should be pointed out that he was responsible for the great bulk of the ballets of the middle, and some of the late, Diaghileff period. This marked a change in style and story. Fokine refined and tightened the classical structure of ballet; whereas Massine did much the same sort of thing for what may be called "character dancing" or the forms based on folk-dancing. Briefly, this may be characterized as a shift in emphasis, so far as ballet is concerned, from dancing to theater, from, one almost might say, choreography to drama. Some of these works should be noted despite the fact that, with the exception of two of them, *The Three-Cornered Hat* and *The Fantastic Toy-Shop*, there is small likelihood our present-day layman will have opportunities to see them: *Parade, The Midnight Sun, Russian Fairy Tales, The Good-Humored Ladies, The Gardens of Aranjuez, Pulcinella, The Song of the Nightingale, Le Astuzi Femminili,* a re-working of the *Rite of Spring,* and *Les Matelots.*

For a time, the tendency was towards a visual *cum* literary appeal. *Pulcinella,* mentioned above, is an example, one of the later ballets choreographed by Massine for Diaghileff, about which the late Constant Lambert, presiding musical genius of the Sadler's Wells Ballet, and a critic of rare discernment, has written in his brilliant *Music Ho!*:

> "Stravinsky was by far the best person for Diaghileff to send time-travelling in the eighteenth century because, both temperamentally and racially, he was out of touch with the whole period. A Frenchman or an Italian might have felt some embarrassment about jazzing up the classics, but Stravinsky is like a child delighted with a book of eighteenth-century engravings, yet not so impressed that it has any twinges of conscience about reddening the noses, or adding moustaches and beards in thick black pencil. . . . Yet there is something touchingly naive about Stravinsky's attitude . . . Like a savage standing in delighted awe before the two symbols of an alien civilization, the top hat and the *pot de chambre,* he is apt to confuse their functions."

Farther and farther afield the later Diaghileff ballets wandered in their search for the "unusual." Perhaps the apex of this sort of thing was achieved in *Le Train Bleu,* produced in 1924, with music by Darius Milhaud, the choreography by Bronislava Nijinska, sister of Vaslav Nijinsky, costumes and scenery by Chanel and Laurens and Picasso. The "story" was by no less a literary figure than Jean Cocteau. Let us look at this Cocteau "story" as it was printed in the preface to the ballet provided by Diaghileff for the London performances of the work·

"The first point about *Le Train Bleu* is that there is no blue train in it. This being the age of speed, it has already reached its destination and disembarked its passengers. They are to be seen on a beach which does not exist, in front of a casino which exists still less. Overhead passes an aeroplane which you do not see, and the plot represents nothing. And yet when it was presented for the first time in Paris everybody was unaccountably seized with the desire to take the train to Deauville and perform refreshing exercises. Moreover, this ballet is not a ballet. It is an *operette dansée.* The music is by Darius Milhaud, but it has nothing in common with the music that we associate with Darius Milhaud. It is danced by the real Russian ballet. It was invented for Anton Dolin, a classical dancer who does nothing classical. The scenery is painted by a sculptor and the costumes are by a great arbiter of fashion who has never made a costume."

This flippancy went even further. The French-Scottish composer, jester, and practical joker, who composed the music for the ballet *Parade* for Diaghileff, offered a ballet to the manager of the Paris Opéra, one Bertrand. The ballet was called *Upsude,* and its "cast" consisted of one character only. Monsieur Bertrand had taken no notice of this offer—not even sent Satie the customary formal receipt for the manuscript; and Satie, electing to construe this piece of negligence as a personal insult, had challenged Bertrand to a duel.

This move was embarrassing for the unfortunate manager, because at that time, when refusing to fight a duel, one had either to prove to the satisfaction of a specially appointed *jury d'honneur* that one's challenger was "disqualified" (that is, unworthy), or, if one failed to prove it, became "disqualified" oneself. Fortunately, Satie, mollified upon receiving formal notice that his ballet had been received, duly examined, and found unsuitable, magnanimously withdrew his challenge, and the knotty problem set for Monsieur Bertrand was solved.

There was practically no "story" to *Upsude,* but on the back of the musical score there is printed this truly wonderful announcement:

> *"In Preparation:*
> *Onotrotance, ballet in two acts.*
> *Irnebizolle, ballet in three acts.*
> *Corcleru, ballet in four acts."*

Satie informed an inquirer, slightly astounded, that this was not a joke, and that he had actually carried in his head materials for all three ballets, and had indeed written parts of them down. The inquirer requested particulars. "Let me see," said Satie. *"Onotrotance* . . . I haven't done much on that one yet, but it will be quite good. *Irnebizolle* . . . Oh! There's quite a lot of *that* done. It's a ballet in which no single person appears on the stage. As for *Corcleru,* it exists . . . Oh, yes, it exists all right. There *are* people on the stage in it. It's difficult to explain, though. In the third act there is a miraculous apparition. I'm rather pleased with *Corcleru. . . ."*

To return to our consideration of the story element in ballet of our time, it should be of interest to contrast the methods and changes that have taken place in the United States and in England. In the former, in the general development of the classical ballet, the successor to Leonide Massine has been George Balanchine. Since this book is concerned with opinion as well as with incontrovertible fact, I feel that, distinguished though many of Balanchine's works are, his contribution to ballet has been less varied and much less productive than Massine's. After quitting Europe and taking up permanent residence in the United States, he was instrumental with others in forming and continuing the

School of American Ballet, from which comes much of the personnel of the New York City Ballet.

Balanchine composed a long series of completely abstract ballets for various American companies in the neo-classical abstract style, including *Concerto Barocco, Danses Concertantes, Ballet Imperial, Mozartiana* (previously produced in Europe in 1933), and Bizet's *Symphony in C* (produced by him for the Paris Opéra, under the title of *Crystal Palace*), together with many others. More recently, he has been the moving choreographic spirit of the New York City Ballet with another long list of the same type of creations. Most of these ballets have *no* story or theme of any kind. Balanchine's chief interest would seem to be in dance for its own sake, and the ballets often consist of long passages that almost inevitably have their *longeurs,* since they lack emotional impact despite an undeniable preoccupation with the technique of the classical dance. Balanchine would seem to be constantly experimenting with technique, inventing different combinations of movements and lifts.

There is hardly a Balanchine work (as a matter of fact, I do not know of one) which is not on a high level of craftsmanship, nor a single one that is not intensely musical. On the other hand, it is often difficult, if it were not for the music, or the costumes, or the scenery (when there is any), to distinguish one ballet from another.

Despite their so-called *"chic"* and often an air of general sophistication, many of Balanchine's works seem to me to be little more than a twentieth-century reversion to the spectacle ballet of the nineteenth-century, with variations. Théophile Gautier, nineteenth-century poet, critic and writer, a leader of the Romantic movement, in the mid-nineteenth century wrote: "The important thing in ballet is the movement itself, as it is sound which is important in a symphony. A ballet may contain a story, but the *visual* spectacle, *not* the story, is the essential element." He goes on to say: "Moreover, as in music, the audience should be able to enjoy the movements *regardless* of the story." And then again:

"Choreographic movement is an end in itself, and its only purpose is to create the impression of intensity and beauty."

I have italicized some words in the above quotation in order the more readily to draw the parallel between Balanchine and the nineteenth century.

This Gautier-like, nineteenth-century attitude on the part of Balanchine has influenced a number of his choreographic disciples, young choreographers who imitate his style, but only succeed in turning out even more non-emotional and conventionally patterned works, despite occasional preoccupations with acrobatism.

Balanchine has experimented with two traditional story ballets: his version of Tchaikowsky's classic full-length *Swan Lake,* and a re-staging of the Fokine-Stravinsky *Firebird.* Great liberties have been taken with each so that portions are well-nigh unrecognizable. In the latter, the Russian fairy-tale element on which it is based is almost entirely missing, and the choreographic patterning of the title-role results in dancing of extraordinary virtuosity but an almost utter lack of any poetry or any bird-like quality whatsoever.

There is a definite place in ballet for the abstract; but one is unable to escape the conclusion that the abstract ballet has deteriorated at the hands of Balanchine and his imitators, and has become merely the vehicle for the display of virtuosic acrobatics.

There is one work of Balanchine's, however, that is not only his masterpiece, but a genuine masterpiece of ballet of any place or period. This is *Orpheus,* done to a quite magnificent score by Igor Stravinsky, in a most extraordinary series of settings and constructions by the Japanese painter, Isamu Noguchi. Using the legend of Orpheus and Eurydice, the result is a perfectly integrated whole. Although more recent performances have deteriorated somewhat, the work itself remains one of the outstanding balletic works of our present time.

Balanchine's last creation for the Diaghileff Ballet, Serge

Prokofieff's *The Prodigal Son,* now in the repertory of the New York City Ballet, remains a monument to Balanchine at the very top of his creative powers.

Mention must be made of a number of other works. One that is a truly American "story" ballet was staged by the American dancer and choreographer, Ruth Page, one of the foremost of our progressives, a figure at once artistically curious, forward-looking, and intellectually alive. It is *Frankie and Johnny.* Originally created for the United States Government's only essay into the subsidized theater, the Federal Theater Project, it subsequently entered the repertory of the Ballet Russe de Monte Carlo, strangely enough.

Miss Page's *Frankie and Johnny* is frankly a "story" ballet and has as its base what Carl Sandburg once called America's "classical gutter song." *Frankie and Johnny* is a theater piece, a *genre* about which I shall have something further to say. It is a far cry from such story ballets as *The Nutcracker, Giselle,* and *Swan Lake.* It is, as a matter of fact, a violent and deliberately bawdy melodrama. True enough, the story has its humors, but it is, at base, a thrilling, sordid story of low-life. It has real drama and a keen sense of the theater. There is no abstract miasma about it, no movement purely for the sweet sake of movement. As a love tragedy, not of the *Tristan and Isolde* type but rather of the common public house, it is quite remarkable. Its story is good reading.

"Faithful Frankie loves Johnny. Johnny loves Frankie, too. But immediately after a tender love duet with her, he visits Nelly Bly. Then 'Frankie goes down to the corner saloon to buy her a large glass of beer.' Her friends form a group around Nelly and Johnny to keep Frankie from seeing what is going on between them. However, the bartender takes keen delight in telling her the real situation, which at first she refuses to believe. Now 'Frankie was a good girl as everybody knows' but when she finally realizes that Johnny is actually in love with Nelly, she works herself up into a frenzy of jealousy, and melodramatically shoots Johnny 'root-a-toot-toot.' All their friends have a fine time celebrating at Johnny's wake. Frankie tries to hang herself, but is saved by Nelly. Finally Frankie is left alone with her lover in the coffin, and the philosophic words of the Three Singers are heard in song:

> "*This story ain't got no moral,*
> *This story ain't got no end,*
> *This story just goes to show you,*
> *That you can't put no trust in any man.*"

Here, for story purposes, the choreographer has retold in choreographic terms and sharply focused images of visual power and impact a genuine, popular ballad which touches the feelings and sentiments.

Another of Ruth Page's balletic experiments found her going to Edgar Allan Poe's *The Bells* for her literary inspiration; yet again, in *Guns and Castanets,* to a treatment of Mallarmé's *Carmen* story, used by Bizet in his opera. Most recently she has transferred the Franz Lehar operetta, *The Merry Widow,* into a successful ballet theater piece; and, less successfully perhaps, Verdi's *Il Trovatore* into a ballet called *Revenge.* In the latter, the libretto is certainly less silly than in the opera.

*   *   *

Before continuing with the American scene, let us return for a moment to what has happened to the "story" element in ballet in England since the Diaghileff era.

It is interesting to observe that England's most prominent choreographer, Frederick Ashton, through a long, uneven, but highly distinguished career, has experimented with almost every style of balletic creation, steadily moving, it would seem, in the direction of abstraction, abjuring story more and more, until eventually he seemed to abjure even theme. His vast choreographic product has played a tremendously important part in the development not only of the Sadler's Wells Ballet but of ballet in England itself.

It may be that Ashton's greatest strength lies in his infinite variety of choreographic approach. His abstractions are strikingly different from those of George Balanchine. The Ashton works are softer, less angular, less virtuosic, more lyrical in their approach, freer from stunts for stunt's sake. There is always emphasis on lyricism.

Two of Ashton's most endearing works, both in comedy vein, are *Les Patineurs* and *Façade*. The former has a deliciously sparkling score, arranged and orchestrated by Constant Lambert from operatic works by Giacomo Meyerbeer, and the purely classical series of linked dances (the balletic term for which is *enchaînements*, i.e., linking together) are arranged with consummate skill. There is no "story" as such; but there is a theme. The setting and idea are a skating festival. To a little pond in a bosky park on a sharp, clean wintry day come an assortment of different characters: a pair of sprightly girls in blue, a rather superior and self-assured young man who is obviously the wearer of a string of skating-championship ribbons, a young couple in white equally obviously deeply in love, groups of young boys and girls. Each dances *variations* that serve to stamp the individualities of their characters. There are comedy falls, touches of slapstick, an overall atmosphere of gaiety and joy unrestrained, together with a quite brilliant finale.

Façade, one of Ashton's early works (it was created in 1931), is fundamentally a series of light-hearted parodies, and is as gay and popular, as entertaining today as it was on the occasion of its first performance a quarter of a century ago. It has no story; is not related to the Edith Sitwell poems save by the vaguest sort of reference. It uses the music William Walton arranged and orchestrated from the music he composed to accompany the original recitations. It is not a ballet at all in the accepted sense of the term but rather a series of dances and might more precisely be called a balletic revue. Where more serious and pretentious works have long since been forgotten, *Façade* lives on with undiminished popularity.

A satirist at heart, Ashton's most completely delightful work is *A Wedding Bouquet,* a deliciously funny, genuinely amusing, and sharply satirical work, set to a score by Lord Berners, and the recitation of lines by Gertrude Stein. A choreographic creation of wit, humor and sophistication, it deserves more American performances than it has yet received.

One of Ashton's most successful serious works was created for and is in the repertory of the New York City Ballet. It is *Illuminations,* set to the score for voice and orchestra by Benjamin Britten, and entitled *Les Illuminations;* the words are by the French poet, Arthur Rimbaud, settings and costumes are by Cecil Beaton. Ashton's method here was to present a series of danced pictures. There is a literary, or, to be more precise, a poetic base: namely, the poems of Rimbaud, himself a symbolist, all of whose work was written by the time he was nineteen years old. During the course of the ballet, the soloist in the orchestra pit sings portions of Rimbaud's impressions, underlying the theme that the poet should be a prophet, a visionary, who himself attains a fresh, original quality of illumination from darkness so that he might be able to see the light.

Ninette de Valois, O.B.E., Mus. D., might, in a sense, be called the English Leonide Massine in that this remarkable executive is at her best choreographically when she has either a powerful theme or a good story with which to work. Her finest creations are those with the strongest dramatic impact.

Among such works, which have been seen on the North American continent, are notably the Ralph Vaughan Williams— Geoffrey Keynes ballet-masque, based on Blake's *Book of Job,* the story of which is, of course, that of man's inward struggle, his trials and tribulations, his eventual triumph through faith.

Ninette de Valois' greatest work is perhaps *The Rake's Progress.* It is Hogarthian in inspiration, feeling, and mood, with music by Gavin Gordon, who also was responsible for the well-worked-out "story" for ballet purposes, clinging closely to the earthy realism of the Hogarth original. It is the tale of the Rake who goes a-whoring and gambling, running life's gamut until he winds up a drooling idiot in a madhouse. Not a pretty tale, but it is at all times gripping, alive, sometimes amusing with comic

interludes, tender with lyric passages, and always works inevitably towards its tragic *dénouement*. At the same time, it is an
appalling indictment of the life of a certain section of English
society in the eighteenth century.

Another of the de Valois outstanding "story" ballets is *Check-
mate,* a gripping dramatic work, whose story is based on the
tense drama of a game of chess; still another, *The Prospect Before
Us,* deals with the rivalries of two London theater managers,
which unfortunately did not arouse the interest or excitement it
deserved to stimulate when it was shown in the United States.

The story element in the ballets of the English choreographer,
Antony Tudor, now resident in the United States, is discussed
elsewhere. Some of his English creations, not seen in the United
States, include *Lysistrata,* whose theme is, of course, taken from
the powerful two-thousand-year-old satiric comedy by Aristoph-
anes, dealing with the far-seeing, organizing lady who "organized"
her fellow-women into a revolt against senseless, stupid war by
having them strike against their menfolk until the latter desisted
from fighting.

It would not be an exaggeration, I think, to call Tudor England's most distinguished choreographer product. He has steadily enlarged the subject matter of ballet, which is one of the true
choreographer's most important functions. Later, when we return
to the theater ballet in the United States, we shall examine the
story base of one or two more of the Tudor creations.

One more pair of English choreographers to be considered from
the point of view of their "story" approach will have to suffice,
for considerable selection is necessary.

The dancer-actor (or actor-dancer), Robert Helpmann, is a
genuinely dramatic choreographer. His first important choreographic work was nothing less than *Hamlet.* Here, with Shakespeare's powerful drama as a "story" inspiration, Helpmann did
not choose (and it would seem a wise choice) to re-tell the tale
of the melancholy Dane by adapting Shakespeare's play to ballet.
Rather did he elect to present the highlights of the play as a

series of mad dreams passing through Hamlet's mind as he lies dying. The ballet is prefaced by these lines from the play:

> "For in that sleep of death, what dreams may come
> When we have shuffled off this mortal coil
> Must give us pause."

And so, as in a dream, the events he remembers are telescoped and twisted through the action of the Prince's internal conflicts.

Miracle in the Gorbals, to a commissioned score by Arthur Bliss, is a "literary" ballet that attempts to deal with social problems of the day, using as its setting the Gorbals slum section of the city of Glasgow. Social problems and the general theme of what present-day society would do to Christ if he returned to earth, are its burden. Helpmann has said: "I have always felt ballet should not ignore social problems, but, like the theater, should deal with living human beings of today and not with fairy-tales of the past. It will be a dead art if it does so." I have said *Miracle in the Gorbals* is a "literary" ballet, and it would seem to have gone for its literary source material to such works for the theater as Jerome K. Jerome's *Passing of the Third Floor Back* and Sean O'Casey's *Within the Gates.*

Both these works have been seen in the United States and Canada during the tours of the Sadler's Wells Ballet. A third Helpmann "literary" ballet, which has not been seen in the Western Hemisphere, is *Adam Zero.* Again with music commissioned from Arthur Bliss, the "story" is by the English stage-director, Michael Benthall. The story idea may perhaps best be understood through the choreographer's own program note. He says: "The theme of *Adam Zero* was influenced by the existentialist philosophy of some modern French playwrights." He adds: "The original scenario of the ballet had not suggested the expression of its theme—man's life from birth to death—through this ancient theater technique of shifting scenery, making up, etc., in view of the audience, and the idea of showing man's life through the medium of a ballet rehearsal came later." The choreographer's intent may be further illuminated by one more quotation. "I also tried in *Adam Zero*," Helpmann says, "to parallel the phases of life with different styles of dance—primitive dance for the man's youth, classical for his prime, jazz and jive for his degenerate middle age, etc. The ballet, in fact, was planned as much to show the development of different forms of dancing as to provide an acting role."

Another and younger English choreographer of marked gifts, whose *metiér* is the dramatic, is John Cranko. Among his works known to America are *Beauty and the Beast*, the familiar fairy-tale, set to the music of Maurice Ravel; and his two striking but entirely differentiated in style works, *Harlequin in April* and *Pineapple Poll*. Whether or not the former, as has been suggested, owes any of its literary values to T. S. Eliot, the work—one of fine poetic imagination set to a commissioned score by Richard Arnell and specially created for the Sadler's Wells Theatre Ballet's contribution to the Festival of Britain—tells a contemporary story in terms of classical and mythological characters. Here, once again, are Pierrot, Columbine, and Harlequin, with their symbolism changed.

In their new guise, Harlequin becomes the symbol for mortal hope reborn after the tragedy of devastation. Actually reborn, Harlequin returns to life in April which, despite its flowers, is "the cruelest month." The flowers themselves are self-sufficient, earth-bound creatures, from whom Harlequin succeeds in escaping. It is Columbine whom Harlequin loves, she being the symbolic embodiment of the ideal to which he aspires. There, standing between the two lovers, is Pierrot, the perpetual fool, exciter of risibilities—that is, until he interferes too much.

The second of the John Cranko works mentioned, *Pineapple Poll*, stems straight from a familiar English literary source for its story.

The ballet is the first based on the works of Gilbert and Sullivan: joyful, zestful, and genuinely exhilarating. The ballet's story is based on one of W. S. Gilbert's *Bab Ballads*. The score, arranged by Charles Mackerras from numerous of the operettas

Arthur Sullivan wrote for the Gilbert texts, is one of the musical joys of contemporary ballet.

The ballad chosen by Cranko to retell in balletic terms is the *Bumboat Woman's Story*, the history of Pineapple Poll, who happily reminisces:

> "My cheeks were mellow and soft, and my eyes were large and sweet,
> Poll Pineapple's eyes were the standing toast of the Royal fleet!
> A bumboat woman was I, and I faithfully served the ships
> With apples and cakes, and fowls and beer, and half-penny dips,
> And beef for the general mess, where the officers dine at nights,
> And fine fresh peppermint drops for the rollicking midship-mites."

A bumboat is a small craft carrying provisions, vegetables, supplies, to ships at anchor. Pineapple Poll literally falls head over heels in love with the handsomest of officers:

> "Of all the kind commanders who anchor in Portsmouth Bay,
> By far the sweetest of all was kind Lieutenant Belaye.
> Lieutenant Belaye commanded the gunboat, *Hot Cross Bun.*
> She was seven and seventy feet in length, and she carried a gun."

Determined to win Lieutenant Belaye, tired of her pot-boy swain, and knowing the *Hot Cross Bun* is putting out to sea, Pineapple Poll disguises herself as a seaman.

> "And I went to Lieutenant Belaye (and he never suspected me!)
> And I entered myself as a chap who wanted to go to sea."

The complications are many and amusing, including the marriage of the handsome commander to Blanche Dimple; and, finally, Pineapple Poll goes back to her patient pot-boy, with whom she has really been in love all the time, as Blanche's stoutly British mamma, her ample bosom draped in a Union Jack, umbrella in one hand, trident in the other, a forthrightly ruling Britannia, beams her smiling blessing upon the happy lovers.

*   *   *

Meanwhile, in the United States, there had gradually come into being a new type of theater ballet that was to have far-reaching results and effects, even beyond the confines of ballet.

Some of the earlier works include *Billy the Kid,* based on the life of the legendary highwayman of the American plains, which was created by the American Eugene Loring in 1938. Together with the splendid score by Aaron Copland, it was the first important native American ballet. Its story materials are fundamentally tragic, and the libretto itself by Lincoln Kirstein is considerably more than merely a biographical sketch of William H. Bonney, New York city born, Kansas City bred, who by the age of twenty-one had killed a man for every year of his life. As Billy the Kid, William H. Bonney became an historical American myth.

Unfortunately, the ballet, *Billy the Kid,* was produced ahead of its time and place, before the public, brought up on more easily digested food, was ready for it.

Another American subject, *Ghost Town,* produced in 1939, with a story based on episodes of the Gold Rush days, by the American Marc Platoff, with music by Richard Rodgers, suffered from a too complicated plot.

With these contemporary antecedents as examples, the die was finally cast in 1942, when, to her own story, Agnes de Mille created a Cinderella tale of the American West, in *Rodeo* or *The Courting at Burnt Ranch,* to a commissioned score by Aaron Copland. Its little plot is solidly built on a sure foundation, with its drama sustained to the happy ending at the final curtain.

As Miss de Mille begins her own program note: "The story is basic." It is a tale of a tomboyish cowgirl who awkwardly com-

petes with the very feminine Rancher's Daughter for the attention of the cowboys and the special and particular favor of the
handsome Champion Roper. Since this child of the plains is quite
unversed in feminine wiles, she is unpopular with the boys, and
her mannishness shocks the belles from Kansas City who visit the
ranch. Is it necessary to add that in the end she gets her man?

I have said that this new type of theater ballet was to have
results reaching beyond the confines of ballet. In a way, *Rodeo*
revolutionized the dance in the musical comedy theater. Prior to
1943, there had been such changes in the dull musical comedy
routines and their blighting sameness as the rather sophisticated
ballets of George Balanchine in such works as *On Your Toes,*
with, in addition to its ballet theme, the lively and vivid *Slaughter
on Tenth Avenue;* and, to a lesser extent, Balanchine's dances in
I Married an Angel, Babes in Arms, The Boys from Syracuse;
but it remained for a musical comedy, the dances of which may
be said to have stemmed directly from *Rodeo,* to alter perma-
nently the face of dancing in the popular musical theater.

For the layman's better understanding of how this came about,
a few lines from Agnes de Mille's superlative autobiography,
Dance to the Piper (Little, Brown, 1952) will give an insight
into what happened and why:

"If it is possible for a life to change at one given moment, if
it is possible for all movement, growth and accumulated power
to become apparent at a single point, then my hour struck at
9:40 P.M., October 16, 1942. Chewing gum, squinting under
a Texas hat, I turned to face what I had been preparing for
the whole of my life.

"This was not a great performance; we gave better later.
Neither was it a great ballet. The style, as I always feared, did
break. But it was the first of its kind, and the moment was
quick with birth.

"There was applause on my first exit. An unexpected bonus.
There was applause or response on every phrase. Did the audience laugh on count eight as I had promised in July in Cali-

fornia? They laughed, not just female titters, but real laughing with the sound of men's voices, and the laugh turned into handclapping. This happened again and again. The dancers were elated but not surprised. I had promised them laughs. The pantomime was spaced to accommodate them.

"There were mishaps. At one point, Kokitch grew confused with his new costumes and failed to make an entrance, leaving me to improvise a love scene, without partner, alone, and exposed for sixty-four bars of music on the Met stage. Lines were crooked. Some of the girls clapped off beat. It didn't seem to matter.

"The pace of the performance rushed us like a wind. The audience were roused and urging us on. Great exchanges of excitement and force and gaiety were taking place all around. The dancers rushed and whirled, grabbing the right person, because the right person was there, though unrecognizable in an unexpected dress and hair-do. And throughout the pace which was too quick for me, beyond my understanding, faster than could be savored or appreciated, was Freddie's arm, Freddie's strong back, propelling, pushing, carrying, and Freddie's feet like bullets on the wood. It was beyond endurance. It was beyond help. It was slipping away too fast, too fast. Also my collar was too tight.

" 'Freddie,' I said at the back of the stage, 'I'm fainting. Loosen my collar.'

" 'No time, duckie. Here we go.'

"And as though we were blown out of the mouth of a gun, he propelled me to the footlights. We separated. Bob, bob. All the trumpets and horns threw their shafts between us. We hung on the brink. The music tore open. We rushed. We clashed. We were lifted. And all the girls had faces like stars with their hair dropping over the boys' shoulders. The great curtain fell. There was dust in my nostrils from the dusty lining of the curtain. It was over. It was done. And I had made so many foolish mistakes. So many hasty things had gone wrong. Once more I had been incapable of the perfect effort. 'Oh, Freddie,' I said gasping, 'what a stinking, lousy performance. We must rehearse like demons tomorrow.'

"I looked at him wistfully but we were walking forward and we were all holding hands and bowing. A large bunch of American corn was put in my hands tied with red, white and blue ribbons. More flowers came, more flowers. The Russians did things this way. They also clapped and called out. Hadn't I stood grinding my teeth at the back of the house for years while they cheered bogus nonsense? We bowed and bowed. At the eighth bow, I looked into the pit. The fiddlers were beating their bows on their instruments. The others were standing up yelling. No one gets the union boys to do this easily. I looked at Freddie in amazement. 'Freddie,' I said, 'this is not a claque. This is not Libidins's contriving.'

" 'Darling, darling,' said Freddie, kissing me, 'this is an ovation. This is the real thing. Take it.' He pushed me forward, and all the company backed away to the edge of the stage and stood there clapping.

"We had twenty-two curtain calls.

"The grips and members of the company helped me carry my flowers to the dressing room. They filled half the floor space. The doorman could not hold my friends in check.

"In the hall between dressing rooms, I met Massine. He bowed formally, and then apparently thought he must say something. He stared at me with his binocular eyes. 'You have done a characteristic ballet.' I struggled to follow this. 'And in Europe I think it will have success.' We bowed.

"Mary Meyer sat at my dressing table crying and crying. 'I can't stop,' she said, mopping her nose. 'It isn't that this is the most wonderful ballet I've ever seen. I've seen better. It's just that I can't stand you making a success after all these years.'

" 'Aren't you proud of her?' said friends to Mother. And Annie drew herself up to her shoulders and looking at them steadily with her penetrating blue eyes answered, 'I've always been proud of her. Always. When no one hired her. I'll go home now and start the coffee.'

"And in the lobby Billy Rose was marching up and down shouting, 'But where has she been? Why haven't we known about her? How could we have overlooked this talent?'

"And Terry Helburn was phoning in a wire to Western Union: WE THINK YOUR WORK IS ENCHANTING. COME TALK TO US MONDAY."

Terry Helburn is Miss Theresa Helburn, a director of the Theatre Guild, which owned a play by Lynn Riggs, called *Green Grow the Lilacs,* an American folk comedy which had had a mild success as a play, and which was in the process of being adapted into a musical comedy by Oscar Hammerstein II and Richard Rodgers. It may be taken for granted that the Messrs. Hammerstein and Rodgers, together with Miss Helburn, harbored no revolutionary thoughts but were concentrating on trying to make the work over into an entertaining musical piece and a commercial success. It is to be doubted that they were at the time being motivated by any sense of embarking on an epoch-making experiment. As had long been their wont, they were engaged upon making a workmanlike, careful, and competent adaptation of the manuscript of a spoken play into terms of the musical theater of Broadway. Agnes de Mille was engaged to do the dances in their adaptation of the Lynn Riggs play, with its poetic but somewhat unwieldy title truncated to *Oklahoma!,* because presumably Hammerstein, Rodgers, Helburn, and company had discovered that Miss de Mille's *Rodeo* had the authentic flavor of Western Americana, which *Oklahoma!* and the Riggs play required for its setting. It is not to be supposed that Agnes de Mille's long struggle for recognition in the world of ballet, nor the numerous sound choreographic contributions she had previously made to ballet in our time, played any part in her engagement. Nor is it to be assumed that Miss de Mille entered upon her new "Broadway" task with the fixed-eye stare of the reformer or crusader. Rather may it be taken for granted that she went about her business of planning, designing, and rehearsing, of integrating the ballets into the fabric and texture of *Oklahoma!*, as a job to be done, one she was glad to have, bringing to it the fruit of her years of study and labor.

It is a matter of record that in *Oklahoma!* ballet as a regular and accepted form of art entered into the popular musical theater: arrived, was seen, conquered. The thousands who have seen *Oklahoma!* not only across the North American continent but in England and Europe, and the many more thousands who will see it in its film version, accept dance as an integral part of the work without realizing that, in addition to the dance episodes throughout, which serve to carry on the story, it also contains a a fairly long ballet with a literary story content of its own, a work that is, in a sense, quite independent of the Hammerstein-Riggs libretto, at the same time an integral part of the story itself, which was written by Miss de Mille during that period of gestation before rehearsals were actually started, thus giving Rodgers, the composer, opportunity to compose the music for it. As an example—and an important one—of this new form for the musical comedy theater, this bit of "story" conceived in terms of visual movement producing emotional reactions and conflicts, is well worth reproducing.

LAURIE MAKES UP HER MIND

An original scenario, by Agnes de Mille; ballet from *Oklahoma!*, with music by Richard Rodgers

Scene: Hilltop—in the sun

"Laurie sits under a tree musing. She is worried. 'If I married Curley . . . ,' she says several times.

"Downstage left she appears to herself, dressed in her own dress, but with a wreath on her head. The music changes to *Beautiful Morning*—very lyric in the best Shubertian style. The dream Laurie advances and stands in the center of the stage, radiantly happy, aware of all the beauty around her.

Betrothed. While she is moving about in her morning, taking possession of her world—the real Laurie sitting on the revolving stage is turned slowly out of sight—or as an alternate, she moves downstage, stands for a second by her dream projection —and then moves softly out.

"(I prefer this method of accomplishing the transition, but for purposes of production the other may have more element of spectacle.)

"Two of Laurie's young friends enter—very young friends, about fourteen. They have a bouquet of field flowers for her. They are shy. She has become strange to them because she is betrothed and special. One of them bursts into tears with nerves.

"(The dancing throughout is lyric, non-realistic and highly stylized, but salted with detailed action that is colloquial, human, recognizable. If by any happy chance the dancers are used as minor characters in the other scenes their main characteristics must be maintained in the ballet.)

"Another young girl runs in, waves her sunbonnet and calls to the people who are following . . . to a very gay triumphal tune. Perhaps a full development of the Morning Song.

"Aunt Ella and the young woman enter—they are carrying the wedding clothes and the gifts. Laurie is stripped to her shift—and then dressed in great starched petticoats, corset, camisole, something blue, something old—all the little ceremonies are observed. The women who are not actually dressing her keep up a lace-like pattern rushing around, talking, busy (strict choreographic form) while the skirts are shaken out, tossed out and rushed up to the bride. The actual dressers are intent, busy and efficient in the gentle ceremony.

"Laurie is dressed in her new starched dress. The veil is borne in— Suddenly (*a cappella*) the men are heard offstage as they come up the hill——

"The bride stands waiting in her group of women. No one moves.

"The bridegroom and his men enter. They take off their

hats—and move into formal positions across the front of the stage—backs to the audience—the bride stands center downstage waiting—the women form an alley to the back of the stage. Laurie appears on Aunt Ella's arm—then advances alone between the women. The groom steps forward and lifts the veil—he kisses her—she stands transfixed—the whole scene freezes with horror— Suddenly she doubles up and tries to run. It is not Curley but Judd whom she has married— No one moves— She runs between them in nightmare terror. Judd does not move either. He waits for her to realize that the unavoidable has happened— She faces him panting—the women sneak away and abandon her—she throws herself for help into the men's arms—they have no faces—they start to leave——

"He has her by the wrist in the middle of the stage. She is dropping with dread. He takes out his postcards—(The postcards enter . . . They are the real thing . . . right off the *Police Gazette*).

"They proceed to dance around the stage in a kind of Whore's Parade— This dance will involve all the best Music Hall steps—it will be dirty, lusty, dreary and funny— They dance with the cowboys who go through the proceedings in a kind of somnambulistic state and still faceless— The leading girl of the troupe pulls Laurie to her and pushes her around in the parade, ripping her dress off her shoulders in a businesslike way. When the girls have had enough they depart like a company of glutted spiders, turning before they go over the crest of the hill for a last appalling salute to their partners. The men stand huddled together somewhat dazed—they leave— not altogether triumphantly.

"Laurie kneels on the stage, dress torn, exposed, ashamed, exhausted. The sky darkens as with thunderstorm. A woman with skirts and sunbonnet blowing runs terrified across the background as though to escape a tornado. Judd rushes on Laurie—swings her over his head and runs.

"(If it is possible to suggest a rape accomplished in midair in the heart of a hurricane, I want that there.)

"The action is brutal, violent, melodramatic and reminiscent of all the old woodcuts of the villain doing the heroine in, including the drag across the ground by the hair of her head. That the movement will be also beautiful is my chief concern.

"In the moment of extremis, Laurie throws back her hands and finds Curley standing beside her. She is not alone. He is with her as she needs him.

"He pulls out his gun and shoots Judd. Judd is not killed. Curley shoots again and again. Judd continues to advance. They struggle and Judd strangles Curley to death.

"Laurie crouches by Curley. Judd comes towards her. —The stage is dark with a yellow thunder light—Judd comes on. She cringes by the body of her lover, trying to seek protection from his dead useless hands— Judd is still moving——
"Quick dimout
"The real Laurie is discovered not feeling her freshest."

One might have thought that the enthusiastic reception accorded to the *Oklahoma!* ballets would have caused the producers to reflect on the significance of what had been accomplished. The artistic significance was passed over as just another formula. To be sure, it was a *new* formula, one which, because it was a success, would supplant the old one. As a result, every musical comedy from then on had to have, for better or for worse, a ballet or ballets, and there had to be a "choreographer." Many of the ballets were pretty awful. But, on the other hand, at least two things happened: dancers, of whom there is a plentiful supply, were able to find employment in greater numbers; and young choreographers of genuine talent, such as Jerome Robbins, Michael Kidd, and Helen Tamiris, were given opportunities to do constructive work in such diverse pieces as *Annie Get Your Gun, High-Button Shoes, On the Town, Finian's Rainbow,* and others; while Miss de Mille went on to works like *Carousel, Brigadoon, Paint Your Wagon,* and others.

There is little question that ballet has been brought to a new and wider audience through its introduction into the commercial musical comedy theater. What its long-range effect on ballet as a whole may be is another matter.

The fact remains that in many musical comedies today the layman is being exposed to more ballet than ever before, and for the present that is all to the good.

)9(

Stages of Ballet Enjoyment

Many considerations: casting problems, costume changes, scenery-hanging facilities, and others, have to be taken into consideration in building programs. Other considerations, less realistic (more, shall we say, psychological) have to be borne in mind when ballet programs are being arranged to attract audiences not too familiar with ballet, and they will vary according to the type of audience, the size and facilities of the stage of the theater, and even the towns or cities concerned. While any audience that is more general than a narrow coterie will object to any obvious attempt at balletic education, it will object no less to an undisguised "playing down," a sure sign of the ballet director's or manager's contempt for his audience. At such times as a program may be designed for an inexperienced audience it is important to provide it with an introductory "friend," the name of which they recognize and which they have heard favorably discussed. However, this work may cease to be the primary attraction when compared with the other items, and this may be an excellent thing; it is indeed one of the first steps in a balletic education.

For any audience, it would seem that there are one or two

136

ballets that never fail to satisfy, whatever the critics may say, whatever the attitude of the *cognoscenti;* like Shakespeare, they have something to offer to every man. It is indeed this richness of appeal which is a proof of ballet's universality, and the many levels at which ballet can be enjoyed is relevant to the whole question of ballet appreciation.

The first essential to the enjoyment of ballet is just this and no more; the auditor must enjoy himself when he looks at and listens to ballet. This sounds trite, but a little honest avowal on the part of many ballet-goers will give it greater importance. Young people enjoy ballet wholeheartedly and almost entirely from an emotional angle. They rarely have the training or the technical knowledge necessary for a complete concentration on what they are seeing and hearing, but as a first stage the purely emotional response is healthy. It is a stage of balletic innocence much to be envied; like most innocence, it is too soon lost and is eternally regretted.

The next step is a purely intellectual one; the inquiring member of the audience will cease to be satisfied with standing outside the mysteriousness of the art, and although he may have only the scantiest knowledge of ballet technique, or none at all, he will want to know what makes ballet tick and by what laws it is controlled and guided. Here lies the greatest danger. From now on he is not satisfied to look and listen and feel what the ballet has to communicate; he begins to think, and between feelings and thoughts on ballet there is an antagonism and an antithesis which must be resolved. The usual result of thinking about ballet, one of the most complicated of all the arts, is a denigration of its emotional possibilities, an attempt to define and restrict it within arbitrary laws. This attempt to sound the unfathomable depths of choreographic intuition is apt to become little more than mathematics, something that can be deadly dull.

Those who are at this stage must guard against preferences and prejudices, which will erect barriers between them and ballet. They will try to maintain an objectivity in their judgment that may rob them of the true pleasure of what they are seeing and hearing; they will go to a performance with opinions ready made, and will struggle to maintain them against the ever-diminishing whisper of their earlier innocence.

The vast majority of regular pre-war ballet-goers belonged to this kind, and they are a problem. Many critics can be found among them, and their grudging attitude is the program builder's load of mischief. Not for them the unalloyed enjoyment of ballet for its own sake. A program of ballets will never be taken simply for the pleasure it provides; each item will be judged by new and often inadequate standards with a fatal finality of opinion. When this is but youthful priggishness little harm is done, for there is still the time and vitality to struggle through to the third stage, where emotional pleasure and intellectual knowledge fuse into a synthesis which is the highest form of balletic appreciation. The ideal balance of thought and feeling makes it possible to find the true value and meaning of a work, irrespective of period and mode of expression. This stage is far more than a matter of balletic knowledge or experience, and calls for the complete integration of the personality of the auditor.

An example of the three stages to which I have referred can be taken from the common type of reaction to the ballets of Petipa and Tchaikowsky.

Newcomers to ballet, with no specialized knowledge and no pretensions, can be found more often in the hinterland than in our larger metropolitan centers; the Petipa-Tchaikowsky ballets offer no difficulties to them, but provide a pleasurable emotional experience. At the second stage the auditor finds the Petipa-Tchaikowsky ballets (even Adolphe Adam's *Giselle*) rather trite and obvious; he looks for works that display more overall brilliance, which break more rules and introduce more subtleties and which are beyond the comprehension of the common man. He is the person who has given up plain food and wanders about looking for exotic dishes, for Chinese cooking, Hungarian wines, and other restoratives to a jaded palate. But if he is wise, he will treat these adventures as a complementary experience, and sooner or later will return to the heart of things. He will find much that he seeks in the great classical ballets, and now will be able to appreciate the simplicity of these master works with a heightened power. He has reached a higher plane of aesthetic enjoyment, and will set out on new adventures with no danger of losing himself.

With those who have reached this high point of development we need not concern ourselves. The programs of the wiser ballet companies are not made for them. It is the newcomers and those who have a little and dangerous knowledge whom ballet companies seriously interested in spreading appreciation of· ballet are trying to attract and please. And there is a serious division between them. Often enough, when a list of forthcoming programs is submitted to ballet-goers of a little experience, they consider the items with a deprecating smile.

"Are they still playing those old things over and over again?" they inquire superciliously. "The number of times I've seen *Swan Lake* and *Sylphides!*"

Such critics overlook the very important fact that for many members of the audience the performances they are dismissing so lightly, far from being the *n*th performance of a hackneyed work, are the doorway to a new world of wonder and delight. They forget that everyone has to see this or that work for the first time, and that what is tiresome to them may be an unforgettable experience for someone who is only just discovering the wealth of the balletic treasury. In their superiority, these folk are apt to forget how much they owe to the works they treat so contemptuously.

This plea on behalf of the standard works of ballet must not be taken as an excuse for humdrum program-building, for an audience, like an individual, progresses steadily if the means are provided. If modern ballet audiences at the Metropolitan Opera House and the New York City Center were treated to the programs offered them two decades ago they would rightly either jeer or stay away. But even the highest point of development at any time will not satisfy the most enlightened section of the audience, and those who compose it will look for something beyond the honest-to-God performances which are all that can be reasonably demanded from run-of-the-mill ballet companies. They will come to expect more subtlety and art both in interpretation and technique, and having outgrown the plodding ballet companies and their programs may look back on them with disdain, forgetting that their very power of deeper appreciation constitutes the finest compliment they can pay to the indefatigability of these hard-working organizations.

So it is that those responsible for the designing of ballet programs must allow for the more advanced members of their audiences, while not forgetting to base their plans on the unassailable classics of all time. This will save them from the fault of offering complete and indigestible programs of exclusively modern or abstract ballets to any audience except one composed of specialists; it will also save them from devoting all their attentions to lesser Tchaikowsky and Rimsky-Korsakoff. The chronological path may be profitably followed, although not too rigidly, and it is important to demonstrate that modern choreographers and composers —apart from experimentalists—do not create their works upon new foundations but carry established principles to a further stage of development.

How is the ballet-goer—not the specialist, not the devotee— but the ordinary ballet-goer, to tell a good program of one-act ballets from a bad one beforehand, from the mere look of it in a newspaper announcement? Broadly speaking, he will make up his mind without difficulty whether it contains works worth seeing.

The introduction of new and unfamiliar works creates many difficulties, particularly in the case of a ballet company (and this embraces most of them) which labors under the necessity of having to make productions "pay for themselves." However progressive a ballet organization may be, it is wrenched back into the rut by financial considerations, and its attitude to the encouragement of young choreographers and composers is governed by these sordid details. Extra rehearsals, for example, will often mean the financial failure of a production and as a result the first performance of a work on which the reputation and future of the

choreographer and composer may depend is inadequately prepared.

Music has a great deal to do with this, plays a tremendous
part, as a matter of fact. For everywhere there is a natural gravi-
tation not only to works that are already known, but to music
or composers of reputation, in the sense they are already ac-
credited; everywhere, I regret to say, there is this flight from
creators of our own time. Unless some clear, honest thinking is
done about this problem, we may lose in the end the benefits of
the progress that has been made in bringing ballet to the people.

In addition to the small audiences which are so often the fate
of new works, there are other financial considerations to be taken
into account. The introduction into the repertoire of new works
brings with it one of the commercial sides of ballet-making. The
composer, if the work is commissioned, or if he is still alive, or
his immediate heirs, will not unnaturally expect to receive some
compensation for his gifted labors. This is covered by a fee paid
for the right of performance, and there are Performing Rights
societies, the chief of which in the United States is ASCAP,
which deal with this aspect of the question, and guarantees the
interests not only of the composer but of the publisher, who
may have hazarded a considerable sum of money in preparing an
edition of a new orchestral score. The hire of the musical material
is also a heavy charge, in addition to performing rights, and one
of the obvious contradictions of our present system is shown
when a house of music publishers will go to lengths to persuade
a ballet organization to utilize a new work, and then send a
bill which is likely to cure the organization of any desire to
repeat the expense, at least in the immediate future. This is the
reverse of the "song-plugging" methods of "popular" music,
about which so much has been said and which, if we are to believe it all, provides a solid encouragement to entertainers and
organizations of a certain type to present new works.

In these days of extreme uncertainty, any sensible ballet
organization will have its eyes turned to the future, and we can
therefore afford to ignore material difficulties and concentrate

upon the task of attracting large audiences by well-balanced programs. The aesthetics of program-building need not concern us unduly: that is a question for the specialist.

What we must do is to remember that every audience includes many of those to whom a ballet performance is a complete novelty and who must not be allowed to go away disappointed. Those whose experience of ballet has given them a healthy curiosity for more advanced movements in ballet and music and painting must not be forgotten, and the perfect ballet program will be the one which achieves the impossibility of pleasing everybody.

) 10 (

Critics and Program Notes

There is something to be said for seeking guidance from professional criticism which, though varyingly competent, need not be entirely despised on principle. The one way of reading it unprofitably is to make up one's mind to agree with it on the assumption, too readily made, that after all the critic, who is bound (or at least so it is hoped) to have had some kind of training, naturally knows better and more. So he may; but even the best critic sees things only from his own angle, and it is precisely the best who would not dream of asking anyone else to agree with him all the time.

What the reader of ballet criticism should ask first is that it should be stimulating, not that it should be right. One critic may write entertainingly without being in the least convincing; another may be judicious and informative but comparatively dull to read; both will be worth attention, and if their views are diametrically opposed, all the more so. Even if the reader disagrees with both, he will still profit from his writing because he will have been compelled to articulate his dissent, if only to himself. In other words, he will have used his brains, which never does any harm.

Criticism, however, comes after the performance, which has the advantage of at least not sending anyone to a first performance with a bias, but does not do everything for the layman that writers on ballet might do. Especially where it is desirable to read something about the ballet seen, the music heard (and professional ballet critics, with a few exceptions, are woefully prone to pay little enough attention to the musical aspect of ballet), rather than the way in which the work is presented, it would often be a great advantage to do so beforehand.

There is not enough opportunity of this sort. Newspapers are reluctant to help the ballet public in this way. Radio is equally uncooperative in this respect. Only the few critics in the country who are still fortunate enough to have a weekly column set aside for them at the week-end in which they may deal with any subject they please are able to write an occasional piece on an important work before its appearance or reappearance. Such articles ought to be eagerly looked for by the public and as eagerly read when found, unless they reveal themselves as mere pieces of news or propaganda or press-agentry.

Propaganda in all its forms had better be distrusted. The hitherto obscure choreographer from the hinterland who has suddenly been discovered by his townsmen for his work with the local Ballet Guild as a great creative artist need not be taken on trust any more than the young New York choreographer about whom another young New York choreographer writes an enthusiastic article. It may be, in the former case, that the obscure choreographer from the hinterland happens to have shown himself to be a good friend of one of the local directors who was influential with the press and who also was amenable to all the desires of his Board, and in the latter case, it may be that both choreographers are graduates of the same school of choreography and imitate the same master and mentor.

Of all questions which ballet can present to its devotees that

which asks "What is good and what is bad?" is the most permanent and the most agitating.

At the level of mere entertainment the professional critic, as
I have said, does not bother very much about the actual quality
of the music in ballet, provided it does not impede the main
business, which is to him the dancing. In fact, if the music is too
good it may draw undue attention to itself and so lay itself open
to the legitimate criticism that, being too good for its purpose,
it puts form and matter out of adjustment with each other. But
it far more often happens that the music for a ballet is not even
good enough for its profound purposes, and it is in such cases
that public opinion generally fails to observe the difference between good and bad. If in such a case the public has enjoyed
the ballet—and it is astounding what the public can delude
itself into enjoying by means of good food and the company of
the opposite sex, alcohol and still more alcohol—it resents the
criticism that the music is poor or the performance equally so,
though uneasily conscious that music and performance, like the
food and the female companion and the beverage, do vary in
quality.

Is there such a thing as bad ballet? Besides incompetent ballet,
feeble ballet, insincere ballet, and ballet of low intensity, there
are other ballets with equal claims to be called bad. But critics
do not dismiss ballets as bad merely because they happen to dis-
like them. Likes and dislikes form the bases of our judgments,
but mere likes and dislikes are not in themselves criticism. The
critic must give his reasons, and even in the frankly subjective
criticism sometimes described as "the adventures of the soul
among masterpieces," mere rhapsody and sheer damnation will
not suffice. The critic forms a scale of values, his own and not
necessarily endorsed by others, but still an organized and considered scale. His judgment may still be opinion, but it is a
considered opinion. And this is the nearest to certainty to which
we can attain.

Scientific criticism is a chimera, except in so far as it means a more exhaustive analysis of the facts. A quasi-statistical statement about the technical features of a dancer's style *may* provide a safer basis for estimating the artist's value than one's native intuition (though it is doubtful), but a scientific computation of worth is impossible—the subject does not permit of it.

But if we cannot attain either certainty or unanimity there is still no need to despair of the value of criticism. The word "criticism" is derived from the Greek *kritikos,* to judge, and it means judgment; the critic is asked to give his judgment on what he sees and hears. How does he do it? In exactly the same way as he makes a judgment about anything else. By sizing it up and striking a balance—not by means of a slide rule, a pressure gauge, or a chemical analysis. We all of us every day of our lives make moral judgments, and, what is more, act on them. As Aristotle said, the judgment is in the perception; it is immediate, a moral intuition.

As in morals, so in ballet. Most people who go to ballet and some of them who perform it (though usually the latter make poor critics) become as expert in forming judgments on the worth of a ballet as they are ready to return a verdict if called upon to serve on a jury or make a rough-and-ready judgment on any moral issue. What they find is that they employ a sliding scale of values, just as they do in morals when they excuse an insult on grounds of ill-health or acquit a murderer on account of provocation.

In criticism it is possible to exaggerate the extent to which cultivated opinion differs. You may read in the *New York Times* that Miss A's performance was lacking in the deeper perception of the part and in the *New York Herald Tribune* that Miss A sacrificed some of the purely dancing values in order to emphasize the characterization and the inner meaning of the role— anyhow, both critics have agreed in finding the performance wrong—but you will not find any critic saying that Pugni was a greater man than Tchaikowsky, that *Esmeralda* is a better work than *The Sleeping Beauty,* that Fokine is outmoded and an exploded force.

You do not even get much division of opinion among the critics on which performances are first class, though personal taste probably enters more into estimates of performance than into evaluation of works. There is quite enough agreement on essentials to make ballet criticism as reliable as the law and a good deal more reliable than the opinions of economic experts. What is asked of the critic is not certainty or science but opinion. The critic is paid for his opinion, precisely as the lawyer, preacher or politician is paid. The essence of criticism is that it is opinion. The critic speaks dogmatically not because he has a belief in his infallibility, but because expressions like "in my view" or "my opinion for what it is worth" spoil his literary style and convey the impression that he has little confidence in his own judgment. It matters not that another critic takes a diametrically opposite view. No one grumbles because the political editorials of the *New York Times* and the *New York Post* draw opposite deductions from the same set of facts. On the contrary, the clash of opinion is regarded as thoroughly healthy.

Criticism then is opinion, but it is not mere preference. What are the canons which a critic can employ to justify his preferences and raise them to the rank of considered criticism? The first we have already discovered—suitability of size and emotional congruity to the artist's purpose and the matter in hand. A choreographer must not aim at a *divertissement* and attain an epic, must not conceive a reverie and bring forth a drama. In ballets which avoid these miscalculations but are still bad, a similar disharmony is the root of the trouble. The complete work of art is the product of three factors: Imagination × Selection × Technique, or expanding the formula—formal arrangement of subject matter in a chosen material. In the complete work of art these elements are fused; it is impossible to separate the content from its formal presentation, the imagination from the technique with which it works. Failure in a work of art is due to incomplete fusion, to disharmony among the constituent elements. Imagination and technique may be defective, one or both, subject-matter may be incompletely digested or it may be too trivial for the high purposes of art. It would seem, however, that nothing whatever is outside the range of balletic treatment from morbid psychology, from low life to the higher lunacy—Antony Tudor's *Undertow* to Frederick Ashton's *A Wedding Bouquet*.

In the end, the essence of taste lies in discrimination, and the critic's function is to make fine discriminations between works of different and finely graded values. His primary qualification should therefore be sensibility, and every man of sensibility should be his own critic of ballets he sees. The professional critic brings to his task, in addition, a very wide experience of ballet and dance of all kinds and the ability to write—he must in fact be an artist in words himself. He should also be a scholar, so that everything he writes is seen in perspective against a wide background of knowledge. The mere scholar, however, is not always a writer and some excellent writers would lay claim to no very extensive scholarship. It is more important that a man who pronounces judgment on balletic matters of all sorts— ballets, books, performances—should have a wide-ranging knowledge of the arts as a whole than that he or she should be themselves practicing experts in one branch of the art, such as, for example, dancing. Set a dancer to catch a dancer and one sometimes gets illuminating technical commentary, but since it is ultimately an aesthetic rather than a technical judgment that is sought, it is on the whole more desirable that dancing shall be judged by standards drawn from the whole field of ballet.

Besides being an authority in matters of taste and knowledge, the critic must also do a certain amount of exposition and comparison, and it is sometimes claimed that he should be a crusader. The difficulty of crusading is that it is not easy to keep it in step with judging. The practicing critic is, from the nature of his calling, in front of public opinion, though he is not often up alongside the latest enthusiasm of choreographers. If a word from him will help the public to a new experience, well and good, and if that helps the choreographer to recognition, that is a further subsidiary good. But the prime duty of a critic is not to the criticized but to the public, and seeing that propaganda has in these times made itself suspect by its very vehemence, it is more probable that a critic can help in the development of the art by his judicial pronouncements, which will command public confidence, than by himself unfurling a banner and waving it like a partisan. He will at times wish to write frankly of his private enthusiasms, which, after all, are based on his judgments, and then he can adventure his soul among the masterpieces and give his readers expository criticism of high literary quality. There are also occasions when controversy is warranted, and if it is well done a duel provides excellent fun for the onlookers, but it may be doubted whether it is as beneficial to ballet as the more persistent and sober clash of divergent opinions in the day-to-day expressions of the antagonists.

In sum, every man acting as his own critic should make judgments of value. The nature of these judgments depends on discrimination, in the last resort on perception. The field for the exercise of discrimination ranges from the sublime to the fairly, though not absolutely, bad.

Meanwhile, we must have all seen at some time a passing thrust by a well-respected writer at "those people who always seem to seek novelty above all things." And if we have been in our normal self-righteous mood, we have all mentally applauded the thrust. On the other hand, we must all have wondered in moments of disillusionment and disappointment why we have been able to watch and listen to this intangible stuff, ballet, so often without realizing what a ridiculous illusion it is. Fortunately, such moments are usually of very short duration, but in them we have no difficulty in finding authoritative confirmation of our opinion.

Here, for instance, are some of the remarks made when well-tried ballets seem for no reason to have lost their attraction. First, a comment made by a distinguished critic after a performance of *The Sleeping Beauty:* "It is not true that the delights of this work are inexhaustible. I can really say I never want to see it again." Second, by another critic: "The more one sees ballets one knows, the less one feels the desire to see them again, because one knows that nearly every performance is an absolute misrepresentation." Third, the remark: "Most critics hate ballet," made by a very superior and scholarly member of that breed.

When to the weight of these dicta (and that of my own experience of ballet-reviewing) and of my observation of the fact that the greatest master of ballet criticism in America in both historical and aesthetic matters—the reader may put whatever name he thinks fits—is almost never to be seen at a ballet performance, I do not find it difficult to convince myself that ballet pleasure is not what I used to think it was.

But surely there are no two answers to the question, "What is ballet enjoyment?" There may be different versions of the same answer, but they all boil down to the same thing—an emotional experience of some kind. It is not my intention to enunciate a philosophy or ethic, or to give an objective summary of other people's views on ballet. I am trying to be completely personal, subjective and unashamed, writing as one who enjoys ballet.

I admit that, as a youngster—knowing little if anything about it, with few facilities for seeing it anyway—I imbibed a notion that ballet (classical ballet, that is), was somehow "uplifting." From this strange idea I proceeded to the notion that ballet people were rather "better" people than others, of finer fibre. Later, I discovered, as part of that bracing disillusionment which is called education, that my early acquired unexamined assumptions were not even sensible. I came to know ballet people of all kinds: dancers, choreographers, musicians, and discovered that they are just as "human" as actors, sailors, tailors, plumbers, or even writers: often more so. They do not appear to have been necessarily improved as men and women by their experience as artists. Contact with the arts has not made them "good"; at least, not any better than they were *au fond*.

My subsequent years of ardent, constant ballet-going have induced in me the conviction that ballet has no "purpose" at all. It is not intended to make a better world. It is not meant to make bad men good and good men better. It has nothing to offer a distracted democracy or a defeated oligarchy in the way of solu-

tions to current problems. True, it may make you forget a tooth-
ache—so will a sharp attack of lumbago. It may give you a feeling
of exaltation—so will good wine. It may soothe harassed and
jangled nerves—so will any reliable sedative.

Ballet is an art (and science, too). It exists for its own sake. In
that sense it attains to the stature of the other allied arts of music
and painting. The fact that the music of *Tristan* makes some
people feel erotic and Beethoven's Ninth Symphony makes some
people feel spiritually elevated does not make Wagner's music
erotic or Beethoven's morally reformative.

In the philosophical sense, therefore, there is no purpose to
ballet; it is not "for" anything; it is not a useful instrument for
the fabrication of saints. Of course, the artist, especially the great
creative artist, works under aesthetic and personal compulsions
of which we may know little and about which little that is en-
lightening may be deduced from his work. The impulses and
processes of creation are obscurely hidden; they vary in different
men; they vary from time to time in the same man. But even
when a choreographer writes an article to explain his relationship
to God, or man's place and significance (or insignificance) in the
cosmos, it does not follow that it is the intention or design of
ballet as an art to do so.

The liking for ballet also appears to exist for its own sake. In
watching and listening to a ballet I am not conscious of purpose,
in the sense that I am when I climb a hill in order to get to the
village on the other side of it, or when I take up a difficult book,
say, on some aspect of economics, and sweat over it in order to
try to understand the theory of rent.

This disinterested quality, this absence of all purpose beyond
itself, is an essential characteristic of all art, and of ballet even
more than the others which are occasionally engaged in doing a
useful piece of work, as when a sculptor commemorates a battle,
and a painter illustrates a book or designs a carpet.

Our own individual attitude to ballet has a close connection
with, and is conditioned by, our views as to its purpose (or pur-
poselessness). I go to see a ballet for "pleasure." I want to see

certain works; I am interested in how certain artists do certain roles, certain works; I am eager to get to know better this or that ballet (there is a limited purpose here, but purely subjective).

In other words, ballet becomes Entertainment. In the hinterland of the United States it is not sufficiently regarded in that light. The heavy frown of the Puritan still commands a self-conscious, if more reluctant, attention. Our auditoriums are usually fashioned more in the style of mausoleums than as halls of pleasure. It would seem audiences have to be disciplined by gloom and hard chairs into a proper appreciation of great art.

But surely ballet is to be enjoyed precisely like fine cooking or a vintage wine or a lovely sunset (what is *that* for?) or a sonnet by Shakespeare or a rolling, tossing sea viewed from a headland.

Don't let us be highbrowbeaten into solemnity, into turning artistic fun into a religious rite. We should take our ballet as naturally as we take a glass of beer with a friend. What is the "purpose" of our beer and our conversation? What is the "purpose" of our appreciation of a beautiful woman? I have no idea.

In the various sorts of bad ballet, the crude, the rudimentary, the ephemeral, the failures and the others we have looked at, the prime cause of badness is the lack of heat in the choreographer's imagination. Bad ballet is in fact underdone ballet, ballet not properly cooked by fire, but merely damped, smoked or warmed, ballet not wholly composed.

The only gauge for testing the heat is critical opinion, which is not a scientific instrument, but an instrument which works when one knows how to use it equally as well as that opinion which governs us in all the major concerns of life. Criticism is not a science, since science after all is concerned not with living but only with the means thereto. If opinion is expressed in formal writing, criticism then itself becomes an art, a parasite art it is true, but an art none the less, in which sensibility and knowledge combine to provide the artist with external standards by which he may measure his or her own aspirations, achievements, and indeed their own exacting standards.

It should be fairly obvious to the layman who seeks guidance that what is needed is information and criticism of the right kind. Now, what is the right kind of information and criticism? An easy question to ask—and, in the case of information, easy enough to answer. For there are objective tests by which the rightness of information can be judged; even though the facts may sometimes be difficult to verify with reasonable certainty, there is at least some conceivable way of doing so. In the case of criticism, on the other hand, the situation is very different: when we make an evaluation of a ballet, there are no objective tests by which we can judge whether we are right. The nearest we can get is a sort of Gallup poll; if a large majority of reasonably cultured people like the ballet, we can be fairly certain that the ballet is fairly good. But we really cannot hope for more certainty than that; the ballet's value, though real enough, may be ephemeral—the qualities may be tied in some way to the contemporary background of culture and have no timeless appeal.

Composers have been, for the most part, poor judges of other composers; ballet-masters and choreographers have shown the same failing towards the works of their colleagues. In the case of choreographers, the judgment is perhaps inevitably biased, sometimes by jealousy, more often by the strongly subjective feelings of creative genius. But there is ample evidence to show that, although no such bias is expected in the opinions of professional critics, they are almost equally erratic; they vary too much and too violently to afford any reliable standards.

The only real test, then, of a ballet of importance is that it should be liked by several generations of cultured people. Unfortunately, when a new work is in question, this test takes an inconveniently long time. Without it we are left very much in the air.

The problem of the subjectivity of critical opinion is one that has played a very odd part in the history of art. In some contexts this subjectivity is accepted without demur: "there is no disputing about tastes," we say with a shrug. But in other contexts it is passionately denied—if not openly, at any rate by implication. As it happens, recent work by such students of the functions of language as the semanticists and logical positivists has tended to confirm the view that subjectivity must be accepted. And, as will already have become obvious, I am assuming that the view is correct—that there are no absolute standards in art and that criticism is therefore mainly the expression of personal feeling, not the assessment of objective fact. There are, it is true, many people who still take the opposite view. But for practical—as opposed to philosophical—purposes, this opposite view may, I think, be ignored, for the following reason. Take, for instance, the age-old question as to whether there is a "true" meaning of the word "beautiful" when applied to art in general and music in particular. By this I query whether a critic has the right to assume that in some absolute sense there are works that are truly beautiful and some which are not. Even if we allowed that there may be such a True Meaning, it does not help us, for we have no way of finding out what it is.

However, to say that there are no absolute standards is not to say there are no standards at all. Clearly, in any one community and in any one fairly continuous culture-pattern there will be a certain amount of agreement in practice on what is valuable.

We do get wide agreement about the greatness of certain creative artists, though even then the agreement is on a very broad and vague base. Everybody agrees that Fokine is a great choreographer; but that is after the event—after the judgment of at least a generation. Even now there is considerable disagreement as to his relative greatness compared (say) with Balanchine, and even more disagreement over the merits of individual works.

For practical purposes, then, and in dealing with new works, we may as well accept the view that criticism is largely the expression of personal feeling, not the assessment of objective fact. There is, of course, some objective basis for judging standards of performance: most people will agree on whether a dancer dances in time, whether the dancer's technique is smooth, or whether a male dancer "lifts" gracefully. But when it comes down to interpretation, and to the actual merits of the work being interpreted, the problem is made particularly difficult by two factors:

first, unlike that of poetry or painting, the medium of communication in ballet uses no signs or symbols which have much practical connection with every-day life and thus with the words invariably used in criticism; second, there is no utilitarian purpose (as there is, for example, in architecture and sometimes in painting and poetry) which will give the critic an opportunity at least to talk about comfort or logical clarity or accuracy of representation. Ballet, in fact, serves purposes and communicates emotions which cannot be expressed (or even referred to with any accuracy) in words precisely because they cannot be expressed in words.

If this is so, what can the ballet critic hope to achieve? His main object, of course, is to try to tell us not only whether we would like a ballet if we were to see it but whether it is worth our while to persevere with it even if we find it difficult to appreciate at first. In attempting to achieve this purpose, he cannot attempt to describe the emotional content of the ballet and then leave us to judge, for no words can do this. Nor can he say with reasonable certainty that everybody will feel pleasure on seeing this ballet, pain at watching that dancer, and passion on regarding another work. Much less can he describe what *kind* of feeling, whether of pleasure or pain, he thinks everybody will experience. However, what he can do is very much better than nothing.

He can try to suggest the kind of feeling he himself experienced, while at the same time showing what kind of person he himself is, so that other people can guess whether they are likely to have the same sort of feelings about the same sort of things. And he has two methods of doing this.

One is to describe directly, and as evocatively as possible, his own feelings. The value of this method depends partly on how clever he is in comparing balletic feelings with other more easily described feelings, partly on how completely his style of writing indicates his own emotional make-up, and partly on how much his readers already know of his reactions to ballets they themselves have seen (a powerful argument, by the way, against anonymous criticism).

The other method is to show the relation between the feelings he got from other ballets already known to his readers; in other words, to compare the new work with older ones and those of other choreographers. Then, in addition to expressing his own feelings, he can of course try to indicate what position the new work takes in the main stream of ballet. This kind of criticism is relatively objective, since it does not involve judgments of value; it can explain what form the work takes, whether it is dramatic, classical, abstract, neo-classic, and so on. (It is this technique which is the basis of most historical scholarship.)

If a critic can manage to do all this, he will be making a valuable contribution to our appreciation of ballet. There is surely no need to feel that, because he is forced to talk mainly about his own feelings rather than about objective fact, his observations are useless. And yet that is what many people feel. They appear to think that we cannot reject absolute standards of art without destroying all standards.

Here we come to a point which clarifies the main purpose of this chapter. As a rule, anybody who argues that ballet criticism is mainly—and inevitably—subjective is regarded as trying to debunk the whole subject. This is by no means my purpose, though I admit I hope to debunk some kinds of ballet criticism. On the other hand, assuming it to be true that criticism of ballet is more often subjective than it is in any of the other arts, it follows that a lot of unnecessary and futile argument results from a failure to acknowledge the fact. My purpose, therefore, is to try to clarify the position—to show when the objective approach is appropriate and when the subjective is not only appropriate but valuable. I wish to establish the value and scope of subjective opinion—not to denounce it as merely subjective.

The most prolific source of confusion, it seems to me, lies in our tendency to imagine that when we ourselves think something is good, the majority of right-thinking people will—or at any rate ought to—agree with us. This is, after all, a very natural tendency. When two people are arguing about the value of a work, and when we ourselves have no particular feelings either way, we may be prepared to admit that the question is one of taste—that there is no criterion which would both decide the issue and, more important, be accepted as final by a decisive majority of cultured people. On the other hand, when our own feelings are involved, we should be more than human if we did not feel that our opinion was worth something on its own merits. And this means that we are powerfully tempted to overlook the actual subjectivity of our own standards of taste. In other words, we wish to believe that our opinion has some objective validity— that there really is some absolute standard which lends it authority and makes it something more than a mere expression of personal liking. (With most people, by the way, this standard is connected with tradition, because too complete a break with tradition is too difficult to understand.) Few people, surely, can be quite content to admit that when they say a work is an artistic success, their observation has the same kind of critical value as when they say they like a good, thick, rare steak.

Of course, no one need quite admit as much as this. Naturally the professional critic is particularly unwilling to do so. The result has been a tendency throughout the history of all the arts for criticism to disguise its subjectivity as much as possible, not only from its readers but also from its writers. A further result has been that, since the critics have done most of the writing about the arts, they have, so to speak, molded their language to their own purposes; it has become a peculiarly effective instrument of disguise.

Obviously, there is not space here to go into the whole question of how language can be used for purposes of deception. We must therefore concentrate, rather baldly, on those aspects of the subject which can help to distinguished between bad and good criticism—"bad" criticism for our purposes being criticism which pretends to be more objective than it really is. Let us take a few examples, some of them from the closely related art of music.

First, "Schönberg's music (*Pierrot Lunaire*) is the last word in cacophony and musical anarchy." There is, this statement implies, universal agreement on the correct definition of "cacophony" and "anarchy" in relation to music; it further implies that this correct definition is the one used by the writer himself. Actually, of course, no such universal agreement can be assumed; the writer's self-deception, therefore, consists in imagining what he means by cacophony really is cacophony in some objective sense. In this case, however, the baldness of his assertion makes it an ineffective disguise; it is easy for us to realize that it means no more than "I hate Schönberg's music."

But what about this on Schönberg's *Five Orchestral Pieces?* "Schönberg's music . . . is a collection of sounds without relation to one another. It is the reproduction of the sounds of nature in their crudest form. Modern intellect has advanced beyond mere elementary noise: Schönberg has not." Substantially the same criticism is made in this example as in the first: the music is condemned as being cacophonous and anarchical. But here the writer has remembered the injunction given to him when he first tried to write essays: he has given his reasons. And the result is that he has at least partly defined his terms. Where the first writer merely used a vague word with derogatory associations, the second has been more precise; he has asserted that there is no relation between the various sounds and that the sounds themselves are crude. The questions still remain though. Can we say objectively that there is no relation between the sounds? Anyway, what exactly does the critic mean by "relation"? And is there any universal definition of "crude"? In other words, is the critic justified in assuming that where he finds no relation other people will similarly find no relation, and that what he finds crude is really crude in some objective sense?

There is the closest relation between ballet and music criticism, and I have taken examples from criticism of Schönberg's music for the special reason that this music is still regarded by many intelligent people as unsuccessful in the sense that it fails to communicate the composer's intentions. It would have been easy to find examples of furious criticism of ballets which are now generally agreed to be valuable, but this would not have illustrated my point so well, because it would have been too obvious that the criticisms were merely subjective. What is interesting about the case of Schönberg's music is that, though the relations between his sounds are usually perceptible on paper, many people still find it impossible to perceive them by ear. It seems unlikely, therefore, that the two criticisms quoted were entirely wrong— by the test of later experience. Nevertheless, they pretended to be more objective than they really were.

It is interesting to compare these criticisms with a discussion by the British critical writer, Edmund Sackville-West. Brief quotations unfortunately cannot give the feel of Mr. Sackville-West's argument. Those who have not read it must therefore take it on trust that it gives a general impression of openly acknowledging the subjective nature of art appreciation while at the same time appealing to what may be called the "majority" argument. That is to say, instead of insisting that Schönberg's music is ugly or bad in some absolute sense, and then concluding that people will not —in fact, *ought* not to—like it, Mr. Sackville-West approached the problem from the opposite direction: he takes as his starting-point the fact that many people cannot understand it, and then tries to explain why this is so. "Even those," he says, "who have grasped the very complicated theory of 'serial' composition usually find the results in practice as baffling as the Etruscan language." Again, later: ". . . there is an absolute cleavage between the printed score and the actual sound. However complete our intel-lectual possession of the former, the latter seems to have no relation to it." (Notice the "seems.") And so on. Finally, he attempts to suggest by analogy the sort of mentally confused feel-ing which results from trying to appreciate the musical sequence of Schönberg's ideas:

"It is like plunging naked into a gorse bush and then trying to follow the pattern of the prickles."

These examples serve roughly to illustrate three different kinds of attitude towards the job of criticism. Still using the same musi-cal analogy, we can bring out their distinguishing features by means of simplified caricatures—with headings which will explain themselves later:

(1) Pseudo-Objective

These orchestral pieces break a fundamental rule of true musical form; their composer has misunderstood the essential nature of the relation between musical ideas. This relation, properly speaking, is organic; it cannot depend on a mere haphazard throwing together of notes.

This kind of criticism is more deceptive than a mere assertion that a piece of music is atrocious or that it is the last word in cacophony. For it uses unemotional language, and it implicitly claims to be judging by objective standards. However, as the caricatured example suggests, there is one fairly reliable way of spotting the deception. This is to look out for words like "fundamental," "true," "properly speaking," "mere," etc., which indicate that the critic is using a vague but "sweet-smelling" word in some particular sense of his own and at the same time persuading himself that this sense is the "true" sense. (The trick depends on the belief, already mentioned, that words like "beautiful," "poetry," "music," "organic," and so on have one and only one correct meaning.) For instance, in the first sentence we at once suspect the words "fundamental" and "true." What *is* true musical form? This, of course, is a question about which argument is possible—and it has been argued for hundreds of years—without coming to an agreed decision. Therefore, by the words "true musical form" the writer means "the kind of musical form which I myself approve of and which I think everybody else ought to approve of as well." The same sort of analysis applies to "fundamental rule." In fact, to make an honest sentence of this assertion, we must translate it as: "These orchestra pieces break a rule which I consider extremely important to the kind of music I like."

Of course, both in ballet and music one seldom comes across a piece of criticism which is quite so over-stuffed with suspicious words as is this caricatured example. As a rule, these words are used in moderation, as in this comment on Gustav Mahler, distinguished Viennese composer, on his death in 1911: "In his treat-

Erratum: read "Janet Reed" for "Nancy Reed" in caption of dancers in *Fancy Free*.

ment of the simple melodies of his symphonies he was utterly inconsiderate of their essence." Sometimes even the key words are not used at all for whole stretches of an argument, but are silently implied, as they were in the original example about Schönberg's *Five Orchestral Pieces*. In such cases it is often difficult to detect this influence. I will return later to an example of this kind.

The second kind of attitude towards criticism may be called:

(2) Objective Explanation of Subjective Feeling

I think many people will find this insufficiently moving (or difficult to understand—or too reminiscent of the Rhapsody in Blue). *I do myself, because* . . . etc.

This type of attitude covers nearly all criticism that is potentially objective. For although the reasons why the critic disliked the reminiscence of George Gershwin may be subjective, the *fact* of the reminiscence can usually be established without fear of serious disagreement. Similarly, one can, as does Mr. Sackville-West, give reasons which adequately explain why the critic, at any rate, finds himself emotionally unmoved. Here is another example of substantially the same attitude towards atonal music: "Another objection that will have occurred to most readers is this: music is primarily a means of expressing things imagined or felt. Calculation plays a part in creation as in performance: the glowing imagination, the warm heart, must be controlled by the cool head. But in twelve-tone music calculation is pretty well everything."

As it happens, this example is perhaps rather near to falling into our first category—into self-deception. For, although this critic has given us some indication as to the reasons for his valuation of twelve-tone music, we do not know exactly which processes in composition are supposed to be "calculation" and which "warmth and imagination." And to that extent his valuation sounds more precise and therefore more objective than it really is. However, this amount of "pseudo-objectivity" is almost unavoidable in any criticism which is reasonably concise and well written. The reader would be bored by a writer who spattered his criticism with hundreds of modest phrases like "I think," "it seems to me," or "my feeling was," and who always explained precisely what he meant. Life is too short for such pedantry. We have to write and speak to some extent *as if* our own values were absolute values and as if things were simpler than they really are. And of course this does not matter, provided we are aware of the *as if* and of how difficult it is to find the happy mean between conciseness and preciseness.

Here is an example which does, I think, achieve this. It is on Paul Hindemith's *Ludus Tonalis:* "The general impression I get from this composition is of Hindemith's strong traditional sense and great cultivation of sensibility. His music is eminently civilized, European and Classical. The material he uses can be traced right back to the source of the entire classical European tradition. . . ." And so on, in reasonably precise detail.

The third attitude towards criticism may be called:

(3) Purely Subjective

This music gave me certain vivid feelings. Since they were musical feelings, they cannot be expressed in words. But I will try to suggest what kind of feelings they were by using simile and metaphor—by describing other feelings which they resemble and which can be expressed in words. I hope you will be able to guess, from this, what your own feelings are likely to be.

It would, of course, take a book longer than this to analyze the technique of writing which this attitude demands, for it is really the technique of the prose-poem. In any case, it is openly subjective, so that it does not greatly concern us here. Should anyone be curious, there can be found in some of our larger public libraries an extended example in *Musical Pilgrim's Progress* by J. A. M. Rorke.

Here are two further short illustrations. The first, by the late M. D. Calvocoressi, is about Béla Bartók's *Cantata Profana:* "It is all a matter of spirit and color, point, economy and fitness. The tone is incisive but restrained, forcible but quiet." (Notice that these two sentences are almost entirely made up of metaphor drawn from non-musical activities and feelings.) "The lines have the simplicity and clarity of definition of a picture by Braque or by Paul Nash—or of the Altamira bison." The second illustration is from a comment by that dean of music and ballet critics, Ernest Newman, on John Ireland's *Legend* for piano and orchestra. "It is heavy-muscled, slightly clumsy, and decidedly attractive in its rough honest way. This music . . . gives out a glow that is light rather than heat, and a north light at that; but what it lacks in warmth it makes up for in bracing power."

I think it is clear that the most valuable kind of criticism is that which combines the attitudes and the kind of language that has been illustrated in the second and third of these categories. The most dangerous, because most misleading, kind is that in the first category—the kind which deceives both reader and writer about its objectivity. As I have suggested, this pseudo-objective criticism will sometimes produce long stretches of argument which are particularly deceptive because they do not actually use such words as "true" and "essence," but only imply them.

I remember reading a magazine article some years ago, wherein a critic argued that Schönberg's music ought really to be called traditional. In my opinion, the thread of the writer's argument depended upon the writer giving the word "traditional" a specially restricted meaning (as applied to "the progressive and ever-increasing use of dissonance" in the history of the art) and then ingeniously implying that this meaning is an essential part of the "true" meaning of the word, thus persuading one to feel that Schönberg's music really *is* traditional in some objective way. This seems to me to destroy the word's practical value. For there is a generally accepted usage which applies it to the music of, let us say, Rachmaninoff or even Vaughan Williams; and it cannot have any usefully precise meaning if it is to be applied both to Rachmaninoff's and to Schönberg's music. But the writer has a special reason for calling Schönberg's music traditional; "traditional" is for him a "sweet-smelling" word, and if a thing is "properly speaking" traditional, it must, he assumes, embody "the essential principles of musical composition." Throughout the article, the writer is in fact implying that the "traditional" he is talking about is the "true" one. However, only once does he openly say so; and, since we may easily miss this one occasion, he has disguised the subjectivity of his views very effectively. "Being in the true sense traditional," he writes, "he (Schönberg) also became an innovator (innovation as we have seen being essentially a traditional quality in all great composers)."

I do not want, in making these comments, to suggest that the main content of this critical argument is valueless. On the contrary, I myself found it a most illuminating exposition of Schönberg's theory and technique of composition as compared with that of (what I myself call) traditional composers. In fact, the *information* it contains is excellent. And the evaluations, coming from a composer-critic who clearly has this subject at his fingertips, are also a useful expression of opinion. (I am not trying to be ironical.) But I think this opinion is misleadingly stated. For example: the critic mentions "the fundamental and constant laws of logic, coherence and clearness applied to the organization of the musical material." He speaks of "real" composers. Finally he asserts that Schönberg "has made the world aware of the authentic laws of musicianship." In a nutshell, he thinks that Schönberg's music is good. He has, of course, every right to state that that is his opinion, and also to give the reasons which helped to form it. But he seems to me to confuse the issue (and the unsuspecting reader) when he tries to suggest that this opinion is quite objectively valid.

It should be the definite duty of the professional ballet-goer—the critic—to protect and guide the public from wasting its time and from mediocre performances. It is not good enough just to read in the daily newspapers that the X ballet company gave a brilliant performance of *Swan Lake* or that the Y company gave an indifferent interpretation of *Giselle* the previous night, if the layman, a newcomer to ballet, did not attend the performances. I feel that the critic could be more helpful to the ballet-goer if he makes use of his knowledge of past performances, and writes on the possible merits of future performances.

A well-informed balletic journalist should be able to forecast to some degree for his readers where, what, and why they should go to see a particular performance. This helpful guide would assist a newcomer to ballet in saving time and money. Money in these matters is not of secondary importance to a great many ballet-goers. The not-so-well-off can easily lose heart, and the ballet world cannot afford to lose their enthusiastic support, because they represent the majority of the public.

A ballet journalist should have better use for his space than to imitate the cheap blurb that is applied to the doings of popular motion-picture and television stars who appear to have nothing more to recommend them than appearance in the latest fashion in sweaters!

There are others whose didactic writing would lose quite a lot of its length and grandeur if they refrained from airing their personal biases and prejudices and devoted their space to simple, direct observation.

The newcomer to ballet can only look for guidance from the critic when he finds him easiest. The layman is not asking Cyril Beaumont and John Martin to come down to his level but to lead him gently and kindly up to their own.

*   *   *

It has been the custom since, I suppose, something best called "time immemorial" that the printed programs for ballets contain program notes, in addition, unfortunately, to scads of advertisements.

One way of obtaining information about a work to be performed, or about an entire program for that matter, is to read program notes beforehand. Generally speaking, they are usually only available in the printed program from the usher as you take your seat.

Now, to scan program notes hurriedly in the half-light of a theater, opera house, or illy-lit barn of an auditorium just before the lights are suddenly lowered and the performance begins is not very helpful, and the sight of people actually trying to read them during the course of the performance is a distressing one. It is too obvious that they can take in neither the work nor the annotations properly, and certainly the balletic impression cannot merge with the literary commentary. The temptation to do so much as glance at program notes during the performance should be firmly resisted. Even when the plot, idea, or theme is obscure and the notes have made some attempt to elucidate its mysteries, no exception should be made, for although the notes may conceivably contain a technical analysis with indications of action and meaning, nothing could be worse for the ballet-goer than to glue his eye to the text and wait until what he duly expects pops up for the first time on the stage, then to lie similarly in wait for the next idea, and so to the end. He will be highly elated, perhaps, over the clever piece of detective work he has done, but he will certainly not have seen or heard the ballet.

It depends, of course, very much on the quality of the notes whether they do the auditor a service or not. If he finds that they tell him nothing he needs, he may put the program down without compunction and hope that the ballet may do without help. It must also be said, in fairness to the writers, that the best ballets do not by any means call forth the best commentary. An action ballet that may have a poorish plot but an excellent musical score, may be quite exciting to write about, whereas a fine abstract work, speaking for itself alone in terms of movement and design, may yield nothing beyond a competent formal analysis. Sometimes notes on the most poetical ballet imaginable make dull reading, because the poetry should not be interpreted in definite terms, lest they fail to express the meaning of the choreographer, who may never have intended to be definite.

It does not do to praise or condemn program notes for their literary merits or shortcomings. They are not meant to be satisfying primarily as literature, but as signposts on a balletic journey of adventure. Signposts are prosaic objects showing the way into a land where one hopes to find beauty.

) 11 (

On Audiences

Almost all creative artists, and certainly all dancers, find an audience an essential part of their life. Even while preparing for the performance of a work, an imaginary audience exists in the background of their mind; although their own artistic standards may be the final arbiter of their work, auditors are needed to ratify those standards.

There is an interesting parallel in music. For example, there is no more deadly work than broadcasting or recording for any sensitive musician; the unfeeling and unobtrusive microphone is no substitute for a living group of people, and while a single speaker may have some conception of the listeners who are following his words—and perhaps the telephone has prepared him for that—the musician, especially if he is playing in a concerted body, will miss the reaction of an audience which is such a valuable contribution to the performance.

I know of a certain distinguished choreographer who provides a striking instance of the truth of this remark so far as ballet is concerned. When he is rehearsing with a company on the stage alone he will go through the work to be prepared with an apparent lack of enthusiasm; but place *one* spectator in the body of the auditorium, and the atmosphere changes at once. The rehearsal suddenly becomes interesting, subtle effects are obtained, and the accented sparkle of his wit flashes like electricity.

Even our mythical layman will gain something from being one of a number of people all concentrating, even subjectively, along the same lines. The positive presence of other ballet-lovers deepens and justifies your concentration.

So we may accept an audience as a body of people who, in addition to being interested in and moved by ballet, have it in their power to affect the performance by their effect on the artists themselves.

We are inclined to take an audience as being a static body, a mass always unified and turned in a certain direction. This is wrong. A group of people does not become an audience, properly speaking, until the ballet and all the elements that go to make it up have gone to work upon its individual sensibilities and molded it into a collective body. When the applause greets the entry of the conductor, the audience takes its first steps towards having an existence *per se,* and the strength of its cohesion will depend on the power of the ballet, and even more, it must be regretfully admitted, on the power and personality of the leading performers to weld the numerous different personalities and temperaments into a unanimous whole.

During the intermissions there will be a tendency to break away, and if the appeal of the ballet has been slight the sense of being one of a group will be lost to the individual. No one will have the feeling that he has a right to speak to anyone he meets in the corridors and to take it for granted that his fellow has been through the same emotional experience as himself. When the performance is really fine, when the sincerity of the artists is equalled by the sincerity of the work, the audience will cease to be a collection of varying human beings, and will become one indistinguishable whole. Even the critics will lose their customary objectivity and themselves in the general response.

Audiences capable of exercising genuine discrimination are

very rare, and in any discussion of audiences the question of applause has to be faced. There are, to be sure, two points of view: that of a member of the audience who might have said all I have written up to this point, and that of the company or the individual artist to whom the applause is offered. The second point of view may profitably be subdivided into the ballerina or soloist and the member of the *corps de ballet,* and I venture to place more value in this connection on the opinions of the latter, who does not merely hear the applause as they enter and who is conscious of it ringing in his or her ears as the exit is made. The *corps de ballet* also has the opportunity, as they stand and wait, of covertly watching the audience go through the whole gamut of the audience's feelings. They will notice some curious things.

Applause is largely imitative, and it has a strange power of auto-excitement. With similar audiences, results will differ. The faithful *balletomanes* (ballet fans: a word coined in Russia early in the nineteenth century where the suffix *mane* is used to indicate a person having a strong liking for something—e.g., a *musicomane* is a person with a strong liking for music, an *Anglomane* for things English; it carries with it the implication of an unreasonable liking for something to the exclusion of everything else) those *balletomanes* who gather every night when a ballet season is on have built up a tradition of applause. Not only are works frequently interrupted by applause, but the curtain will merely have to flutter—not even start to descend—at the conclusion of a work and that flutter will be met by a sudden, full-strength burst of clapping, and although some of these may not be classed among the most discriminating, the length of the applause and the amount of extraneous noise brought in to add strength may be taken as indicating the depth of appreciation felt by those enthusiasts, if not solely for the ballet, at least for the favorite personalities who have been seen in it.

In the Italian operas, as in ballet, the whole continuity of the work may be interrupted at a given point—in Italian opera it is usually indicated by an overheld top note of the tenor or soprano; in ballet by an overheld and precariously sustained *arabesque* of

an exhibitionistic ballerina. There are, I regret to say, opera companies where this is followed by an encore of the aria which has
aroused the audience. If the character represented by the popular
singer is thus made to die twice, it is little matter. The plot has
been forgotten for the time being. In the earlier operas, where
each number was complete in itself and a short break was made
before the next, as is the case in purely conventional classical
ballets with a series of independent *variations,* there was, it is true,
a certain excuse for such behavior, but in more modern works,
where the composer has been at pains to write music which
carried the story right through, it is little better than vandalism,
although to hope to correct it at this time of day is sheer tilting
at phantoms.

The intelligent ballet-goer could do much to help rescuing
applause from the silly convention it has unfortunately become.
One would think that applause ought to have something to do
with the public's reaction to a performance, but only too often
one suspects it is a purely mechanical response. At certain performances which attract a select audience—I mean balletically
select—differences in the quality of the applause may sometimes
be detected which an analytical ear may bring into accord with
the quality of the performance; but too often the same thick, non-
descript noise of hand-clapping greets any and every sort of dancing and induces one to ask despairingly whether audiences are
really as dense as they seem or merely misguidedly kindhearted.

Occasionally one has cause to suspect the latter more strongly.
It is a psychologically interesting if artistically distressing fact
than when for once in a way an audience in this country goes
to extravagant lengths of generosity in the matter of applause, it
is usually after some ghastly blunder on a dancer's part, some
accident too obvious to have escaped even the most imperceptive
auditor, such as a stumble or an actual fall. Our American spirit
of sportsmanship, admirable even when it is grossly out of place,
asserts itself on such occasions with a fervor that is touching, but
both ludicrous and exasperating from an aesthetic point of view.
Where sports are concerned nothing could be finer than the

principle that approbation should be offered for an attempt
rather than an achievement, and indeed such a principle may
well be applied to ballet performances by amateurs at a ballet
school recital. But professional performers are to be judged only
by the results of their work and on no account by shows of pluck.
An attempt not carried out is simply a bad performance, and
there is no excuse for applauding this from any consideration
whatever. It is an excellent rule for any ballet-goer to regulate his
outward response entirely by the impression which the performance as such makes on him and not by the artist's or performer's
personalities. And he ought to take the trouble to train himself
to measure his applause by what he feels about the ballet and the
performance itself. If he is stirred to the point of wanting to shout
for joy, let him shout; but if he is left cold, no mere sense of
politeness should move him to stir a hand. Much less ought he
to be induced to clap merely because others clap and it seems
rather churlish not to join in. Enough goes on at ballet performances, goodness knows, at which one *ought* to feel churlish.

These remarks on the subject of audiences and applause may
have seemed rather unkind, but much might have been said of
well-behaved audiences who, while not lacking in enthusiasm,
are sensitive enough to know when and where to relieve their
emotions and display their appreciation. The source of the trouble
really arises in the fact of applause. To applaud or not to applaud
has often been discussed, but since applause is such a well-estab-
lished fact, and one which even the influence of Bayreuth cannot
always restrain, any such discussion is purely academic. What
would be more useful would be to recognize that if appreciation
may legitimately be shown by clapping, the lack of it, or more
positive disapproval, might be no less justly displayed. Some time
ago an enlightened member of one audience showed his distaste
for what he had seen and heard in no uncertain manner. He
seems to have been reproved by all and sundry. I should like to
see a Congressional medal struck in his honor, and a society of
courageous ballet-lovers formed who would not hesitate to demon-
strate exactly their reactions to certain works and certain perform-

ances. There can surely be nothing said in favor of applause which cannot also be put forward on behalf of any expression of displeasure. At least it would give a value to applause which it does not now possess, and might make it at length possible to exercise criticism in the ballet theater. A unanimous audience might subsequently be more difficult to attain, but the artist or company which achieved it would recognize its triumph.

Funny things, audiences. They have their own distinctive personalities. Some are restless, some are garrulous, some, as I have pointed out, are inclined to excessive clapping of the hands. Yet, there is error in the opposite. As I said at the beginning of this chapter, audience response is absolutely essential to the artist. There is a disturbing tendency, outside of metropolitan centers, not to applaud at all. Applause, intelligently placed, is a valuable and necessary contribution to the artist.

Despite all I have written, there are times when I look at what I can only term a typical ballet audience I find it difficult to be dogmatic about its reactions. Through all weathers they have come. Discomfort does not matter, even at the over-crowded, over-heated, uncomfortable top of the house, where rapt young girls and concentrated young men are still as still. And during the intermissions the buzz of their volubility rises to the ceiling and bounces back again.

Those who live in the big metropolitan centers who, for economic or other reasons, have not taken the precaution to secure their seats in advance, and have to content themselves with standing-room, queue up hours in advance of performance time, and stand and stand and stand. How they do it I don't know. Their endurance is almost incredible. When I look at the queues I usually find a large percentage—if not the largest—consists of young women who are not abashed by the rigors of the New York and Chicago climate or the tedious hours of waiting.

In looking at them I find it hard to dogmatize about audience reactions.

) 12 (

Subsidy Must Come!

It is too easy, and not nearly enough, to say, as so many do, that the place of the performer is exclusively and only on the stage. A much truer method of situating the performer in ballet is half-way between the choreographer and the audience. The performer is the channel through which the ideas flow: the transmitter of the original balletic compositions of the choreographer, and, like all transmitters, the less distorting the better.

Yet there exists in the minds of a large number of people a considerable confusion about the place and function of the dancer as performer; and especially there exists a confusion between "performance" and "interpretation."

Let us first cut away some of the dead wood from this equivocal, obscurantist, multiform word, "interpretation." The *Concise Oxford Dictionary* gives its main sense (under "interpret") as to "expound the meaning of (abstract words, writings, etc.)" and later "to act as interpreter." An interpreter is "one whose office is to translate orally in their presence the words of a person speaking different languages." Is dance a foreign language to be translated? Or an obscure gospel needing exegesis? The big

Oxford English Dictionary defines "interpretation" as "the representation of a part in a drama or the rendering of a musical composition according to one's conception of the author's idea." The only quotation given in the *Oxford English Dictionary* is from the *Athenaeum* of 1880; so we may take it on authority that the word never occurred before in English literature, and then only in a Victorian critical journal.

There are two sorts of critics today: the armchair critics and the peripatetic critics, who have to ramble from theater to hall, whenever ballet seasons ridiculously overlap in large metropolitan centers, and to cover dance recitals *nearly* every night (I believe they get a night off now and then), seeing very often the same works and the same dancers in our so restricted repertoire, or what they have time to see of them, in order to hasten back to the office or to the telephone to provide "copy" for next morning's breakfast table. Small wonder that the ambient critics, the "professionals," write about "interpretation." After the first few years, there is little left that one can think up in the late evening to write about. Having been a critic myself, I do not hint at blame. But those armchair critics who compare performances of our thin repertoires and tell us practitioners of ballet from a splendid height, about "interpretation"—well, them I condemn.

Of all the creative artists, only the playwright, the composer, and the choreographer need performers. Painters, sculptors, poets, novelists perform their own works with their own hands. Anyone who mixes up drama and music and ballet in his critical mind is wrong. When Jan Peerce sings *Bohème* at the Metropolitan Opera House, he is not "interpreting" the part of Rodolfo—he is quite simply "performing" Puccini's music as Puccini meant it to sound, with a fine understanding of the nationality and idiom of the composer's invention. That is musical performance, not interpretation. When Margot Fonteyn dances the role of the Princess Aurora in *The Sleeping Beauty,* the same thing is true balletically; she is not "interpreting" the role.

That dictionary quotation of 1880 is extremely important, for it accurately dates the life, so short, of this misconceived word "interpretation." It is a Victorian invention and survival. It is post-Romantic almost to the pitch of being a part of "the Romantic agony." It comes from the "Brahmins" and their adoring tradition; it is a part of the virtuoso-dancer craze, a part of the jealousies of the 1850-1939 period.

By the eighteenth century the performing artist had become more important than the work performed. By the mid-nineteenth century, she (and he) were becoming adored figures; with the rising motion-picture the performer became supreme. We go, it seems, to see Miss X or Mr. Y in intolerable rubbish that no artist could stomach. We go to see Miss Z dance in the same old ballets. Crowds flock to hear Mr. A conduct the same old war-horses and listen to them on the radio. If another conductor puts on an unfamiliar work of genius, without a "star," the house will be empty, the home listeners will turn off their receiving instruments. The public's thrill at success does not cover its ignorance of real worth. For it is easier to fool the public as a performer than as anything else in the world. It is as true in ballet as it is in music, where it is very true indeed. Let me give a musical example: A pianist can give showers of wrong notes, but "we like his interpretation of Chopin"—we can say "we like his (or her) Chopin," as if Chopin were a puppet worked by a skilled ventriloquist of charming platform manners. That is, I submit, a rubbishy point of view.

Who can imagine, for example, William Byrd fussing about "interpretation" when a motet by him was performed at the Chapel Royal in London? Obviously, he did not expect clowns to sing his religious music any more than he expected the "Gentlemen and Children of H. M. Chapels Royal" to do trapeze acts or horse-training. But that is style, not interpretation. Did Bach fuss about his "inner meaning" at Cothen or his "soul" at the Thomaskirche? Was Purcell anxious about being properly interpreted in his Act Tunes for the theater? He was probably more interested in whether the bawdy jokes in his Catches written for the Coffee House got a good resounding laugh above the clatter of pots and bottles and plates! There can have been no attempt at "interpretation" with Schubert's amateur orchestra, and little more, save for a general, smiling, benign humor, with Haydn's band at Esterhazy.

The answer is that these great persons were practicing professionals, not armchair critics. Look at the Köchel catalogue of Mozart's works, and you will realize that it left little time in thirty-six years for bothering about his "soul." The "soul" came in with Goethe and Wordsworth, flourished on Tennyson and Matthew Arnold, and became dominant with Freud and Schönberg.

Ballet is activity. It is something done by breath and body, hands and feet. The real performer is, first, a dancer. A good performance is a matter of good texture, for ballet moves in time as the muscles move in space. The performer is necessary in ballet because no choreographer can dance his own patterning or convey his ideas by himself. The dancer has his (or her) "part" to perform. He has been taught this "part" by the choreographer. Now this "part" is, actually, a series of instructions, of demands for action, from a more dominating and more creative mind; it is nothing else. The performer does not "interpret" that; with his technique, his innate sense of balletic practice and custom, his skill of movement, muscle and breath, his working-in with his colleagues, he transfers into balletic patterns, literally and without any personal intrusion, the directions of the creator of the work. If he is a good performer, he will have understanding of the choreographer's intentions. But also he will use no false effects. He will realize his responsibility to the directing mind of the choreographer, and find his joy, his life work, in serving it.

Any form of personal intrusion in the performance of a ballet is an insult to the choreographer and a barrier between choreographer and audience. Choreographer and audience are, in my mind, very near; the first wants to express his emotions in ordered patterns, the second to receive them in the simplest and most direct form possible.

Interpretation? No! Performance? Yes! That is the study of a lifetime for the real artist.

*   *   *

Again we come to the question of assistance for ballet, for all the arts, in some practical way. It will have been seen already that from the time of the foundation of ballet some form of subsidy has always been necessary. The subvention may have come from one of a variety of sources: from a king or prince who had a taste for the arts or a desire for display, as in the instance of Louis XIV and Lully; from a municipality or central government; from the coffers of a wealthy man with ambitions; from a group of business men who for more obscure reasons—tax relief among them—think this a good way of spending money. The euphonious name for this sort of financial assistance for the arts is patronage.

Art or the arts is the name given to the activities of those who express themselves not in the limited medium of words, but in the more imaginative forms of music, ballet, the visual arts, the drama, and certain types of motion-pictures. Whichever of the forms is chosen for self-expression, there will be two distinct approaches to the art, namely, the function of the creator and the function of the performer; and in any discussion of State assistance for the arts, it is essential to think of these functions separately.

In the United States, some municipalities apart, faith has always been pinned to private enterprise; groups of socially-minded and generous people have pooled their resources, and by means of their organizations have helped. Such organizations have seldom operated on lines broad enough to make a permanent ballet company possible, although with the help of interested business people, an air of permanence has been given to some companies from time to time.

Both running expenses and the cost of new productions being in excess of actual income in most cases, ballet is obviously a deficit enterprise. Ballet offers no investment to the cautious investor; for in the long run considerable money must be lost, just as it is "lost" on education, art galleries, museums, public parks.

From this it is obviously but a step for all those who consider

the arts to be an essential part of our cultural life to say that the
Government should find the money. In Great Britain during
the last decade-and-a-half valuable advances have been made in
this direction. Since patronage, as I have pointed out, has always
existed, it is not even a new idea that the Government should be
patron. Up until the eighteenth century, it was the Government
in the person of the Sovereign who was always a patron of the
arts. In Germany the history of opera is the history of patronage,
first by the petty sovereigns of the numerous states and after the
debacle of 1918 by the patronage of municipalities and the national government. During the difficult between-wars period
eighty-one opera houses and companies in Germany were subsidized, Berlin at the top receiving over $1,000,000 a year.

In Britain, for the first time, the arts are receiving financial
assistance from a democratic state. The wartime organization of
the Council for the Encouragement of the Arts (ENSA), set up
as a permanent body under the title of the British Arts Council,
provides the machinery for distribution of State aid. It should be
emphasized that no professional artist, be he musician, painter,
dancer, or actor, questions the desirability of the subsidy. It has
been left to the amateurs, the connoisseurs, the theorists, and
the reactionaries to doubt the possibility of a healthy growth of
national culture activity which must look to the Government for
its patronage. And even those doubters do not question the need
for patronage, but rather doubt the ability of the Government
to create an adaptable enough machinery.

There have been even deeper reasons for the official neglect of
the arts. Government circles in the United States have never
displayed any great sympathy for the arts. As a democracy, the
United States has been blessed with no princelings who, with
their eyes turned towards some New England Versailles, have
used the ballet, opera, and music as a medium for an ostentatious
display of wealth, power, and culture. Although the motive for
such expenditure may have been fundamentally vague, artists
whose glory far outshines that of their patrons produced mag-

nificent works as a result, displaying their own splendor rather than the tempered brilliance of those whom they served.

Deprived of such exalted assistance, American artistic organizations have languished. Perhaps one could scarcely expect cultural sympathy from coal and iron ore owners, steel magnates, and the higher middlemen of commerce, and it is only now, when the upward rush of industrialism has eased, that their descendants, standing somewhat aloof from their family origins, have had the leisure and desire to form foundations and trusts to interest themselves in more polite activities. Thus it is that we find occasional benefactors to whom a few thousand dollars as a gift to an artistic enterprise is not considered ill-spent money. To such people, whose number is being rapidly diminished by taxation, these organizations have been grateful, and the practical value of such help cannot be denied. But it offers no sure foundation for a permanent ballet company. The wealthy donor may be whimsical and capricious, may change the object of his favor at any moment, like the generous captain of industry who, after having partly erected a handsome Episcopal church at his own expense, suddenly turned Catholic and left the unfinished ghost of his former sympathies to mock his infidelity.

The patron has always been deemed an integral part of the provision of the arts and especially for the support of work of that small section of the artistic world that must be ahead of the main development of its own time in order to become the main growth of the future.

The fundamental cause for uneasiness of opinion lies in the anxiety regarding the human factor in the administration of the Government subsidy when it eventually comes. On the one hand is the knowledge that Government patronage involves the spending of the tax-payers' monies, and that the expenditure must be accounted for. On the other hand is the little appreciated but essential condition that the arts cannot give a short-term account of themselves. The ideal conditions of Government aid will assume the principle that Government subsidy for the arts is acceptable to the people: that the distribution of the funds must be left unreservedly and without interference from the Government (which *is* the people) and any of its departments, in the hands of administrators chosen for their knowledge, their powers of judgment and discernment; that there must be no call, no request, no demand, not so much as a thought for short-term results; and that there must be ample allowance for a considerable margin of error.

So far the problem of Government aid has been discussed in general terms from the point of view of the public. In practise it is likely to be found that each art will require particular consideration, although, finally, similar principles are applicable to all.

The economic problem facing the creative artist arises, as we have seen, first out of the need for a prolonged and specialized training, and eventually out of the time lag, which may last to the end of his life, between the first steps towards creation and the sale of the work. The entrepreneur, impresario, manager, or agent, what you will, who acts, after a lapse of time can indeed make a considerable fortune by the circulation of the great creative works. Musicians do, as I have pointed out, obtain a very small performing right fee for a period, but this, together with the cost of publishing and printing, defeats its own purpose by making the cost of performing the works of living composers greater.

The solution of the first problem can and must be overcome as a part of a sound long-term education policy of the country at large. The second problem, that of covering the time-lag, will involve the granting of financial assistance and substantial aid direct to the individual, a solution which, if accompanied by conditions and qualifications, could bring in its train more evils than at present exist. It is a truism that no generation can be the judge of contemporary creation. But as there is no absolute standard in creative art, there is no test by which a potential artist can claim to qualify for subsidy. It appears, therefore, that until such time as the whole population is on a minimum subsistence rate, personal subsidy must be made for creative artists and the chance of error must be risked.

The element generally disregarded by the alarmist who would warn us against such a procedure is that the quantitative sum of such claims for subsidy, when taken in proportion to the total population, would be minute. At the same time it would be a salutary comparison if the alarmist looked up the cost to state and local governments, to say nothing of the national government, of supporting lunatics and mental deficients.

For the performing function of the arts, the duty of the Government is far more obvious and far easier of execution, because results can be shown in very much shorter time. Again the first problem is even more prolonged and specialized training to produce the executant and the future administrator. Again the solution is to be found in an appreciation of the problems peculiar to this type of training, and its inclusion in the country's general education policy is imperative. A step in this direction is the New York City School of Performing Arts, where, as a part of the city's public school system, the adept and talented pupil is given training for a career in the arts.

The gradual reduction of the higher incomes must in any case cut down the number of potential private patrons, but, even in the heyday of private patronage, no single person or organization could have met such a demand as is at present waiting to be met. Only the vast resources of the Government itself can provide the special facilities requisite for cultural activities by the provision of theaters that are modern and well appointed, auditoriums worthy of the name, halls that are something more than storage warehouses, and art centers functioning otherwise than as roosting perches for countless pigeons. Perhaps the difference between cultural activities in the past and in the future lies in the new conception of decentralization from metropolitan centers like New York, Chicago, San Francisco, to the country at large, from the "upper classes" to the whole public, from certain intermittent occurrences to daily activity.

Far from stifling art, Government aid has become essential to the very existence of the arts. As to whether Government aid will improve the standard of the arts in this country, it must be generally assumed that that will depend to what extent patronage can be left free to grow with the temporary and ever changing need in the artistic world, free of any and all conditions and qualifications; and to what extent the country itself can produce an administration capable of building a living tradition of patronage.

Those who fear possible political meddling in the arts and the wielding of force through government subsidy might well bear in mind the power wielded by today's private patrons. It is possible under the democratic system to vote the interferer out of office. Nothing can remove the unintelligent private patron; so long as the patron calls the tune, the artist must dance to it.

) 13 (

Ballet in America

In this volume, intended to bring to the layman something about what he may look for in order to derive from ballet the greatest amount of pleasure, I have from time to time expressed some of my dissatisfactions with some of ballet's practices and some of our ballet institutions. Some readers may have wondered at the drift of the arguments, whether I have been hitting out in all directions or whether the blows were aimed at a single target. At the risk of boring the more discriminating and certainly the more discerning, who will have seen through all my strictures against ballet managements and administrations, dancers, choreographers, patrons, and so on, I must endeavor to correlate my opinions on these and similar matters, if only to satisfy myself that I have not scribbled a few unrelated chapters to relieve the grudges of many years.

Someone has wisely pointed out that "the only true prophets are those who carve out the future which they announce." That we should go on being displeased with things as they are, long after the rebellious twenties have passed into history, is an excellent attitude and was never more necessary than today, but such feelings should be the prelude to hard thinking which in its turn will be of very little use unless it leads to a plan of action combined with a determination to put the plan into operation.

Few people will disagree with this as far as it goes, but most of us are so occupied with quotidian details that we may almost be excused if we lose sight of the aim we originally made for. But now the world changes before our very eyes; institutions, prejudices, and hampering traditions are crumbling around us, and even while we attempt to resist or control these changes, hoping in either event to save ourselves from becoming engulfed in the ruins, we have unexampled opportunities of planning and erecting the structures which are to take their place. And from the falling edifices we can select certain bricks and beams and stones which may usefully be employed in our new buildings, and the best of the past will serve other and even better purposes.

It would seem well to review concisely what has been accomplished in ballet in the United States in the little more than two decades since its revival, at the risk of and with the intent of repeating for purposes of emphasis certain facts which have been touched on earlier.

Ballet. What is ballet? *The Concise Oxford Dictionary* says quite simply, "Combined performance of professional dancers on the stage. (F, dim. of *bal,* BALL.) *Webster's* Dictionary volunteers the information, adorned with the usual cabalistic signs, that the word ballet is derived from "*It. balleto;* dim. *ballo—* dance. An artistic dance performed as a theatrical entertainment, or an interlude by a number of persons, usually women. Sometimes, a scene, accompanied by pantomime, or dancing."

Which, of course, is all right as far as it goes. Ballet, like most words we use in everyday conversation, has enlarged and changed its meaning through the ages. Some balletically illiterate people still use the word in its now obsolete connotation of "toe-dancing."

For purposes of summary, so far as ballet in our time in the

Western Hemisphere is concerned, it would be well to remember that, late in 1933, to the St. James Theatre in New York—a playhouse of the Broadway type that was by coincidence a decade later to serve as the long-time home of the musical comedy, *Oklahoma!*—there came, almost unsung and unheralded, a European ballet organization known as Colonel de Basil's Ballet Russe de Monte Carlo. At one of its performances, the gross receipts totalled $48.

Late in 1949, this time to the Metropolitan Opera House in New York, came, widely heralded, the Sadler's Wells Ballet of London. Practically unknown to the Western Hemisphere, after four weeks in New York and five of touring the hinterland, it gathered some $500,000 from the sale of tickets.

In 1933, such meagre support as ballet had came from a handful of people composed of those who knew from experience what ballet was, a few who were sufficiently curious to wish to investigate, and a tiny, hysterical fringe of idolators from whom stalwart men flinched.

In 1956 the enormous audience that storms the doors may fairly be described as a cross-section of the American public.

In 1933, ballet was a highly speculative, dubious, but high-hearted and courageous venture, looked upon sceptically and, since it seemed something foreign to the temper and taste of the American people, generally regarded as being without a future. Today there is certainly no question about its popularity; any fear there may be for its survival springs from other sources than its public appeal.

What has happened to change the attitude of the people of the Western Hemisphere from one of either passive disinterest or active distaste for ballet to one not only of acceptance but in many cases of genuine enthusiasm?

The reasons are numerous and opinions varied. There is, of course, the fact that certain ballet companies are a "must" in the sense that to see them is "the thing to do." Another reason would seem to be that the people have found for themselves that ballet is not foreign to their temper and taste, but that it is, both as an art and as an entertainment, first-rate theater: satisfying and exciting.

All this did not happen over night. During the years since 1933, a great deal of valuable spade work has been done in the garden. Ballet has had its able apologists, its impassioned and vocal devotees, its talented if sometimes misguided propagandists. Yet none or all of these would have succeeded by mere power of words. The only value of writing or talking about any art is to induce people to look at it more intelligently or listen to it with a more sensitive ear. Writing or talking cannot teach one to look or listen. None of what has occurred could have happened had not the people themselves out of their natural curiosity gone to see and discover ballet for themselves. This they could not have done had it not been for hardy, pioneering souls who, for one reason or another or a combination of them, continued to make ballet available. Ballet had to be cultivated, and the only possible cultivation was by exposing the people to it at something like its best.

It is safe to assert that, by and large, the average American had preconceived notions about ballet, gathered partly from hearsay and partly from the occasional Classical, Spanish, or Oriental Ballets that popped up in the stage shows of movie houses the country over, in the days of silent films, where frequent hippy ladies and occasional hippier gentlemen pirouetted about the stage until it was time for the feature picture. The retort of those brought up on that diet could only be some variant of "Even if it was good, I wouldn't like it."

What was required was that the people of the Western Hemisphere should be exposed to ballet as often and as continuously as possible. Through the media of various ballet companies of varying qualities this has been done with considerable consistency since those not-so-far-away days of 1933, until names of certain organizations, certain individuals, have become as familiar and as newsworthy as movie stars, athletes, and some congressmen. While it is regrettable that quality has by no means always kept pace with popularity, on the whole North Americans have been offered a good deal of ballet.

The late war had a stimulating effect on ballet, particularly in the field of audience growth. Because the revival of ballet occurred during the pre-war depression years, there were economic reasons why a considerable section of the public was unable to investigate its delights. With the lush years of high employment, money became more plentiful and there was more to spend on entertainment. A large new audience cautiously tasted and found the dish to its liking. It was not uncommon during the war to observe, for example, at a Los Angeles premiére of a ballet season, with Hollywood publicity-seekers tripping over one another to exhibit their plumage, spotted throughout the audience, dungareed, tin-helmeted citizens, who would leave hurriedly at the end of the performance for their stretch on the swing-shift.

The performances given by the various touring companies for military encampments and hospitals gave many a service man his first taste of ballet. The communications phrase, I believe, is a "captive audience." More often than not, on his return to private life the service man, thus exposed, became a supporter of ballet.

So, the rank and file of the people of the United States and Canada having been exposed to it, liked it and in turn became the best of all propaganda agents; for the old adage that the best customer is the satisfied customer still holds true.

*   *   *

Thus far our summations have been almost exclusively with the financial and popular aspects of ballet in the Western Hemisphere.

This is perhaps as it should be. However, there are those to whom ballet is a necessity. To these people ballet is something more than entertainment. It is a great art. Surely, there is no reason why a great art cannot be a great popular art.

While this is not the place for a detailed history of theatrical dancing on the Western side of the Atlantic, it will not be amiss to point out that from the earliest beginnings of the American democracy the dance of the theater has figured in its annals. However, the early history of ballet in America is made up chiefly of records of performances of European ballets and dancers. It is only very recently, historically speaking, that American and Canadian companies and American and Canadian dancers have begun to appear.

One reason for this, no doubt, is that ballet for the performer, as pointed out before, requires long and arduous training. This training can be had only in schools which, thanks to state subsidies and endowments, have existed throughout Europe for years. Unless there are permanent companies, providing an outlet for the trained products of these schools, the latter are of little practical value.

On the other hand, history shows us that Americans have always, in greater or lesser degree, been receptive to ballet. The first recorded ballet performance on American soil dates back to 1791; and James Hewitt's *Tammany,* one of the earliest American operas, featured a ballet based on American Indian dances. Practically all the great so-called Romantic ballets were seen at one time or another, and the apex was probably reached when in 1840 the Viennese Fanny Ellsler came here for what was to have been a brief visit and remained two years to the delight of American audiences, causing Congress to recess when she danced in Washington; she was officially received by President Van Buren and his entire Cabinet, and won the respect of such a discerning intellectual as Ralph Waldo Emerson. Following Ellsler's departure, interest remained high for a decade or more, to lapse only as quality lapsed.

To many still living, for years ballet was synonomous with the name of Anna Pavlova, the great Russian ballerina, who visited American almost annually, carrying her fine individual artistry and her own particular and personal conception of ballet to a generation which had never seen any sort of ballet performance.

During the First World War, the famous Russian Ballet of

Serge Diaghileff gave America its first viewing of a new art of the theater, where music, settings, costumes, and dance itself were as if informed by a single mind. The result was a revelation, the impact of which had repercussions not only in the theater, but in women's clothes and in the decorative schemes of American homes.

After the Diaghileff return to Europe, there were half-hearted attempts to keep ballet alive in the United States, but from the date of Anna Pavlova's final American appearance, in 1925 until December 21, 1933, when the de Basil Ballet Russe de Monte Carlo first appeared at the St. James Theatre, there was what amounted to a balletic drought, relieved none too successfully by the movie-house presentations aforementioned.

So, December 21, 1933, may be said to mark the rebirth of ballet in America in the sense of its presentation at the hands of a professional and reasonably permanent company, giving attention to all its details, music and setting, together with dancing.

The subsequent reawakening of interest in ballet, the nationwide tours of the various "Russian" companies, the formation of Ballet Theatre, and, more recently, the New York City Ballet, the development of schools, and the emergence of native dancers and choreographers, with the beginnings of what may be called a native adaptation of an international art—all these go to make up the pattern of ballet in North America today.

The really important thing is that ballet has at the same time developed a wide and seemingly ever-growing audience, one that is becoming increasingly informed and, therefore, more intelligently discriminating. In many towns and cities of the United States and Canada, ballet is the only form of "live" theater the public sees.

*   *   *

Half a decade ago, when the British Sadler's Wells Ballet first visited America, the demand for seats struck the uninitiated as unprecedented and inexplicable. Particularly was this true of the commercial vendors of Broadway amusement. The response was, of course, phenomenal; but it should be borne in mind that since 1933 one or more ballet companies have been giving annual seasons in New York, and have toured the country from end to end, without interruption even during the war years.

A considerable measure of credit for much of this pioneering spade-work must go to a round-faced, cherub-like impresario, S. Hurok, himself a curious mixture of sentimental idealism and shrewd commercialism, who at one time had managed Anna Pavlova's American tours, and who in 1933 sensed that the time was ripe for a renaissance of ballet interest.

It was the late Charles Frohman, dean of American theatrical producers, who laid down the dictum that a new generation in theater audiences arrives every seven years. Exactly seven years elapsed between Anna Pavlova's final American performances and Hurok's introduction of Colonel W. de Basil's Ballet Russe de Monte Carlo to the American shores. Convinced of the validity of his own hunch that now was the time, Hurok persevered, giving the entire country annual ballet seasons up to the point where for a long period his name became in the minds of many synonymous with ballet.

I have taken pains to point out earlier that the very nature of the art, the costs of new productions, the high level of operating expenses, all of these preclude the possibility of ballet being commercially profitable, of even paying its own way, despite its popularity and its wide audience. However, one does not suggest Impresario Hurok is poorer for this three-decade association with the art.

Political, financial, personal, and artistic differences caused a split in the Ballet Russe de Monte Carlo ranks in 1937, when the Russian de Basil's Ballet Russe de Monte Carlo was supplanted in America by the Russian-American Denham's company bearing the same name, containing many of the same "personalities," and headed by the same artistic director and choreographer, Leonide Massine. It still appeared under the Hurok banner. Those were the days when all ballet had to be "Russian" at all costs. The behind-the-scenes political and financial shenanigans leading to internal schism were of little interest to the general public, which wanted to have and was entitled to have ballet at its best.

From 1933 to 1940, ballet in North America was almost completely under the domination of the so-called "Russian" companies, although their ranks were increasingly filled by English, American and Canadian dancers, frequently masquerading under pseudo-Slavic names to maintain a deception which with the passing of time eventually deceived no one save the deceivers.

In 1940, largely through the enterprise of an idealistic young American, Richard Pleasant, and the substantial financial backing of a wealthy American widow with dancing ambitions, Lucia Chase, Ballet Theatre was founded. This was what may be called the first thoroughly professional American ballet company. In its early seasons it made ballet history, not with any accent on chauvinism but with a broad, catholic, international repertory and the best available artists from the international world of ballet; at the same time it gave opportunity for native dancing, musical, choreographic and designing talent. Conceived on a grand scale, its costs were mastodonic.

Political and financial schisms apparently being one of the more unfortunate aspects of ballet, the Hurokian sponsorship of the Denham Ballet Russe de Monte Carlo was terminated in 1942. Hurok, determined not to be balletless, and still persuaded that unless ballet was "Russian," it could neither be ballet nor popular, assumed the booking and promotional direction of the more or less native Ballet Theatre, loading it down with the unwieldy and untrue slogan, "The Greatest in Russian Ballet."

Meanwhile, the Ballet Russe de Monte Carlo struck out on an independent booking course, and with assets consisting principally of a trade name that had been effectively publicized, a repertory of old war-horses considerably the worse for wear, and a ballerina of international renown but no longer in the first flush of youth. Year in and year out, the company barnstormed to enthusiastic audiences presumably of a remarkable lack of discrimination.

Meanwhile, as early as 1934, two Americans, Lincoln Kirstein and Edward M. M. Warburg, founded the School of American Ballet, and in December of that year the School's Producing Company presented its first public program at the Avery Memorial Theatre, Hartford, Connecticut, with George Balanchine as ballet-master, artistic director, and choreographer.

From this sprang the American Ballet, which, in turn, became the Ballet Caravan, which toured extensively from 1936 to 1939, until the war interrupted its activities. Immediately after the war, in 1946, Lincoln Kirstein announced the formation of the Ballet Society, a "non-profit membership organization for the encouragement of the lyric theatre by the production of new works." Its program was ambitious:

1. *Presentation of new theater pieces, including ballet, ballet opera and chamber opera, either commissioned by the Ballet Society or unfamiliar to the American public as well as individual concert dancers. 2. Cooperation with other educational and cultural institutions to enable the production of performances, exhibitions, and publications difficult to accomplish alone. 3. Publication of books, prints and articles which will award to the dance a serious and consistent attention long enjoyed by painting, sculpture, architecture and music. 4. Production and circulation of ballet companies, individual dancers and national dances as well as experimental films using dance as a main element. 5. Publication of record albums of music used in the performances of the Ballet Society with photographic documentation and full program notes. 6. Awards of fellowships to enable talented young dancers and choreographers to work by themselves or with groups of dancers to develop technically and professionally.*

One of the strongest features of these activities was that the organization was coupled with a comprehensive academy of ballet for the first time in the United States. From this school and its associated public activities have come a number of leading American dancers and young choreographers. Much of the work has been highly experimental, some of it valuable, some of it seemingly capricious; but it may be said that Kirstein has done more than any other individual for the development of the art of the ballet on these shores.

Kirstein's present non-commercial venture, the New York City Ballet, which with Ballet Theatre and the Ballet Russe de Monte Carlo go to make up the trio of big ballet companies in the Western Hemisphere, in the opinion of many is potentially the strongest, with the greatest likelihood of eventual survival in a highly competitive field.

*   *   *

According to the Charles Frohman theory of the seven-year generation cycle in the world of entertainment, ballet in America, since its revival in 1933, had in 1949 entered its third generation. New audiences had been attracted, its drawing power had increased. However, so far as the so-called "commercial" companies were concerned, its quality had deteriorated considerably. A tonic was called for.

It was provided, surprisingly enough, by the visit to these shores of the Sadler's Wells Ballet of London. Superbly organized, offering the attraction of novelty in the form of full-length ballets requiring an entire evening for performance, whereas the custom in America had heretofore been to present a program consisting of several shorter pieces, and with productions that were tastefully, carefully, thoroughly prepared in every department, it showed American audiences how good ballet can be when it is at its best. The chief value of the Sadler's Wells visits therefore may be said to have been educational.

It is an open question if American and Canadian audiences, after exposure to the quality of the Sadler's Wells productions, will be content with anything less than that. This could have two possible results: either our American companies will be forced to pull up their individual and collective socks, or else risk losing a public which has heretofore been content with an inferior product without realizing its inferiority.

This naturally raises in the lay mind the very obvious question why our native companies do not immediately heed the warning and take steps to remedy the situation. The answer, as the reader may have gathered, is simple. It is a matter of money. Why should it be a matter of money if ballet is so highly successful at the box office? A successful play makes a profit for its investors while giving a livelihood to its participants; why, then, are funds lacking with which to improve quality and pay for new productions?

Some of those intimately associated with ballet, to whom these questions present a recurring nightmare, point out that Sadler's Wells is able to make productions of high quality and to maintain a permanent company employed the year round, something that is essential to the sound conduct of any ballet company, because it has the benefit of a government subsidy from the British Treasury allotted through the governmentally associated British Arts Council. There is some truth in the assertion, but it is not the whole story. However, the fact remains that ballet is not a profit-making enterprise, in the sense that a business venture is profit-making. Ballet is of essence non-commercial. Its function is no more money-making than it is the function of libraries, colleges, universities, art museums, opera companies, symphony orchestras to show profits.

While ballet can and often does show a profit on its actual running operation, it is impossible to earn enough to amortize the cost of new productions and the rehabilitation of old scenery and costumes.

It must not be overlooked that Sadler's Wells was an established and distinguished private institution, paying its own way long before it was helped by the government. Subsidy in one form or another from one source or another is necessary; yet there are those who strongly feel that wise and sound direction, something that has never been a conspicuous feature of ballet in America, will go far towards helping to solve ballet's difficulties.

To highlight and sum up these more mundane aspects of ballet in the Western Hemisphere, it should be noted that the Ballet Russe de Monte Carlo has had the helping hand of private subsidy for nearly two decades; that the Marquis George de Cuevas, a brother-in-law of John D. Rockefeller, Jr., poured what is estimated to have been close to $1,000,000 into a two-months season of ballet in New York in 1944; that Ballet Theatre is said to have cost Lucia Chase, its New England Yankee founder, well in excess of $2,000,000 in the decade and a half of its existence. These monies are no longer available in such quantities. The result has been that corners have been cut, personnel reduced in size as well as in quality, productions neglected and new ones made only with economy in mind, fewer new productions being the end result. But this end result can only lead ultimately to dissatisfied audiences; and dissatisfied audiences all too soon become nonexistent audiences.

Since the cultural life of a democracy is as important as any phase of its existence, it is of prime importance that these problems be faced squarely.

*   *   *

These problems, germane and important to an understanding of ballet in America today, are those of management, and are not primarily the concern of that vast audience that derives such pleasure from attendance upon ballet performances. Yet, such is the hold ballet has today on the imaginations and the affections of the American public, it therefore becomes a matter of news when in its uncertain career Ballet Theatre announces a suspension of its activities for financial reasons; and becomes a matter of even bigger and more important news, when its directors, Lucia Chase and Oliver Smith, were able to announce a resumption of the organization's activities, and that two successful and discriminating theatrical producers, the late Dwight Deere Wiman and Blevins Davis, had become associated with the management.

Ballet, then, is a cultural entertainment and an exciting one that the American people have demonstrated they want. It has been pointed out that ballet audiences today represent what may well be termed a cross-section of the American public. These audiences are made up of business men, business women, housewives, lawyers, doctors, white-collar workers. The entertainment expenditures of a considerable number of those who go to make up these audiences are carefully budgeted. While it is true that there was an effete, lunatic fringe of idolators, these have been quietly but firmly put in their place and overcome by sheer force of numbers. Ballet's chief audience regards ballet, it would seem, in the light of sound entertainment, an entertainment in direct competition with the neighborhood movie and the Broadway show-shop. Their first exposure to it may have come about in a variety of ways: the reiterated newspaper appeal of a star name, the enthusiastic press response to a modern work in the jazz idiom. They have tried it, and found to their own surprise that they liked classical ballet, too. They have gone to it again and again, and have gradually come to formulate standards of their own, and from these standards often have become choosey, differentiating between artist and artist, ballet and ballet, company and company. They have their individual favorites, argue heatedly among each other about the virtues and defects of various artists, particularly the leading figures. For while the perfect whole is the thing most sought after in ballet, unfortunately, ballet, like the so-called "legitimate" theater, eventually stands or falls very largely by the star system. It is deplorable, but, like taxes, it goes on, because no one has yet thought of anything better. Moreover, the star system, regrettable though it is, is almost a law of nature.

A case in point is the democratically conducted Sadler's Wells ballet company, which harbors no stars *per se*. Yet it took but a single performance in New York City for Americans to discover that in one of their leading figures, Margot Fonteyn, they possessed an outstanding artist and personality, who took the country by storm, attained the coveted cover of a topical weekly news review magazine, and threatened to become the "woman of the year." Margot Fonteyn possesses a magnificent technique. But it was not technique alone that singled her out. What the audience recognized was that, in addition to technique, she possessed an exceptional personal charm, and that, moreover, she

had intelligence, something often lacking in dancers, and, rarer
still, a true sense of humor.

Our American ballet companies are, on the whole, extremely
competent. Competence, unfortunately, is a word that savors
more of trade than of art. To carry out duties, to make useful and
concrete things. It is all a matter of carrying out definite duties.

But art is another matter. "We can," says Oscar Wilde, "forgive
a man for making a useful thing so long as he does not admire
it. The only excuse for making a useless thing is that one admires
it intensely. All art is quite useless." Ballet, therefore, so intensely
admired, is an art, but the merely competent dancer turns it into
a business and ruins it.

The competent dancer, and he and she are legion, comes onto
the stage like a workman. His role is not an artistic or emotional
creation; it is a piece of work to be performed satisfactorily. He
does his job. It is all part of the day's work. He is dependable,
but he is never exciting; and ballet is nothing if not exciting.
Something more than competence is required, and competence,
ironically enough, may serve to contribute to ballet's decline and
eventual extinction.

This is by no means to suggest that America has not produced
ballet artists of the first rank. The list is considerable. Space per-
mits mention of only a few. Nora Kaye, particularly in Tudor's
Pillar of Fire, reached sublime heights. Janet Reed is a soubrette
of major caliber. Maria Tallchief, Rosella Hightower, Mary Ellen
Moylan are on the upper rungs of contemporary ballet.

Two of the chief needs of ballet in America today are a higher
production-and-performing standard, and new choreographers.
The whole essential atmosphere of ballet, the splendid orchestra,
the settings, the costumes, the lighting, the highly trained *corps
de ballet,* all serve to enhance the brilliance of the soloists, who
are the apex of carefully built triangles. But orchestra, *corps de
ballet,* and soloists are inarticulate puppets until the choreographer
comes to put them into motion. The proportion of great dancers
is small enough, but the number of great choreographers is
minute. An enormous number of the older ballets have disap-

peared completely and probably justly, the names of their choreographers dying with them. Among the old works that are lost
in any art the proportion that deserved to be saved is usually
negligible. Therefore, the young choreographer is to be guarded
and nursed.

A minor effect of the awakened interest in ballet has been to
give wide circulation to the words "choreography" and "choreographer." Even such a mass-produced form of entertainment as
the motion picture takes full cognizance of them. The dances in
films formerly were "arranged by the Dance Director." Today we
find "choreography by Mr. X or Miss Y."

Every television station worthy of its electricity today has at
least a part-time choreographer on its staff, and there is little
doubt that, as the medium develops, choreography and the choreographer will play important roles in television.

It is a rare gift the true choreographer possesses, and we should
be thankful that we have so much talent in that direction already,
and watch carefully to discover and foster more.

*   *   *

An even wider ballet audience was made possible in the United
States by the extension of the balletic form of dance into the
popular musical comedy theater. For as long as the memory of
the oldest living inhabitant, dance in musical comedy was of a
routine and highly incidental nature, where a line of comely
lassies, introduced by some such inspired utterance from the
laddies as: "Look! Here come the girls!," entered and performed
painfully routined steps and kicks, sometimes supported by wasp-
waisted gentlemen, the while emitting equally routined lyrics.

It was in 1935 that a revolution in musical comedy dancing
took place. The occasion was a Rodgers and Hart musical piece
having a ballet company's activities for its background, entitled
On Your Toes. It contained, as an integral part of its story and
action, two ballets, one a satire to end all Oriental spectacles, and
the other a thoroughly American dance theater piece provocatively
titled *Slaughter on Tenth Avenue*.

There was an eight-year lapse before the introduction and establishment of ballet in the musical comedy theater actually became an accomplished fact. Agnes de Mille, one of America's outstanding choreographers, having succeeded with some difficulty in getting a genuine American work into the repertory of the Ballet Russe de Monte Carlo over its Slavic-minded management's opposition, made history in the native theater with the ballets she staged as an integral part of the action of the Rodgers-Hammerstein *Oklahoma!*, in the very same theater where the rebirth of ballet in America had taken place ten years before.

The die was cast, and since then musical comedy, through the works of de Mille, Helen Tamiris, Jerome Robbins, Hanya Holm, Valerie Bettis, and Michael Kidd, Americans all, has found dance assuming an increasingly important and often a major place in its affairs; not as incidental routines but as a part of its very web and woof.

The invasion of the musical comedy field by ballet undoubtedly increased the general public interest in ballet itself, although there are those within the field of ballet itself who feel strongly that ballet as ballet is at its best only within its own frame. There are those who insist that dance, even integrated dance, in musical comedy is not ballet at all, but a hybrid growth imposed upon quite another form of theater. However, the fact remains that the Webster definition still holds.

A question frequently raised these days is where the line of demarcation should be drawn between low-class ballet and high-class musical comedy dancing? Low-class ballet is, of course, any ballet that is not ballet at its best. A great balletic work becomes a low-class ballet when it is presented at anything less than its best in any of its interrelated components: dancing, scenery, costume, music, and, of course, artistry. It may be appropriate to cite an example: one of the most striking of the one-time revolutionary ballets, *Schéhérazade*, an Oriental spectacle, with a tale dealing with a Sultan's favorite wife who dallies with a Negro slave during her husband's absence, ending in the bloody slaughter of all the harem inmates and the favorite wife's suicide on the husband's return, while the latter weeps over the debacle. *Schéhérazade* was in its day with its striking opulent Oriental decorations, the frenzied dancing of the legendary Nijinsky, the seductive atmosphere of the harem, and the voluptuous coloration of the Rimsky-Korsakov score and the Bakst decorations, a ballet of powerful and suspenseful excitement. As presented today, with faded settings, jaundiced musical performance, and young American dancers fresh from the classroom, it is both ludicrous and lamentable. That is low-class ballet.

One is compelled to admit, however, that even in its present desiccated form, it manages, Heaven alone knows why, to retain its popularity, and would seem to have a mass appeal to a public that is still without any realization of what first-class ballet it could be if it were properly presented.

In striking contrast to the sleazy productions given many so-called "masterpieces" of ballet today by our touring companies, the fresh, bright, exploratory ballets of present-day musical comedy come as breaths of fresh air. In no department of the theater does the American so excel as in the slickness of its production, the smoothness of its operation, the smartness of its *mise en scene,* the artistic effectiveness of its lighting. As ballet is presented up and down the Western Hemisphere today, these are features conspicuously lacking. It is true that in their New York seasons, occasionally in Chicago and San Francisco, extra pains are taken and there is at least a gesture made in this direction.

If ballet in America is to survive, if it is to retain its present hold on the imagination and affections of the American people, if it is to fulfil its potential as a vital art and entertainment medium, then America, *all* of America, not one or two metropolitan centers alone, must be given ballet at its best, with no corners cut, no pennypinching, no cheating.

*   *   *

Ballet in the Western Hemisphere, then, has a large, loyal audience, growing in size as it is in taste and discrimination, and, as a result, demanding an increasingly higher standard of production, presentation, and performance.

The American ballet companies are confronted with the problem of providing this higher standard, if they are to survive. The Sadler's Wells invasions have been disturbing to the equanimity of their managements, and they realise that something must be done to match the quality offered by the visitors from overseas.

Lack of subsidy is but one of the stumbling-blocks. An enlightened and informed management is quite as important as it is to have those qualities in the audience. There is no question that much of the direction of ballet in America has been inefficient and almost entirely devoid of any policy save one of expediency; and this is not confined to any one company or organization. Fantastically large sums of money have been wasted through lack of knowledge and judgment and of interdepartmental lack of coordination and cooperation. Bookings involving doubling backwards and forwards across and over the continent unnecessarily consume fortunes in railway fares; non-consecutive bookings resulting in non-playing days have meant only mounting costs and nonexistent revenue. Productions not thought through to their completion and lacking in coordination with all elements concerned have too often resulted in the abandonment of one set of plans and the substitution of another after the first has been completed, thus doubling the costs. From an artistic point of view, ballet is all too frequently booked into halls and theaters and auditoriums where it is physically impossible to give anything other than the crudest travesty of the art.

One of the most conspicuous and happiest features of the operation of the Sadler's Wells ballet is the perfection of its organization, its well-ordered conduct of its affairs, its interdepartmental coordination and cooperation, with nothing left to guesswork, nothing to chance.

Our British visitors have the advantage of a permanent home, year-round employment, artistic and economic security for personnel, the time as well as the means for long-range planning. They perform for long, uninterrupted seasons in a single, well-equipped theater, to which is attached a school where a rounded educational curriculum, in addition to dance instruction and training, is provided for the students. The dancers are not subjected to the rigors of long one-night-stand tours, as are their American colleagues.

Perhaps, of all the problems confronting ballet on the Western side of the Atlantic today, none is more serious than the lack of security and continuity. Economically ballet in America is suicidal in all its branches. Only sound and enlightened management, with either private or public subsidy sufficient to ensure a reasonable flow of new productions, can provide for the continuation of all the companies currently before the American public.

The artist is worthy of his hire and is entitled to his share of this security and continuity. Many dancers and other workers in ballet today lack not only continuity of employment, but because the ballet operating company is a non-profit corporation, they are sometimes denied the benefits of social security and unemployment insurance. This sort of hand-to-mouth existence provides little incentive to the artist and no opportunity for new talents to develop or gain that experience so necessary to their professional growth.

The answer to the survival of America's new popular art may well lie in the reduction of the number of companies currently presenting ballet, in the development and maintenance of the highest production and performing standards, in the inclusion of the widest possible variety of styles of choreography, choreographers and themes, with, over all, a wise and discerning management capable of maintaining economy of operation without either cheapening or cheating.

Then, and then only, will we have ballet at anything like its fullest and finest, without self-seeking, but with that pervading and comforting sense of discipline that is the hallmark of our British visitors. Then and then alone will we have ballet that has nothing of the amateur in the tone of the performance, no playing at dancing, no slackness, no carelessness.

It will be good ballet, because it will be a serious professional venture.

*   *   *

And now, what does all this reading about various aspects of ballet amount to for those who have sought enlightenment from this volume? The possession of facts means a craving for their application, even if only negative or amateurish, and so I have tried to give a series of indications to those who go to the ballet as to how they may see it and hear it to the utmost possible advantage, though without any professional insight on the one hand or professional detachment on the other.

There follows a glossary of general terms, with illustrations. The terms are French; for it is the language of ballet.

Any thoughts, as differentiated from facts, which I have tentatively put forward are, of course, things that hardly can be done in a day. Another five years or so, uninterrupted by war, might well astonish us. Government subsidy must come. The cost of international misunderstanding directs economy at our cultural work and millions can be spent on methods of destruction, with nothing for constructive efforts. Our art is the strongest sanity in a world of imaginary fears, where the enjoyment of life has been forgotten. Those who believe in the arts must demand against all other claims the means to continue along the developing path. Here is the United States, a nation once derided for its lack of cultural power, with a splendid living school of composers, ballet artists comparable with the best, with symphony orchestras we are now proud to send abroad, to Europe and to the Orient. Are we to let them languish, these arts of peace, dependent upon private charity, while all our thoughts are turned to destruction and the means whereby to accomplish that destruction?

We are faced with a double struggle: to eliminate all that leads to a belief that war follows peace as night follows day, and at the same time to preserve those eternal verities which some leaders would scrap in a misguided confidence in material powers.

But the immensity of all that is at stake, the vision of all that may be lost, is awakening thousands of people to a recognition of the treasures they possess. The arts offer them relaxation, renewed strength, a touchstone to show they are truly alive—a reassurance that the future can be wide enough to hold their hopes.

If our artistic future has never been more promising, it has never been more in danger. We must build and build, preserve what we have inherited and establish it upon a foundation that will withstand the unimagined shocks to come, upon a foundation not of stone but of strong roots, the roots of a tree which may bend and shake, but which will endure and spread its branches giving shelter and refreshment to humanity throughout the ages.

) APPENDIX (

Glossary

In this volume designed for the layman, I have reiterated my belief that an understanding and appreciation of ballet is not contingent upon an understanding of the intricacies of the technique of ballet; that such an understanding is by no means a prerequisite to an appreciation of the art or the enjoyment of it as an entertainment. I have tried to avoid explanations that involved technique *per se;* and also as much of the mechanistic side as possible. Such explanations are not necessary to the layman, and are the province of the specialist: the dancer, the choreographer, the pupil, the teacher.

However assiduously I have tried to avoid the use of technical jargon, the use of certain terms in the language of ballet has been unavoidable. The glossary that follows defines such terms as have been used, which have not been clarified in the text. I am indebted to Dmitri N. Vedensky, Jr., for the excellent drawings that illustrate the Glossary.

ADAGIO: From the Italian. As in music: leisurely. In ballet, a succession of slow movements, performed with consummate ease apparently, and with a maximum of fluidity, with the body (in most cases) being supported on one foot. Above all, it emphasizes balance.

ALLEGRO: From the Italian. As in music: lively. In ballet, it is the antithesis of *adagio*. Under this general heading are included all the steps of elevation, referred to later, for example: *balloné, echappé, entrechat, cabriole, et al.*

ARABESQUE: From the French, Arabian plus *esque*. There are a number of *arabesques;* but the basic and fundamental *arabesque* is the position of the body on one leg, with the other leg extended to the rear, with one arm extended forward and the other towards the rear, thus forming the longest possible line one can make from the tips of the fingers to the toes. The accompanying drawing shows the first *arabesque.*

ASSEMBLÉ: French. A step in which the two feet are brought together for the Third Position. (See Five Basic Positions.)

À TERRE: French. Literally, "on the ground." Generally applied to steps performed on the stage as opposed to those performed in the air.

ATTACK: English, from the French *attaquer*. In ballet it has the meaning of the deliberation behind the performance of the various steps.

ATTITUDE: French, from the Italian *attitudine,* fitness, posture. In ballet, a quiet beautiful pose, originally developed by Carlo Blasis (see text) after the famous statue of Mercury by Jean Bologne. There are several *attitudes*. One of the most common (and most beautiful) is shown in the accompanying drawing.

BALLET: (see text).

BALLET BLANC: French. Literally, white ballet. Applied to traditional ballets in which the dancers wear long, delicate white costumes. The second act of *Giselle* (see text) is an example. Fokine's masterpiece, *Les Sylphides* (see text), is an outstanding *ballet blanc*.

BALLET D'ACTION: French. Literally, a ballet in which something happens. That is to say, something happens besides dancing for dancing's sake; in other words, a ballet with a story or a plot.

BALLET MASTER: From the French, *maître de ballet*. The term has undergone a number of changes with the passage of time. At first, the *ballet master* was the choreographer. Even today, in Russia and France it is used in this sense. However, today in England and the Western Hemisphere, the term is used (with *ballet mistress* for the feminine counterpart) as the title for the person responsible for company discipline, for the daily lessons, for the rehearsals of works already produced and in the repertory. The *ballet master* (or *mistress*) may or may not be a choreographer. In Russian Ballet, the permanent choreographer is often called the *ballet master,* and the teacher-rehearser-disciplinarian is known as the *régisseur,* sometimes the *régisseur-general*.

BALLETOMANE: From the Russian, first introduced into the English language by the English critic, Arnold Haskell. (See text.)

BALLETOMANIAC: A ballet "nut."

BALLON: ·French, handball or balloon. A term generally used to describe the quality of springiness in a dancer.

BARRE: French, bar. A bar or rail (round) extending along the walls of a dance studio or rehearsal room (see text), which the pupils and dancers grasp during the first exercises of the lesson, in lieu of the hand of the partners. It is usually installed about 3′ 6″ from the floor.

BATTEMENT: French. There are various types of *battements,* the simplest form being performed standing at the *barre,* extending the foot in front on the floor, or back, or in a semi-circle. (See drawing.)

BATTERIE: French. A general term used in ballet for all movements involving the beating of one foot against another.

BRISÉ: French, broken. Literally, a broken movement.

CABRIOLE: French, to caper, leap. A movement of elevation.

CENTRE: French, middle. The second part of the ballet class, in the middle of the floor after the exercises at the *barre* have been completed.

CHOREOGRAPHER: (see text).

CLASSIC: (see text).

CORPS DE BALLET: (see text).

DANSE D'ÉCOLE: French, dance of the school. In ballet, the classic dance.

DANSEUR NOBLE: French. A classical male dancer; the partner of the ballerina.

DÉVELOPPÉ: French, to develop, reveal, unfold. In ballet, a gentle and gradual unfolding of the leg as it is raised from the floor, eventually to be fully extended in the air. (See accompanying drawing.)

DIVERTISSEMENT: French. A series of disconnected dances.

ÉCHAPPÉ: French, to escape. A step in which the dancer escapes or slips from a closed to an open position.

ELEVATION: French. The ability to jump.

EN ARRIÈRE: French. To the rear.

EN AVANT: French. To the front.

ENCHAÎNEMENT: French, linking. The sequence of steps, linked together.

EN DEDANS: French. Inwards.

EN DEHORS: French. Outwards.

ENTRECHAT: French. A jump involving changing positions of the feet while in the air—four, six, or eight times. (See text.) Exhibitionistic dancers sometimes change as many as ten. This latter is purely a freakish stunt.

FIVE POSITIONS (BASIC): The fundamental root of ballet dancing, these basic positions of the feet, from one or another of which every movement is ballet starts and in one or another of which all movements end. (See accompanying drawings.)

FIRST POSITION: (see drawing).

Heels together, feet turned out to make a single straight line.

SECOND POSITION: (see drawing).

Feet are turned out, thus forming a straight line, with the heels separated by an open space approximately the length of one of the feet.

THIRD POSITION: (see drawing).

Both feet are turned outward as they are in the First Position; but with one foot placed in front of the other. It will be noted that each heel is touching the middle of the opposite foot.

FOURTH POSITION: (see drawing).

Actually a transition position. Note that the feet are turned outward, and that one of the feet is placed in front of and parallel to the other. The distance between is approximately twelve inches. Also to be noted is the fact that the toe of one foot is in line with the heel of the other. When in transition there can be two variations, known as *croisé* (crossed) and *effacé* (literally, shaded).

FIFTH POSITION: (see drawing).

The feet are turned outward, with one foot placed in front of the other. The heels and the toes are touching so that neither big toe projects. Thus the feet are, in effect, boxed in. There are corresponding positions of the arms, as will be seen.

In *adagio* practice, these positions are utilized to the fullest, and their execution involves steps which, in turn, invoke the following terms: *Croisée devant,* French, crossed in front; *À la quatrième devant,* French, to the fourth front; *Ecartée,* French, thrown wide apart; *Effacée* (as above), French, shaded; *À la seconde,* French, to the second; *Epaulée,* French, shouldered; *À la quatrième derrière,* French, crossed back.

FOUETTÉ: French, from *fouetter,* to whip. Turns on one leg, in which the other leg is used as a whip to propel the dancer. These turns should be performed on one spot. This movement is often provocative of the most undiscriminating, violent, and prolonged unnecessary applause on the part of the audience.

MOVEMENTS IN DANCING: Basically there are seven:
Plier, French, to bend.
Étendre, French, to stretch.
Relever, French, to raise.
Glisser, French, to slide.
Élancer, French, to dart.
Tourner, French, to turn.

GLISSADE: French (see *Glisser* above). A sliding movement from the Fifth Position to an open position and back. This is usually made as a step in preparation for a jump.

JETÉ: French, from *jeter,* to throw. This is the long jump, in which the dancer throws the weight of his body from one foot to another. The *jeté* is not to be confused with other *small* jumps in ballet, such as *assemblés, changements, échappés,* and others. The *grand jeté* is the large aerial jump with a fleeting pose held in flight, landing softly on the other foot from that which has served as the take-off foot. (See drawing of *Grand Jeté.*)

LIBRETTO: Italian, diminutive of *libro,* book. The story of a ballet. In the plotless ballets discussed in the text, the *libretto* may be said to be its theme or idea.

NOTATION: From the Latin. The term given the setting down of dances on paper by any method sufficiently intelligible to make their accurate reproduction possible. There have been many and varied attempts at forms of dance stenography, none of them seemingly completely satisfactory. The most recent development, based on a system devised by Rudolf von Laban, has been carried on in the United States by Ann Hutchinson, whose book, *Labanotation,* published by New Directions, 1954, is a definitive work. An even more practical system is said to have been recently developed in England.

PANTOMIME: From the Greek. Dumb-show in significant gestures. In contemporary ballets it is seldom, if ever, used; but in the Romantic ballets such as *Coppélia, La Fille Mal Gardée, Giselle, The Sleeping Beauty, Swan Lake,* it is used extensively, and it would be well for the layman to be able to recognize some of the basic mime used in carrying on the story. A few examples will suffice:

THANK YOU: The head is slightly inclined, and one hand, placed on the chest, is brought down and extended towards the recipient of the gratitude.

YOU: Pointing to the person with the hand open. Only when angry is the index finger used in pointing thus.

TO INDICATE OR DESCRIBE A CHILD: The hands are raised in three progressive steps, with the palms downwards. The idea is as if measuring the varying heights of a growing child.

BEAUTIFUL: Appropriately enough the mimetic gesture for beautiful is the same as to indicate a girl. The face is circled gently with the back of the hand, permitting the back of the middle finger to outline the face.

SLEEP: The head is inclined against the back of the hands.

TO INDICATE A ROYAL PRINCESS: The arms are lifted and the hands held just above the top of the head, as if gently grasping a crown.

TO INDICATE A KING: The right hand is raised above the head with a flourishing gesture, the idea being to indicate the feather commonly worn in the bonnets and crowns of royalty.

TO INDICATE A QUEEN: The index finger of the right hand touches the top of the forehead at the points where the crown rests.

DANCE: The hands are circled round each other above the head.

DIE: The arms are brought up to the side of the head, and then brought down quickly so that the hands with fists clenched are crossed in front of the body.

KISS: The lips are touched with a finger.

BLESS: The head of the person to be blessed is touched with the hand.

LOVE: Both hands are held over the heart.

FRIENDS: The hands are clasped together on a level with the waist.

MARRY: The wedding-ring finger of the left hand is pointed to with the index finger of the right.

REMEMBER: The temple is touched with the index finger.

FORGET: The hands are held out loosely with the palms upwards at the same time as the head is shaken slightly.

ME: The middle fingers of both hands are simultaneously pointed at oneself.

STOP: The hand is upheld, palm outwards.

OBEY: A determined pointing towards the floor.

ANGER: The arms are raised above the head, elbows projecting forward, with the fists shaken.

NO: The arms are first held at the side, then crossed in front of the body as the head is shaken in the negative.

SAD: The fingers trace imaginary tears as they run down the face.

BEG MERCY: The arms are held out with palms pressing against each other, as if in an attitude of prayer.

WEEP: The face is hidden in both hands or at other times the eyes are rubbed with clenched fists.

PAS: French, step. (See text.)

PAS DE DEUX, PAS DE TROIS, PAS DE QUATRE, etc.: (see text). There is a great variety of *pas: Coupés, Gargouillades, Pas de Bourrées, Pas de Chat, Pas de Cheval.* The layman will quickly learn to identify some of them; but, from the point of view of enjoyment of ballet, such identification is by no means necessary.

PAS DE BOURÉE: This is one of ballet's most effective and beautiful steps, being a sequence of very small, even steps on the *pointes.*

PIROUETTE: French, to turn. A complete turn of the body on one leg. There are various types of *pirouettes.* Well performed, they are dazzling. They include *pirouettes en arabesque, pirouettes en attitude, et al.* Rapid turns executed in the air are called *tours en l'air.* The accompanying drawing illustrates the most common type of *pirouette.*

PLIÉ: French, *plier,* to fold, to fold up, to bend. A classic ballet fundamental. Simply explained, it is a bending of the knees with them wide open and the feet turned outwards. Its function is that of a spring in the development of a true elasticity. The half-bend of this type is called the *demi-plié;* the deep-bend is known as the *grand plié.*

PORT DE BRAS: French, literally, the carriage or movements of the arms.

RELEVÉ: French, from *relever:* to life again. Balletically, the raising of the body on to *pointe* or *demi-pointe.* (See *Sur les Pointes*).

RÉVÉRENCE: French, a low, deep bow.

ROND DE JAMBE: French. The rotary movement of the leg, in which the dancer describes circles on the floor or in the air with the pointed toe of the working foot. One of the early basic exercises and often utilized on the stage.

SAUTÉ: French, from *sauter,* to jump. In ballet, the term is used in connection with others, indicating that a jump is involved. Examples: *échappe sauté, sauté en arabesque.* The meaning is self-evident.

SUR LES POINTES: French, on the toes. Dancing on the toes is dancing *sur les pointes.* All ballet dancing is by no means *sur les pointes;* therefore it is quite wrong to refer to ballet dancing as toe-dancing. The ballet dancer's foot can be *sur les pointes* (on the toes); *à terre* (on the ground); *à quart* (with heel slightly off the floor); *sur la demi-pointe* (on the half-toe); *à trois quarts.*

TOUR: French, turn. (See *Pirouette.*)

TOUR EN L'AIR: French, a turn in the air. In ballet, a complete aerial turn from the Fifth Position, landing precisely where the dancer started. These *tours* by skilled dancers may be doubled or tripled for excitement's sake, but three complete, true turns in the air is the maximum.

TURNOUT: This, perhaps more than any other single thing, may be said to be the outstanding characteristic of the classical dancer. The knees that face forward in an ordinary standing position are turned out at the hip at an angle of ninety degrees. This may be easily observed by studying the drawings of the Five Basic Positions.

TUTU: French, a nickname for *tunique,* tunic. The ballet skirt.

VARIATION: In ballet, a solo dance.

A Discography of Music
of and for the Ballet

More than once in this volume I have pointed out that it is through its music that the layman may quite well come to know and love ballet. This following section of music of and for the ballet to be found on records is preceded by a glossary of technical terms for those who wish to know and familiarize themselves with something of the technique of ballet. Let me repeat, this knowledge is by no means essential to the layman's enjoyment of ballet. It can help. Six and one-half decades ago George Bernard Shaw, a critic of remarkable sanity, wrote of critics: ". . . The indiscreet revelation of how a critic with no artistic sense of dancing may cover up his incapacity by talking about *ronds de jambe, arabesques, elevations, entrechats, ballonés,* and the like threatens to start a technico-jargonistic fashion in ballet criticism . . . The critics will make as much as possible of any ugly blemish (the teetotum spin, for instance), provided they can thereby parade their knowledge of its technical name."

What was true of critics in 1890 is equally true today not only of certain professional critics but of far too many garrulous *balletomanes.*

Through the music of and for the ballet, the layman may, if he wishes, enjoy the music for its own sake in his own home. After a few visits to the ballet he may be able to visualize movements he has seen done in ballets to the music, reconstruct the action, relive the story, and re-create the pleasures of the performances he has seen. He may be stimulated by listening to the music to want to see works he has not yet visited.

In most cases, the musical performances listed hereinunder on records, are vastly superior to those heard in many theaters with ballet orchestras. For seven years I regularly conducted a radio program, the first of its kind, called *Music and Ballet,* during which time it was conclusively proved to me by a large correspondence that the public was attracted to ballet through its music.

In the following Discography, where there are several recordings of a work available, I have indicated the ones I prefer. This recommendation is made on the basis of (a) its balletic values, as regards *tempi,* cuts, etc., and (b) on the quality of the orchestral playing and gramophonic reproduction.

The hope is that this list of preferred recordings may serve to increase the layman's enjoyment of ballet in the performances he visits, in reconstruction of the pleasures in his own home, and to whet his appetite for ballets he has not seen and heard, arousing a sense of curiosity and expectation. It will not be out of place to preface this Discography with the following quotation from *Ballet Profile,* a book I wrote in 1936:

"THE EARS HAVE IT"

"Since Ballet is Audible as well as Visual, and although at the Ballet the Eyes have it, it is the Ear that will awaken memories and arouse recollections when the Personalities are no longer in our midst. Therefore, there is appended a list of the best available recordings of Ballet Music; and of music which has, in one way or another, become associated in the ballet-lover's mind with the art of the ballet. As that exacting musician, critic, and champion of the new ballet, Ernest Newman, says, 'It is now possible, by virtue of the new methods of recording that have come into use, for the gramophone listener to get the thrill of the real thing . . . At last an orchestra really sounds like an orchestra. These records bring with them the very blood and nerves of the orchestra and the theater.' And, best of all, there will be no audience save ourselves, our memories, our imaginations, our retrospect, our hopes (if we wish to invite one or two understanding friends, we may; but we should exercise care in selecting the elect); and no vulgar barbarians to slam down seats; to walk on our feet; to chatter about some cocktail-or-dinner-party; or firmly to mispronounce names, incorrectly to identify dancers, or to regale companions with whispered morsels of unauthenticated gossip. There will be only the disembodied work of the composer, pouring its melodies and sonorities into our receptive and quickened senses."

ADAM, Adolphe (1803-1856)

GISELLE

Blareau—Orchestra de l'Opéra. 12" London LL-869.
Fistoulari—London Symphony. 12" Capitol P-8306.
Irving, Royal Opera Orchestra. 12" Victor LM-1092.
Lambert, Royal Opera Orchestra. 10" Columbia LM-2117.

Although abbreviated, the best recording is the Constant Lambert—Columbia ML-2117. The fullest and genuinely complete version with first-class orchestral playing and tempi and fine sound is the Richard Blareau—Paris Opera recording: London LL-869.

ANTHEIL, George (1900—)

CAPITAL OF THE WORLD

Levine, Ballet Theatre Orchestra. 12" Capitol P-8278.

In this recording the Spanish foot-and-heel work and the fingers of the dancer, Roy Fitzell, are heard. Quality excellent.

A ballet by Eugene Loring in the repertory of Ballet Theatre.

ARBEAU, Thoinot (1519-1595)

The name is the anagrammed pseudonym of Jehan Tabourot, a French priest, who wrote one of the earliest treatises on dancing, *Orchésographie*, giving dance tunes in musical notation. *L'Anthologie* Sonore, vol. 1 (78 rpm), contains dances from this famous work. It is not presently easy to secure, and is a collector's item.

ARNELL, Richard (1917—)

PUNCH AND THE CHILD

Beecham, Royal Philharmonic Orchestra. 12" Columbia ML-4593.

Superbly recorded by Sir Thomas Beecham. Quality excellent. A delightful work in the repertory of the New York City Ballet, unfortunately seldom performed.

AURIC, Georges (1899—)

FONTAINE DE JOUVENCE (*Fountain of Youth*)

Leibowitz, Paris Phil. Orch. 12" Renaissance X-41.

An eight-minute ballet, pleasant musically and a novelty.

LES MATELOTS (*The Sailors*)

Kurtz, Houston Symphony. 10" Columbia ML-2112.

This is a suite from a highly amusing Diaghileff ballet by Leonide Massine. The work is not performed today but is pleasant and amusing music.

BACH, Johann Sebastian (1685-1750)

THE WISE VIRGINS: (*Bach, arranged by William Walton*)

Boult, London Philharmonic. 12" London LL-1165.
Litschauer, Vienna State Opera Orch. 12" Vanguard 440.

The Boult version (London LL-1165) is the better from every point of view.
The work, by Ninette de Valois, is in the repertory of the Sadler's Wells Ballet.

CONCERTO BAROCCO (*Concerto in D Minor for Two Violins and Orchestra*)

Barchet, Beh. Davisson, Pro Musica Orch. 12" Vox PL-9150.
Busch, Magnes, Busch Chamb. Orch. 12" Columbia 3ML-4002.
Heifetz, RCA Victor Ch. Orch. 12" Victor LM-1051.
Krebbers, Olof, Van Otterloo, Hague Phil. 12" Epic 3LC-3036.
Menuhin, Enesco, Monteux, Orch. 12" Victor LCT-1120.
Stern, Schneider, Casals, Prades Fest. Orch. 12" Columbia 4ML-4351.

The Heifetz version (playing both parts) (Victor LM-1051) is the most interesting.
This is the musical base for George Balanchine's ballet,

Concerto Barocco, in the repertory of the New York City Ballet.

THE YOUNG MAN AND DEATH (*Passacaglia and Fugue in C Minor*)

There are thirteen recorded versions of this work. The arrangement by Leopold Stokowski, 10″ Victor LM-7033 and 12″ Victor LM-1133, are excellent.

This is the music used by Roland Petit in his ballet, *Le Jeune Homme et la Mort* (*The Young Man and Death*), seen for a season in the repertory of Ballet Theatre.

BALAKIREV, Mily (1837-1910)

TAMAR

Ansermet, Orch. Suisse Romande. 12″ London LL-1068.
Beecham, Royal Phil. Orch. 12″ Columbia ML-4974.
Fistoulari, London Symphony. 12″ MGM 3076.

The Ansermet recording (London LL-1068), being the work of a former Diaghileff conductor of outstanding ability, is by far preferable from all points of view.

An early Diaghileff ballet by Michel Fokine, its sensuousness is patent in its richly textured score. The ballet is no longer performed.

BANFIELD, Rafaello de

THE COMBAT

Levine, Ballet Theatre Orch. 12″ Capitol P-8278.

A ballet staged by William Dollar, which has been in the repertory of the Ballets de Paris, the New York City Ballet, and, most recently, the Ballet Theatre.

BARANOVICH, Kreshimir (1894—)

THE GINGERBREAD HEART

Baranovich, Belgrade Phil. Orch. 12" London LL-1235.

Gay folk work in the repertory of the Yugoslav National Ballet. Points of musical contact with *Petrouchka*. Tuneful and good fun, excellent recording and playing quality.

BARTÓK, Béla (1881-1945)

CAPRICHOS (*Contrasts for Violin, Clarinet, and Piano*)

There are three LP recordings available, of which Columbia ML 2213, with the composer at the piano, Joseph Szigeti, violin, and Benny Goodman, clarinet, is preferred.
Ballet staged for Ballet Theatre by Herbert Ross in 1950.

THE MIRACULOUS MANDARIN (*Suite from the ballet*)

Dorati, Chicago Sym. Orch. 12" Mercury 50038.
Serly, New Sym. 12" Bartók 301.

This is one of Bartók's most striking works, packed with color. Powerful, strong, it makes a frontal attack on the senses. The Dorati recorded performance is at all times exciting and masterly in its presentation of the music. Like all Mercury recordings, the sound is outstandingly vivid.
The ballet, set in a brothel, involving a prostitute and the murder of one of her victims by a gang, a Chinese mandarin being the victim, was banned in Europe for some time. Composed in 1918-1919, its first performance in Cologne was not until 1925, and was withdrawn by orders of the censor after a single performance. In 1951 it was produced by Todd Bolender for the New York City Ballet.

THE WOODEN PRINCE

Pflüger, Leipzig Phil. 12" Urania C-7161.
Süsskind, New Symphony. 2-12" Bartók 308.

An early pantomime-ballet by Bartók, the Süsskind version is practically complete, and is marvellously recorded.

BAX, Arnold (1883-1953)

PICNIC AT TINTAGEL

Boult, London Phil. Orch. 12" London LL-1167.

Ballet created for the New York City Ballet by Frederick Ashton, and in the repertory of that company. The recording of a moving impressionistic score, excellently recorded.

BAYER, Joseph (1852-1913)

THE FAIRY DOLL

Wilhelm Loibner, Vienna Sym. Orch. 12" Epic LC-3102.

Ballet from Old Vienna, produced in America by Catherine Littlefield with the Philadelphia Ballet. No longer performed. It is lovable Viennese music, always danceable and listenable. Recording first rate.

BEETHOVEN, Ludwig van (1770-1827)

THE CREATURES OF PROMETHEUS

Goehr, Winterthur Symp. 2-12" Concert Hall 1063.
Litschauer, Vienna St. Op. Orch. 12" Vanguard 429.

The Walter Goehr-Winterthur recording (Concert Hall 1063) being reasonably complete is preferred.
This only ballet by Beethoven was most recently performed by the San Francisco Opera Company.

224

AT THE BALLET

LA GLOIRE

Dorati, Minn. Sym. 12" Mercury 50017.

This ballet staged by Antony Tudor for the New York City Ballet utilized three Beethoven Overtures: The *Coriolanus Overture*, the *Lenore No. 3*, and the *Egmont Overture*.

SEVENTH SYMPHONY

"Symphonic" ballet by Leonide Massine; no longer performed.
Many excellent recordings of the work exist. The listener may make his own choice.

BERLIOZ, Hector (1803-1869)

THE DAMNATION OF FAUST (*Excerpts*): (*Ballet music*):

There are numerous recordings of these delightful dances, of which the Koussevitzky-Boston Symphony recording, Victor LCT-1146, is decidedly preferable.

HAROLD IN ITALY

Berlin Sym. 12" Royale 1384.
Brittenbach, Moralt, Vienna Sym. 12" Vox PL-6700.
Primrose-Beecham, Royal Phil. Orch. 12" Columbia ML-4542.
Primrose-Koussevitzky, Boston Sym. 12" Victor LCT-1146.
Riddle, Scherchen, London Phil. 12" Westminster 5288.

The Primrose-Beecham version (Columbia ML-4542) is distinctly superior.
The ballet by Leonide Massine was created in 1954 for the Ballet Russe de Monte Carlo, and was seen on tour only.

SYMPHONIE FANTASTIQUE

Balser, Berlin Sym. 12" Royale 1325.
Dorati, Minneapolis Sym. 12" 50034.
Monteux, San Francisco Sym. 12" Victor LM-1131.
Munch, Boston Sym. 12" Victor LM-1900.
Ormandy, Philadelphia Orch. Columbia ML-4467.
Rodzinski, Cleveland Orch. 12" Columbia RL-3059.
Scherchen, London Sym. 12" Westminster 5268.
Sebastian, RIAS Sym. 12" Remington 199-176.
Van Beinum, Amsterdam Orch. 12" London LL-489.
Van Otterloo, Berlin Philharmonic. 12" Epic 3LC-3005.
Von Karajan, Philharmonia Orch. 12" Angel 35202.

Although a transfer from 78 rpm, the Rodzinski-Cleveland recording (Columbia RL-3059) is still my choice, with the Munch-Boston a close second.
An outstanding masterpiece of ballet by Leonide Massine; unfortunately it is no longer to be seen.

BERNERS, Lord (Gerald Hugh Tyrwhitt-Wilson) (1883-1950)

THE TRIUMPH OF NEPTUNE

Beecham, Philadelphia Orch. 12" Columbia ML-4593.

An outstanding recording of a witty, tuneful score. An added advantage is that it is coupled with Arnell's *Punch and the Child.*

A British ballet by George Balanchine, created for the Diaghileff Ballet, and first presented at the Lyceum Theatre, London, December 3, 1926; a work packed with a delicious kind of humor, but unfortunately not seen today.

BERNSTEIN, Leonard (1913—)

FACSIMILE

Bernstein, Golden Sym. 12" Camden 196.
Levine, Ballet Theatre Orch. 12" Capitol P-8320.

The choreographer, Jerome Robbins, called it a "choreographic observation." It was staged for Ballet Theatre in 1946, but is not being performed any longer.

FANCY FREE

Bernstein, Ballet Theatre Orch. 10" Decca 6023.
Fiedler, Boston Pops. Columbia 12" LM-1726.
Hilsberg, Philadelphia "Pops" Orch. 10" Columbia AL-17.
Levine, Ballet Theatre Orch. 10" Capitol L-8197.
Levine, Ballet Theatre Orch. 12" Capitol P-8196.

The Capitol recording (P-8196) is the fullest; but musically both the Bernstein-Decca (6023) and the Hilsberg-Columbia (AL-17) are preferred.
An outstanding contemporary ballet by Jerome Robbins in the jazz idiom in the current repertory of Ballet Theatre.

THE AGE OF ANXIETY (After W. H. Auden)

Foss, Bernstein, New York Philharmonic. 12" Columbia
    ML-4325.

A first-class recording of an important contemporary work. Ballet staged by Jerome Robbins, and in the repertory of the New York City Ballet.

BIZET, Georges (1838-1875)

L'ARLESIENNE

There are some six recordings of this dance music, with the John Barbirolli, Halle Orchestra (Victor 12″ LBC-1047) preferred.

This music is frequently interpolated as ballet dances in the opera *Carmen*.

JEUX D'ENFANTS

Braithwaite, Covent Garden Orchestra. 12″ MGM 3000.
Lindenberg, Orch. Paris Consv. 12″ London LL-871.
Salke, Olympia Symph. 12″ Allegro 3070.

The Braithwaite-Covent Garden version (MGM 3000) preferred.

A ballet by Leonide Massine staged for the de Basil Ballet Russe de Monte Carlo, no longer presented, but still delightful. Another version, by Balanchine, was staged for the New York City Ballet in 1955.

ROMA

Barzin, New York City Ballet Orch. 12″ Vox PL-9320.
Berendt, Philharmonia Orch. 12″ Allegro 3051.

The Leon Barzin, N.Y.C.B.O. (Vox PL-9320) is infinitely superior.

A ballet choreographed by George Balanchine for the New York City Ballet in 1955.

SYMPHONY IN C

Allain, Orch. 12″ Remington 199-31.
Ansermet, Orch. Suisse Romande. 12″ London LL-1186.

Cluytens, Orc. Nat'l Française. 12" Angel 35119.
Leibowitz, Orch. Radio-Sym. 12" Oceanic 33.
Rodzinski, NY Phil. 10" Columbia ML-2051.
Stokowski, His Orch. 12" Victor LM-1706.

The Ansermet-Suisse Romande version (London LL-1186) is far and away the best, with the Rodzinki Columbia (ML-2051) as second choice.
One of George Balanchine's most completely satisfying contemporary works. Now in the current repertory of the New York City Ballet. The music also used by Andrée Howard for her ballet, *Assembly Ball,* in the repertory of the Sadler's Wells Theatre Ballet.

BLISS, Sir Arthur (1891—)

CHECKMATE

Irving, Royal Opera Orch. 12" Columbia ML-4362.

A genuinely fine reading from the musical, balletic, and sound points of view.
Moving and powerful dramatic ballet dealing with a chess-game, by Ninette de Valois, in the repertory of the Sadler's Wells Ballet.

MIRACLE IN THE GORBALS

Bliss, Philharmonic Orch. 12" Angel 33516.
Lambert, Royal Opera Orch. 10" Columbia ML-2117.

The Lambert-Royal Opera Orchestra version (Columbia ML-2117) is to be preferred ˙despite the fact it was transferred to LP from 78 rpm.
Dramatic ballet of life in the Glasgow slums, by Robert Helpmann, for the Sadler's Wells Ballet, with an unusually interesting score.

BLOCH, Ernest (1880—)

THE DESCENT OF HEBE (*Concerto Grosso for Orchestra with Piano*)

Schick, Kubelik, Chicago Sym. 12" Mercury 50027.

Franklin, Steinberg, Pittsburgh Sym. 12" Capitol S-8212.

The Schick-Kubelik recording is the choice (Mercury 50027) if for no other reason than that the other side contains another ballet score, Hindemith's *Metamorphoses.*

Music used by Antony Tudor for his British ballet, *The Descent of Hebe,* not seen in the United States.

BOCCHERINI, Luigi (1743-1805)

SCUOLA DI BALLO (*School of Ballet*)

Dorati, London Philharmonic Orch. 12" Columbia RL-3043.

Excellent transfer of Antal Dorati's brilliant playing this delightful score from 78 rpm to LP.

Gay, diverting ballet by Leonide Massine for the de Basil Ballet Russe de Monte Carlo. No longer performed.

BORODIN, Alexander (1833-1887)

BOGATYRI (*Symphony No. 2 in D*)

Out of some nine LP recordings available, the Antal Dorati-Minneapolis Symphony Orchestra version (12" Mercury 50004) is the definitive recording musically and from the sound reproduction point of view.

This Symphony, preceded by the First Movement of Borodin's *Quartet No. 2 in D,* made up the score for Leonide Massine's Russian spectacle-ballet, *Bogatyri,* for the Ballet Russe de Monte Carlo. No longer performed.

PRINCE IGOR

(*Polovtsian Dances*)

There are no less than twelve LP recordings of this exciting, barbaric music available. From a balletic point of view the Igor Markevitch-Orchestra Nationale Française recording (12″ Angel 35144) is preferred.

Michel Fokine's stirring ballet of a Polovtsi camp, one of the first Diaghileff Ballets, and still seen today in pale and wan imitations at the hands of various companies.

BOYCE, William (1710-1779)

THE PROSPECT BEFORE US

Regrettably, no LP recording is available but there is a superlative 78 rpm of these melodies arranged from Boyce by Constant Lambert on Victor album DM-857, with Constant Lambert, London Philharmonic Orchestra.

Dramatic ballet by Ninette de Valois for the Sadler's Wells Ballet in 1940. Presently in repertory of Sadler's Wells Theatre Ballet.

BRAHMS, Johannes (1833-1897)

CHOREARTIUM (*Symphony No. 4 in C*)

Eleven LP recordings of this, the last of Brahms's symphonies, are available. From many points of view the most interesting is the Leonard Bernstein-Stadium Symphony recording (12″ Decca 9717). From a purely musical point of view, the Weingartner-London Symphony Orchestra version is preferred, despite its age.

This is the music used by Leonide Massine for his second

"symphonic" ballet, *Choreartium,* a deeply moving ballet, no longer to be seen.

VARIATIONS ON A THEME BY HAYDN

From a long list of recordings, I have found those of Igor Markevitch, with the Philharmonia Orchestra (Victor LBC-1010) and Otto Klemperer and the Philharmonia Orchestra (Angel 35221) the best.
Ballet by Bronislava Nijinska for the de Cuevas Ballet, 1944.

BRITTEN, Benjamin (1913—)

LES ILLUMINATIONS

Krebs, Rother, Berlin Radio Sym. 12″ Urania A-7104.
Pears, Goossens, New Symphony. 12″ London LL-994.
Mock, Sokoloff, La Jolla Orch. 12″ Alco Y-1211.

The Pears-Goossens performance (London LL-994) is decidedly superior.
An intensely moving contemporary ballet by Frederick Ashton in the repertory of the New York City Ballet. Commissioned in 1950.

SOIRÉES MUSICALES

MATINÉES MUSICALES

The former: Warwick Braithwaite conducting the Covent Garden Orchestra, 10″ Parlophone (London) PMD 1020; The latter: Edgar Cree, conducting the New Symphony Orchestra of London, London International 10″ W91075. Both are also available with the same artists on 10″ MGM E-117 and 12″ MGM 3028.
These two suites are based on music by Rossini, little songs

and duets Rossini wrote for various parties and published together in 1835. *Soirées Musicales* was composed in 1938, and was used by Antony Tudor for his ballet called *Soirée Musicale*. Zachary Solov staged a work to this music for the Metropolitan Opera Company in 1956. The *Matinées Musicales* was commissioned by Lincoln Kirstein for the ballet, *Divertimento*, by George Balanchine, given in South America in 1941.

Both records, differing in musical approach, are a valued addition to a record library, and the sound is well engineered.

JINX (Variations on a Theme of Frank Bridge Op. 10)

Boyd Neel String Orch. 12" London LL-1123.
Von Karajan, Philharmonia Orch. 12" Angel 35142.

The Boyd Neel performance is preferred; additionally there is a Peter Warlock ballet score on the other side.

This is the music used by Lew Christensen for his ballet, *Jinx,* presently in the repertory of the New York City Ballet.

FANFARE (The Young Person's Guide to the Orchestra)

De Wilde, Swarowsky, Pro Musica Sym. 12" Vox PL-9280.
Dorati, Minn. Sym. 12" Mercury 50047.
Markevitch, Philharmonia Orch. 12" Angel 35135.
Sargent, Liverpool Philharmonic. 12" Columbia ML-4197.
Van Beinum, Concertgebouw Orch. 12" London LL-917.

The Markevitch version (Angel 35135) is preferred.

Music used by Jerome Robbins for his ballet, *Fanfare,* in the repertory of the New York City Ballet.

More recently used by Frederick Ashton for his ballet, *Variations on a Theme of Purcell,* which is the basic theme of Purcell's, used by Britten, from a rondeau in the incidental music to Behn's play, *Abdelazer.*

Music: Brilliant orchestral variations written in 1946 as accompaniment to a motion picture illustrating the make-up of the modern orchestra.

CARPENTER, John Alden (1876-1951)

SKYSCRAPERS

Hendl, Amer. Recording Orch. 12" ARS 37.

Ballet commissioned by the Metropolitan Opera Company and produced there in 1926. This is not literal jazz, but jazz filtered through the mind of a musician who thought in terms of art. A picture of American life.

CHABRIER, Alexis Emmanuel (1841-1894)

COTILLON (*Suite Pastorale*)

Some of the music used by George Balanchine in his ballet, *Cotillon,* to be found in: Braithwaite, Covent Garden Orch. (12" MGM 3000) and Lindenburg, Orch. Paris Con. (12" London LL-871).
The Braithwaite-Covent Garden version (MGM 3000) is the more satisfactory.

ODE A LA MUSIQUE

Fournet, Chorale Brasseur, Orch. 12" London LL-639.

This includes the *Marche Joyeuse,* which forms the overture to Balanchine's ballet, *Bourée Fantasque,* also used in the Roland Petit ballet, *Ballabile,* as is Chabrier's *España.* The *Suite Pastorale* (above) used in *Cotillon,* and also by Ninette de Valois's *Bar aux Folies-Bergère,* Walter Gore's *Light Fantastic* and *Balabile.*
It is an adequate recording of competently performed music.

BOURÉE FANTASQUE

Barzin, New York City Ballet Orch. Vox PL-9320.

The only complete version of an utterly delightful Balanchine ballet, a highlight of the repertory of the New York City Ballet, and, as recording, a must for every collector.

CHAUSSON, Ernest (1855-1899)

LILAC GARDEN (Poème for Violin and Orchestra, Op. 25)

There are eight LP recordings of this work, of which the best is that of Francescatti-Ormandy and the Philadelphia Orchestra (Columbia 10″ ML-2194).
The romantic score utilized by Antony Tudor for his moving ballet, *Jardin aux Lilas (Lilac Garden)*.

CHOPIN, Frédéric (1810-1849)

CONSTANTIA (Concerto No. 2 in F, Op. 21)

Of eight recordings Rubinstein, Steinberg, NBC Sym. (12″ Victor LM-1046) is preferred.
Ballet choreographed by William Dollar for the International Ballet (de Cuevas) in New York, in 1944 also has been presented by Ballet Theatre.

LES SYLPHIDES

Désormière, Orch. Paris Con. 12″ London LL-884.
Fiedler, Boston Pops Orch. 10″ Victor LM-10.
Irving, Royal Op. Orch. 12″ Victor LBC-1078.
Kurtz, N.Y. Philharmonic. 12″ Columbia 3ML-4255.
Levine, Ballet Theatre Orch. 12″ Capitol P-8193.
Levine, Ballet Theatre Orch. 10″ Capitol L-8194.

List, Berlin Sym. 12" Royale 1338.
Markevitch (Collection).
Ormandy, Philadelphia Orch. 12" Columbia CL-741.
Rignold, Royal Opera Orch. 12" Decca 9550.
Sargent, London Philharmonic. 12" Victor LBC-1011.

The finest performance of this extremely pleasant score, which has been orchestrated by Glazounov, Stravinsky, Rieti, and others, is to be found in the Irving, Royal Op. Orch. (Victor LBC 1078).

This "romantic reverie," originally choreographed by Michel Fokine for the Diaghileff Ballet, is to be found in the repertory of the Ballet Theatre, the Ballet Russe de Monte Carlo and in most other ballet companies. Present day performances leave a good deal to be desired, but it takes a good deal to ruin utterly this very lovely work.

CONCERTO NO. 1 IN E. OP. 11

There are twelve LP recordings available, with various soloists and conductors and orchestras, of which the most satisfactory, in my opinion, is that of Friederich Gulda with Sir Adrian Boult and the London Philharmonic Orchestra 12" London, No. LL-1001.

The music utilised for her ballet, *Chopin Concerto,* by Bronislava Nijinska, at one time in the repertory of the Ballet Russe de Monte Carlo.

CIMAROSA, Domenico (1749-1801)

CIMAROSIANA

Braithwaite, Royal Opera Orch. 12" MGM 3013.

This ballet music was arranged by G. Francesco Malipiero for the Leonide Massine ballet of same name, staged for the Diaghileff Ballet.

COPLAND, Aaron (1900—)

APPALACHIAN SPRING

Bath, Hastings Sym. 10″ Allegro 4056.
Koussevitzky, Boston Sym. 12″ Victor LCT-1134.
Litschauer, Vienna St. Op. Orch. 12″ Vanguard 439.
Mitchell, National Sym. Orch. 12″ Westminster 5286.
Rother, Berlin Radio Sym. 12″ Urania C-7092.

The Koussevitzky-Boston recording is preferred, although the Mitchell-National Symphony (Urania No. C-7092) has much to recommend it.

BILLY THE KID

Bernstein, RCA Vic. Sym. 12″ Victor LM-1031.
Levine, Ballet Theatre Orch. 12″ Capitol P-8238.
Mitchell, Nat'l Sym. 12″ Westminster 5286.
Stokowski, N.Y. Phil. 10″ Columbia ML-2167.

The Victor (No. LM-1031) under the composer is preferred over the others, although there are cuts.
This is Eugene Loring's stirring ballet of the American west. It is presently to be seen in the repertory of the Ballet Theatre.

THE PIED PIPER (*Concerto for Clarinet & Orchestra*)

Fiedler, Boston Pops Orch. Victor 12″ LM-1726.
Goodman, Copland, Columbia Orch. 12″ Columbia ML-4421.

Ballet by Jerome Robbins for the New York City Ballet in 1951.

RODEO

Dorati, Dallas Sym. Orch. 10″ Victor LM-32.
Levine, Ballet Theatre Orch. 10″ Capitol L-8198.

Levine, Ballet Theatre Orch. 12" Capitol P-8196.

The Dorati-Dallas is, despite the cuts, the more satisfactory. Victor LM-32.

Agnes de Mille's triumphant portrait of ranch life, now in the repertory of the Ballet Theatre.

TIME TABLE (Music for the Theatre)

Hendl, Am. Rec. Soc. Orch. 12" ARS-12.

Music used by Antony Tudor for his ballet, *Time Table,* produced for the Ballet Caravan.

DEBUSSY, Claude (1862-1918)

THE AFTERNOON OF A FAUN (Prelude à l'àpres-midi d'un faune)

There are available some fifteen recordings (LP) of this work. The Ansermet-Suisse Romande (10" London LD-9031) should be given preference, and the Beecham-London Philharmonic performance on 78 rpm (Columbia 69600) should not be overlooked.

Nijinsky's most famous creation made history. A later and quite different balletic treatment has been made by Jerome Robbins for the New York City Ballet.

BALLADE (Epigraphes Antiques)

Ansermet, Orch. de la Suisse Romande. 12" London LL-992.

The definitive recorded version of this Debussy piano work, orchestrated by Ernest Ansermet, and used in this orchestration by Jerome Robbins for his ballet, *Ballade,* for the New York City Ballet, in 1952.

LE MARTYR DE SAINT SEBASTIAN

Ansermet, Orch. Suisse Romande. London 12" LL-1061.

Magnificent playing and recording of this music incidental to the play, in which the *danseuse-mime,* Ida Rubinstein, appeared, and which she produced.

JEUX (Games) (Poème Danse)

Ansermet, Orch. Suisse Romande. 12" London LL-992.
de Sabata, Orch. 12" Victor LM-1057.

The Ansermet-Suisse Romande performance (London LL-992) is the definitive recording.
Staged within the boundaries of a tennis court this ballet was created by Vaslav Nijinsky for the Diaghileff Ballet in 1913. A version of it has been seen in the repertory of Ballet Theatre.

DELIBES, Léo (1836-1891)

BALLET MUSIC

Marlborough Sym. 12" Camden 119.
Schonner, Austrian Sym. 12" Remington 199-126.

COPPÉLIA

There are nine LP recordings of various portions of *Coppélia* available, of which, though truncated, the Constant Lambert-Royal Opera House Orchestra performance (12" Columbia ML-4145) is far and away the most sensitive performance. The Roger Désormière performance, on 12" London LL-846 is excellently played and reproduced and has the advantage of substantial portions of Delibes' ballet, *Sylvia,* on the opposite side.
One of the stalwart pillars of romantic ballet, this work, created by Louis Mérante in 1870, is best performed today by the Sadler's Wells Ballet.

SYLVIA

Seven LP recordings of excerpts from this ballet are available, of which the Désormière recording (see above) is an excellent performance of this charming French ballet music, and the sound is rich and fine.

This full-evening ballet (three acts and four scenes) was first produced by Louis Mérante at the Paris Opera, in 1876. In 1953 it was given a new production by Frederick Ashton, and is in the repertory of the Sadler's Wells Ballet.

DELIUS, Frederick (1862-1934)

ROMEO AND JULIET

A ballet by Antony Tudor, created for Ballet Theatre, in 1943, utilizes various compositions by Delius. It would be the course of wisdom to list the works used: *Over the Hills and Far Away,* Sir Thomas Beecham and the Royal Philharmonic Orch. (10" Columbia ML-2133); *The Walk to the Paradise Garden* (from the opera *A Village Romeo and Juliet*) Beecham, and Royal Philharmonic Orch. His Master's Voice DB 9316/7 (78 rpm); *Eventyr (North Country Sketches)* Beecham, Royal Philharmonic, (12" Columbia 3ML-4637); Prelude to the opera *Irmelin,* Beecham and Royal Philharmonic, HMV DB 9092 (78 rpm); *Brigg Fair, An English Rhapsody,* Collins, London Sym., 12" London LL-758, also contains *The Walk to the Paradise Garden* (see above). All performances and recordings are especially fine.

NOCTURNE (Paris)

Collins, London Symphony. 12" London LL-923.

A first rate recording, with two additional Delius works for good measure.

This music was utilized by Frederick Ashton for his ballet, *Nocturne,* created in 1936 for the Sadler's Wells Ballet.

DOHNANYI, Ernst von (1877—)

THE SHADOW (Suite in F#, Op. 19)

Irving, Phil. Orch. 12" Victor LBC-1090.
Sargent, London Sym. 10" Columbia ML-2172.
Wallenstein, Los Angeles Phil. 10" Decca 6006.

Sargent, (Columbia ML-2172) is preferred.
Ballet by John Cranko, choreographed in 1953 for the Sadler's Wells Ballet, and seen in America in the repertory of that company.

FIVE GIFTS (Variations on a Nursery Theme)

Jacquinot, Fistoulari, Phil Orch. 12" MGM 3004.
Katchen, Boult, London Phil. 12" London LL-1018.
Smith, Sargent, Liverpool Phil. 12" Columbia ML-4146.

Fistoulari .(MGM 3004) is preferred.
Ballet choreographed by William Dollar for the de Cuevas ballet.

DUKAS, Paul (1865-1935)

LA PERI

Ansermet, Orch. Paris Con. 12" London LL-1155.
Fistoulari, Westminster Sym. 12" MGM 3062.
Sebastian, Colonne Orch. 12" Urania C-7097.

The Ansermet-Orchestra de Conservatoire de Paris recording (London LL-1155) is quite magnificent. However, the

Fistoulari-Westminster recording (MGM 3062) has an advantage to ballet lovers in its coupling with Vincent d'Indy's *Istar.*

Composed in 1912, this *"poème dansé"* has been made into a ballet on numerous occasions: Trukhanova (Paris) 1912; Leo Staats (Paris Opera) 1921; Frederick Ashton (London Ballet Club) 1931; Frank Staff (Ballet Rambert, London) 1938; Serge Lifar (Les Noveaux Ballets de Monte Carlo) 1945, and with the Paris Opera, 1948.

A Persian fairy tale, the Ansermet recording captures the sensuous delights of the score magnificently, and the recording and sound are flawless.

ELWELL, Herbert (1898—)

THE HAPPY HYPOCRITE

Hendl, American Rec. Soc. Orch. ARS 12" 37.

After the story by Max Beerbohm, this was danced by Charles Weidman and the Dance Repertory Theatre in New York in 1931.

EASDALE, Brian (1909—)

RED SHOES

Mathieson, Orch. 10" Columbia ML-2083.

The ballet music from the extremely popular motion picture which brought the ballerina Moira Shearer to international attention.

FALLA, Manuel de (1876-1946)

EL AMOR BRUJO

There are five recordings available on LP. The two outstanding performances are those of Carol Brice, Fritz Reiner, and the Pittsburgh Symphony (10" Columbia ML-2006) and Anthony Collins with the London Philharmonic (London LL-203) the latter being fuller and having fewer cuts. This is a genuinely exciting score. The Reiner version, with many cuts, nevertheless includes some of the vocal parts. The ballet has been choreographed by numerous dancers, including the late Argentinita, Adolph Bolm, and La Meri.

THE THREE-CORNERED HAT

Danco, Ansermet, Orch. Suisse Romande. 12" London LL-598.

Martinon, Orch. Opéra Comique. 12" Urania 7034 and numerous excerpts by others. The above are the two complete recordings.

The Suzanne Danco-Ansermet recording (London LL-598) is complete, exciting, and one of the really thrilling recordings of our day. It is something that should be in every record collector's library, irrespective of the degree of his interest in ballet.

The ballet is Leonide Massine's masterpiece, staged for the Diaghileff Ballet in London, in 1919. Today it is in the repertory of the Sadler's Wells Ballet.

FRANÇAIX, Jean (1912—)

THE EMPEROR'S NEW CLOTHES

Striegler, Saxon State Orch. 12" Urania C-7122.

A ballet created by Ninette de Valois for the Sadler's Wells Ballet.

A LA FRANÇAIX (Serenade for Twelve Instruments)

Françaix, Jochum, Orch. 10" Capitol L-8051.

Long, Martinon, London Phil. 12″ London LL-1058.

A comic ballet by George Balanchine, produced in 1951, and in the repertory of the New York City Ballet.

FRANCK, César (1822-1890)

PSYCHÉ

Seven LP recordings of this Franck symphonic poem are available, of which the Van Beinum-Concertgebouw Orchestra performance and recording on London 10″ LD-9081 is definitely preferred.

This symphonic poem was utilised by Jean Babilée for his ballet *L'Amour et son Amour* (*Cupid and his Love*), produced in Paris in 1948, and seen in the repertory of the Ballet Theatre during the season of 1951.

SYMPHONIC VARIATIONS

No less than ten recordings are available on LP, of which the performance by Walter Gieseking, with Herbert von Karajan and the Philharmonia Orchestra (12″ Columbia ML-4885) is perhaps the performance to own.

Staged as a ballet under the same title by Frederick Ashton for the Sadler's Wells Ballet, in 1946, and in the repertory of that company.

GERSHWIN, George (1898-1937)

AN AMERICAN IN PARIS

From the twelve existing LP recordings, that of Morton Gould with his orchestra (Victor 12″ LM-6033) is, on all counts, the best.

A ballet staged by the American choreographer Ruth Page. Gene Kelly's dance film of the same name was built around it.

RHAPSODY IN BLUE

There are a round dozen LP recordings of this Gershwin work of which the Morton Gould is far and away the best. A ballet to this music was staged by the dancer Anton Dolin.

GILLIS, Don (1912—)

SYMPHONY FOR FUN

Gillis, New Sym. 10" London LS-177

Gay, jazz-tinted work used for an amusing ballet in the repertory of the London Festival Ballet, and seen in America.

GLAZOUNOV, Alexander (1865-1936)

RAYMONDA

Fayer, National Theatre Orch. 12" Vanguard 432.
Festival Concert Orchestra. 12" Camden 166.
Rosenthal, Paris Philharmonic. 12" Capitol P-8184.

The Manuel Rosenthal—Paris Philharmonic recording (Capitol P-8184) is the best of the lot, although cut to a suite as are the others.
A standby as a full-length ballet in the Imperial Russian Ballet, and still in the repertory of the Soviet Ballet. A not very satisfactory cut version was presented in the United States some years ago by the Ballet Russe de Monte Carlo.

RUSES D'AMOUR

Golovanov, Bolshoi Theatre Orch. Colosseum 12" CRLP 165.

Ballet in one act by the composer and Marius Petipa, and first produced at the Hermitage Theatre, St. Petersburg in 1900. Charming music in the post-Tchaikowsky manner.

THE SEASONS

There is but a single recording of this by Roger Désormière and the French Symphony (12" Capitol P-8157).

Another tuneful full-length work from the repertory of the Imperial Russian Ballet. A messed-up version of the music, for a ballet called *The Snow Maiden*, was staged by the Ballet Russe de Monte Carlo, in 1943. The Bacchanale movement from this work was made famous by Anna Pavlova.

GLIÈRE, Reinhold (1875—)

THE BRONZE KNIGHT

Guhl, Berlin Radio Symphony. 12" Urania C-7121.

In the repertory of the Soviet Ballet. Recording Good.

THE RED POPPY

Fayer, National Theatre Orchestra. 12" Vanguard 432.
Gahlenbeck, Berlin Radio Sym. 12" Urania C-7078.
Scherchen, Vienna St. Opera Orch. 12" Westminster 7001.

The Scherchen recording (Westminster 7001), by far the the fullest and best recorded, is preferred.

A dramatic, propaganda ballet in the Soviet Ballet repertory, first performed in Moscow in 1927. A shortened version of this ballet was produced in the United States by the Ballet Russe de Monte Carlo in 1943.

GLINKA, Michael (1803-1857)

JOTA ARAGONESA

Orloff, Orch. 12" Colosseum 10040.

A ballet to this Russo-Spanish music was staged by Michel Fokine in St. Petersburg in 1916, and later was in the repertory of the Blum Ballet Russe de Monte Carlo.

RUSSLAN AND LUDMILLA

Ansermet, Orchestre Paris Conservatoire. 12" London LL-864.

Dances for the opera tastefully played and excellently reproduced.

GLUCK, Christoph Willibald von (1714-1787)

BALLET MUSIC—SUITE: FRÜHLINGSFIER

Keilberth, Prague Orchestra, Steffin, Berlin Orch. 12" Urania C-7018.

DON JUAN (Pantomime ballet)

Moralt, Vienna Symphony. 12" Westminster 5028.

This early ballet to the music of Gluck was re-created in 1936, by Michel Fokine, for the Blum Ballet Russe de Monte Carlo. It is a delightful musical work, although the ballet is no longer performed.

GOLDMARK, Karl (1830-1915)

BALLET MUSIC FROM ACT III, THE QUEEN OF SHEBA

Stock. Chicago Symphony Orchestra. Victor 7474 (78 rpm).

GOOSSENS, Eugene (1893—)

BALLET MUSIC FROM JUDITH (1925)

Goossens, New Symphony Orchestra. Victor 9470 X. (78 rpm).

GORDON, Gavin. (1901—)

THE RAKE'S PROGRESS

Lambert, Royal Opera Orchestra. 12" Columbia ML-4229.

A definitive recording of this interesting contemporary score in the eighteenth-century style as befits the ballet for which it was commissioned.
A ballet based on the satirical set of paintings of the same title by William Hogarth, by Ninette de Valois, first choreographed in 1935, and in the repertory of the Sadler's Wells Ballet.

GOTTSCHALK, Louis Moreau (1829-1869)

CAKEWALK (Ballet suite)

Ormandy, Philadelphia Orchestra. 12" Columbia 3ML-4616.

A definitive recording of this "minstrel show" score, arranged by Hershy Kay from the music of Louis Moreau Gottschalk, American pianist and composer. Gay, nostalgic, and utterly delightful.
The ballet, telling a balletic version of an American minstrel show, was choreographed by Ruthanna Boris for the New York City Ballet in 1951. It is still in that company's repertoire.

GOULD, Morton (1913—)

FALL RIVER LEGEND

Levine, Ballet Theatre Orch. 12" Capitol P-8320.
Mitropoulos, New York Phil. 12" Columbia 3ML-4616.

Recordings of the dramatic music for the Agnes de Mille ballet of the same name (1948), for which it was commissioned. The story of the ballet is founded on the Lizzie Borden story. The recording is excellent. The ballet is currently performed by the Ballet Theatre, for which it was created.

INTERPLAY FOR PIANO AND ORCHESTRA

De Groot, Van Otterloo, Hague Phil. Orch. 12" Epic 3LC-3021.
Gould, Robin Hood Dell Orch. 12" Columbia 3ML-4218.

The composer's own performance of a gay, diverting score (Columbia ML-4218) is definitive.
The music, originally composed for a radio broadcast, was utilized for the gay ballet of the same name by Jerome Robbins for Ballet Theatre in 1945, having first been staged for Billy Rose's *Concert Varieties*. It is in the repertories of both Ballet Theatre and the New York City Ballet.

PARRANDA (Latin American Symphonette)

Hanson, Eastman-Rochester Orch. 12" Mercury 40002.

Brilliant recording and performance of one of the composer's finest works. An addition to any collector's library of gay contemporary music.
The musical base of the Latin-American ballet, *Parranda,*

staged by Willam Christensen for the San Francisco Civic Ballet in 1947.

TAP DANCE CONCERTO

Daniels, Gould, Rochester "Pops." 10″ Columbia ML-2215.

The feet of the dancer Danny Daniels and his taps are an integral part of the composition, used as an instrument.

GOUNOD, Charles (1818-1892)

FAUST (Ballet music)

Six recordings of the extensive ballet music in this Gounod opera are available in LP, of which the Rignold, Royal Opera Orchestra version (12″ Decca 9548), seems to be the most satisfactory.

GRADWHOL, Pierre (1905—)

DIVERTISSEMENT CHAMPÊTRE

Leibowitz, Paris Phil. Orch. 12″ Renaissance X-41.

A ballet presenting a group of townsmen of the 19th Century in the gracious glades of France in a festive summer atmosphere. Each dance is determined by motives played by each instrument in turn.

GRÉTRY, André (1741-1813)

No recordings of the delightful ballet music by this pioneer among ballet composers are presently available on LP. However, the following in 78 rpm may be found by diligent search of collector's shops, in case anyone is interested: *Ballet Music* (unspecified), von Benda, Chamber Orchestra, Gramophone EG 3063; *Danses Villageoises,* The Six Dances in this recording are from *Colinette à la Cour, L'Embarras de Richesses, L'Epreuve Villageoise, Richard Coeur-de-Lion, Rosière de Salency,* Ruhlmann, Symphony Orchestra, Pathé X-96133/4.

Ballet Suite from Cephale and Procris, arr. Mottl. Brussels Conservatory Orchestra-Defauw, Columbia LFX 65.

Ballet Suite from La Rosière Républicaine, Meyrowitz, Philharmonic Orchestra, Pathé PD 7/8.

GRIFFES, Charles Tomlinson (1884-1920)

THE WHITE PEACOCK

Stokowski, New York Phil. 10" Columbia ML-2167.

Music utilized by Adolph Bolm for his ballet of the same name, produced for his *Ballet Intime.*

HANDEL, George Frederick (1685-1759)

THE FAITHFUL SHEPHERD

Beecham, Royal Phil. Orch. 12" Columbia ML-4734.
Engel, Columbia Ch. Orch. 12" Columbia ML-4685.

The former is the distinctive ballet recording.

THE GREAT ELOPEMENT

Beecham, Royal Phil. Orch. 12" Victor LHMV-1030.

Unproduced ballet by Sir Thomas Beecham. Excellent.

The following 78 rpm, excellent in playing and quality, may possibly be found after searching.

ALCINA (Minuet, Musette, Minuet, Gavotte, Sarabande, Gavotte, Minuet, Gavotte, Tambumino).

Mengelberg, New York Philharmonic Orchestra. Victor 1435/6.

THE GODS GO A-BEGGING (*Arranged by Sir Thomas Beecham, 1928*).

Beecham, London Phil. Orch. Columbia 68202D and LX 40.

Excellent recordings of a ballet staged by both George Balanchine for the Diaghileff Ballet and by Ninette de Valois for the Sadler's Wells Ballet.

THE ORIGIN OF DESIGN

Beecham, London Phil. Orch. English Columbia LX-224, 313, 346.

Handel music arranged for the ballet of the above name by Sir Thomas Beecham for the Camargo Society, and choreographed by Ninette de Valois in 1932.

HINDEMITH, Paul (1895—)

THE DEMON (*Ballet pantomime*)

Carraciolo, Scarlatti Orchestra. 12″ Colosseum 1036.

METAMORPHOSIS (*Symphonic Metamorphosis on Theme by Weber*)

Kubelik, Chicago Sym. 12″ Mercury 50027.
Szell, Cleveland Orch. 12″ Columbia ML-4177.

Kubelik (Mercury 50027) preferred.
Ballet by George Balanchine for the New York City Ballet, in 1952.

NOBLISSIMA VISIONE (*St. Francis*)

Klemperer, Phil. Orch. 12″ Angel 35221.
Ormandy, Phil. Orch. 12″ Columbia 3ML-4177.

The Ormandy Record is a splendid recording of a noble work.

The music for the ballet of the same name, known in America as *St. Francis,* a balletic masterpiece by Leonide Massine, choreographed in 1938. Regrettably this work has been dropped from the repertory of the Ballet Russe de Monte Carlo.

THE FOUR TEMPERAMENTS

The music; *Theme and Four Variations*
There are four LP recordings of which that of Lukas Foss, with the Zimbler Sinfonietta (10" Decca DL-7501) is preferred. Music utilized by George Balanchine for the ballet in the repertory of the New York City Ballet.

HOLST, Gustav (1874-1934)

THE PERFECT FOOL

Boult, London Phil. Orch. 12" London LL-1169.

Ballet music from Holst's opera of the same name, written in 1921 and produced at Covent Garden, London, in 1923. Ballet of the spirits of fire and water; excellently played and resoundingly reproduced.

THE PLANETS

Boult, BBC Symphony. 12" Victor LHMV-1002.
Boult, London Phil. Orch. Proms and Choir. 12" Westminster 5235.

The Sir Adrian Boult version (Westminster 5235) is a superb reading of a valuable and exciting work. Staged as a ballet by Antony Tudor in 1934 in London.

IBERT, Jacques (1890—)

DIVERTISSEMENT

Désormière, Orch. Paris Cons. 12" London LL-884.
Slatkin, Concert Arts Orch. 12" Capitol P-8270.

The Désormière version (London LL-884) is preferred.
Moreover, it has a really excellent *Les Sylphides* on the
opposite side.
Music used by Ruth Page for her ballet, *The Gold Standard.*
Not presently in the repertory of any ballet company.

ESCALES (*Ports of Call*)

The preferred performance and recording out of four available on LP is that of Leopold Stokowski and Orchestra on
a 12" Victor LM-9029.
Used for the ballet *Ports of Call,* choreographed by Leon
Woizikowski, and seen in the repertory of the Polish Ballet
at the World's Fair, New York City, in 1939.

D'INDY, Vincent (1851-1931)

ISTAR

Fistoulari, Westminster Symphony. 12" MGM 3062.
Sebastian, Orchestra Colonne. 12" Urania C-7115.

The Fistoulari version (Urania C-7115) is preferred. A ballet
in the repertory of the Paris Opera Ballet.

JOSTEN, Werner (1885—)

ENDYMION

Hafner, Vienna Orchestra. 12" SPA. C-16.

KABALEVSKY, Dmitri (1904—)

TARAS' FAMILY
Kirov Orchestra. 2-12" Classic 3004.

KAY, Hershy (1919—)

WESTERN SYMPHONY
Barzin, New York City Ballet Orchestra. 12" Vox PL-9050.

A successful ballet on an American theme by George Balanchine in the current repertory of the New York City Ballet.

KHACHATURIAN, Aram (1903—)

GAYENNE
Kurtz, New York Philharmonic. 12" Columbia 4ML-4030.
Herman, Berlin Philharmonic. 12" Royale-1294.

The Efrem Kurtz version (Columbia 4ML-4030) is preferred. A popular work in the repertory of the Soviet Ballet.

KODALY, Zoltan (1882—)

DANCES FROM GALANTA
Five LP versions are available of this exciting dance music based on Transylvanian folk dance melodies, of which the Victor de Sabata version, 12" Decca 9518, is preferred.

PEACOCK VARIATIONS
Dorati, Chicago Sym. 12" Mercury 50038.
Solti, London Phil. Orch. 12" London LL-1020.

The Dorati version (Mercury 50038) is superior in every way, and is a genuinely stirring recording.

LALO, Édouard (1823-1892)

NAMOUNA

Martinov, London Phil. 12" LL-1628.
Sebastian, Orch. Paris Conservatoire. 12" Urania 7068.

Ballet choreographed by Marius Petipa for the Imperial Russian Ballet, in 1882. Tuneful, well-played and well recorded.

LAMBERT, Constant (1905-1951)

HOROSCOPE

Irving, London Sym. 12" London LL-771.
Lambert, Phil. Orch. 10" Columbia ML-2145.

The Robert Irving version (London LL-771) contains more of the ballet's music and is better recorded; the Lambert version better played.
Ballet by Constant Lambert, choreographed by Frederick Ashton, for the Vic-Wells Ballet, in 1938.

RIO GRANDE

Lambert, Phil. Orch. 10" Columbia ML-2145.

One of the composer's last recordings of one of his earliest and most effective scores incorporating the jazz idiom. Ballet choreographed by Frederick Ashton for the Camargo Society, London, in 1932, under the title *A Day in a Southern Port*, and later revived for the Vic-Wells Ballet as *Rio Grande*.

LECOCQ, Alexandre (1832-1918)

MLLE. ANGOT SUITE

Gressler, Lamoureux Orchestra. 12" Vox PL-20000.

Kurtz, N. Y. Phil. Orch. 12" Columbia ML-4083.

The Efrem Kurtz recording (Columbia ML-4083) is preferred.

Ballet by Leonide Massine, first produced for the Ballet Theatre, and also in the repertory of the Sadler's Wells Ballet. It is occasionally revived by the Ballet Theatre.

LHOTKA, Fran (Contemporary Czech Composer, living in Yugoslavia)

THE DEVIL IN THE VILLAGE

"Folky" in style, this is a popular, unpretentious score that successfully compliments the action of a folk ballet in the repertory of the Yugoslav Ballet.

LIADOV, Anatol (1855-1914)

CONTES RUSSES (Baba-Yaga, Eight Russian Popular Songs, Kikimora)

Ansermet, Orchestra Suisse Romande. 12" London LL-1068.
Schartner, Berlin Radio Sym. 12" Urania C-7117.

This version by Ernest Ansermet is one of the very superior recorded performances extant. A colorful Russian work (three works, as a matter of fact) which should be in every music-lover's library.

Contes Russes (Russian Fairy Tales) a ballet by Leonide Massine utilizing this music, was choreographed for the Diaghileff Ballet, but is no longer performed.

LISZT, Franz (1811-1886)

APPARITIONS

Music for this ballet by Frederick Ashton in the repertory of the Sadler's Wells Ballet was taken from the works of

Liszt and orchestrated by Gordon Jacob. Two excerpts are available: *Mephisto Waltz, No. 3*, used in the *Cave Scene*, Constant Lambert and the Philharmonia Orchestra (Entré RL-3056) which record also contains the *Galop* from the same work.

DANTE SONATA

A ballet by Frederick Ashton for the Sadler's Wells Ballet to an orchestration of the Liszt piano work from *L'Annèes de Pèlerinage* by Constant Lambert. The recording, a particularly fine one on 78 rpm, has been deleted from the British Columbia catalogue. It may be found as a collector's item: English Columbia DX 967/8.

MEPHISTO WALTZ

Seven LP recordings are available of which the version by Igor Markevitch and the Florentine Orchestra (12" Tempo 2038) is preferred.

Used by numerous choreographers for ballet works. It was the last ballet choreographed by Adolph Bolm before his death, for the San Francisco Civic Ballet in 1948.

LES PRÉLUDES

No less than fourteen LP recordings of this work exist of which that by Paul Paray and the Detroit Symphony Orchestra (12" Mercury 50036) is preferred.

This Lisztian warhorse has been used by numerous choreographers, including Bronislava Nijinska and Roland Petit, for ballet works.

LORTZING, Gustav Albert (1801-1851)

CZAR AND CARPENTER

Loibner, Vienna Sym. Orch. 12" Epic LC-3102.

"The National Wooden Shoe Dance," from the Lortzing opera, is gay in a good solid way.

ONDINE

Music from Act II of the ballet of the water-sprite who falls in love with a mortal and comes to grief.
Both on the same record and an interesting collector's item. Well recorded.

LUIGINI, Alexandre (1850-1906)

BALLET EGYPTIAN

Fiedler, Boston Pops Orch. 12" Victor LM-1084.
Weldon, Birmingham Orch. 10" Columbia ML-2180.

The Fiedler (Victor LM-1084) is excellently played, with first-class sound.

LULLY, Jean Baptiste (1639-1687)

The ballet music of this pioneering composer in the ballet field has for some strange reason been neglected in LP. The following 78 rpm recordings, all of them excellent as of their period, may be found by careful searching: *Le Triomphe d'Amour Notturno.* Stokowski, Philadelphia Orchestra Victor 7424.

MACKERASS, Charles (SULLIVAN, Arthur)

PINEAPPLE POLL

The two best recordings are Robert Irving, London Sym. Orch. Victor LM-1224, and the Sadler's Wells Orchestra under the direction of Charles Mackerass, Columbia ML-4439.

Ballet based on W. S. Gilbert's "Bab Ballads," telling the story of an attractive vendor of sweets and tobacco to the sailors in Portsmouth Point. Staged by John Cranko for the Sadler's Wells Theatre Ballet, 1952.

MAHLER, Gustav (1860-1911)

SHADOW OF THE WIND (Das Lied von der Erde)

Cavelti, Klemperer, Vienna Symphony. 12" Vox PL-7000.
Ferrier, Walter, Vienna Phil. 2-12" London LL-625/6.

The Kathleen Ferrier—Bruno Walter recording is a priceless gem. (London LL-625/6.)
Music used by Antony Tudor for his ballet, *Shadow of the Wind,* choreographed for the Ballet Theatre but no longer in the repertory.

DARK ELEGIES (Kindertotenlieder)

There are seven versions of this moving work available on LP, including one by Marian Anderson and Pierre Monteux. However, again the Kathleen Ferrier—Bruno Walter version with the Vienna Philharmonic (12" Columbia ML-4980) is a recording that should have a high place in every record collector's library. A deeply moving work.
Music used by Antony Tudor for his ballet, *Dark Elegies,* first produced in London for the Ballet Rambert, and later re-created by him for the repertory of Ballet Theatre.

MASSENET, Jules (1842-1912)

LE CID (Ballet Suite)

Five LP recordings of these ballet excerpts exist, of which the Robert Irving—London Symphony Recording (12" London LL-651) is the best played and best recorded.

MENDELSSOHN, Felix (1809-1847)

A MIDSUMMER NIGHT'S DREAM

Sargent, BBC Symphony (complete work). 3 12" Victor LM-6115.

Sargent, BBC Symphony (abridged). 12" Victor LM-1863.

The Robert Helpmann—Frederick Ashton choreographic version for the Old Vic Theatre production was seen in the United States, in 1954.

MENOTTI, Gian Carlo (1911—)

SEBASTIAN

Mitropoulos, Robin Hood Dell Orch. 10" Columbia ML-2053.

Stokowski, NBC Sym. 12" Victor LM-1858.

Ballet by Edward Caton, originally created for the de Cuevas Ballet in 1944.

The Stokowski (Victor LM-1858) is preferred, if only because it is a more recent technical production, the Mitropoulos having been transferred to LP from 78 rpm.

MESSAGER, André (1853-1929)

LES DEUX PIGÉONS

Blareau, Opéra-Comique Orchestra. 10" London LS-647.

Excellent recording of music for the ballet of the same name, choreographed by Louis Mérante for the Paris Opera, and seen in the repertory of that organization in the United States, in 1948.

MEYERBEER, Giacomo (1791-1864)

LES PATINEURS

Five different recordings of this popular ballet are available, of which that by John Hollingsworth and the Royal Opera Orchestra (12" Columbia ML-4362) is preferred.

Highly successful and popular, tuneful ballet by Frederick Ashton to this music by Meyerbeer, arranged and reorchestrated by Constant Lambert for the Sadler's Wells Ballet. A less effective choreographic version, also by Ashton, was offered for a number of seasons by the Ballet Theatre.

MILHAUD, Darius (1892—)

LE BOEUF SUR LE TOIT

Golschmann, St. Louis Symphony. 12" Capitol P-8244.
Mitropoulos, Minneapolis Orch. 10" Columbia ML-2032.

The Mitropoulos performance (Columbia ML-2032) is preferred both from a musical and balletic point of view.

A ballet originally composed as an experimental ballet by Jean Cocteau, staged by George Balanchine in Soviet Russia, and most recently used as music for a ballet called *The Nothing-Doing Bar,* by Willam Christensen, for the San Francisco Ballet Guild.

DARK RITUAL (*Le Création du Monde*)

Bernstein, Columbia Orch. 10" Columbia ML-2203.

This is one of the finest uses of jazz in serious music. The ballet, negro in theme, was choreographed originally by Jean Borlin for the Swedish Ballet; later by Ninette de Valois, for the Vic-Wells Ballet. Agnes de Mille used the music for her interesting work, *Dark Ritual,* with a negro group, in the first season of Ballet Theatre, 1940.

LES SONGES

Music for this early Balanchine ballet may be had, with the Paris Symphony, conducted by the composer, on a 78 rpm recording, Columbia 17638/9.

MINKUS, Louis (1827-1897)

DON QUICHOTTE (*Pas de Deux*)

Fistoulari, New Sym. Orch. 10″ London LD-9108.

A performance-stopping *pas de deux,* of great virtuosic brilliance from the old Petipa ballet of the same name.

MONTECLAIR, Michel de (1666-1737)

LES TENTATIONS DE LA BERGÉRE

This composer is not to be found at all in LP records, but a 78 rpm recording of some of the music of this ballet, originally choreographed for the Diaghîleff Ballet by Bronislava Nijinska, may be found on British Columbia Album—78 rpm—248; and on American Columbia 64830/1D.

MOROSS, Jerome (1913—)

FRANKIE AND JOHNNY

Hendl, Am. Rec. Soc. Orch. 12″ ARS-12.

The complete recording of the score for Ruth Page's striking American ballet, based on the famous "low-down" American song.

MOSSOLOFF, Alexander (1900—)

SYMPHONY OF MACHINES—STEEL FOUNDRY

Music for this early Soviet mechanistic work may be found conducted by Erlich and the Paris Symphony Orchestra, in British Columbia LB-17, and Pathé X-96300.

The ballet was staged by Adolph Bolm for the first season of Ballet Theatre, at the Center Theatre, New York, in 1940.

MOZART, Wolfgang Amadeus (1756-1791)

CARACOLE (Divertimento No. 15 in B Flat, K. 287)

Prohaska, Vienna St. Op. Orch. 12" Vanguard 444.

Music used by George Balanchine for the ballet, *Caracole,* in the repertory of the New York City Ballet. A veritable musical masterpiece.

LES PETITS RIENS

Braithwaite, Royal Opera Orchestra. 12" MGM 3034.

SYMPHONIE CONCERTANTE (Sinfonia Concertante in E Flat, K. 364)

From several LP recordings of this work, the Isaac Stern— William Primrose version (12" Columbia ML-4564) is preferred; but the Joseph and Lillian Fuchs version (12" Decca-9596) runs it very closely.

Music used by George Balanchine for his classic ballet, *Symphonie Concertante,* in 1947; an abstract work which attempts to approximate in terms of movement this exquisite Mozart music.

MUSSORGSKY, Modeste (1839-1881)

A NIGHT ON BALD MOUNTAIN

There are ten LP recordings of this tone poem, of which the choice is that of Ernest Ansermet and the Orchestre de la Suisse Romande (10" London LD-9086) and Igor Markevitch and the Orchestre National Française (12" Angel 35144).

Music used by various choreographers, including, among others Bronislava Nijinska, Adolph Bolm, and David Lichine.

PICTURES AT AN EXHIBITION

Sixteen recordings on LP exist, of which, so far as personal preference is concerned, I would list that of Ansermet and the Orchestre de la Suisse Romande, 12" London LL-956, and that of Antal Dorati, with the Concertgebouw Orchestra, 12" Epic 3LC-3015.

Bronislava Nijinska utilized this music for her ballet of the same name, staged for the de Cuevas Ballet in New York, 1944.

OFFENBACH, Jacques (1819-1880)

BLUEBEARD

Levine, Ballet Theatre Orchestra. 12" Capitol P-8277.

A suite from the ballet by Michel Fokine, with Offenbach's music orchestrated and arranged by Antal Dorati.

Michel Fokine's last ballet creation, choreographed for Ballet Theatre in 1941, and on rare occasions revived by that company.

GAITE PARISIENNE (*Orchestrated by Rosenthal*)

From seven recordings of this joyously gay work available on LP, those of Efrem Kurtz with the Columbia Symphony Orchestra (12″ Columbia 3ML-4233) and the Arthur Fiedler, Boston Pops Orchestra (12″ Victor LM-1001) come closest to the real thing. Kurtz, as a matter of fact, was in on this music from the time of its selection, and was its original conductor.

In some respects, one of the most popular of modern ballets, this comedy masterpiece of Leonide Massine was first presented in Monte Carlo in 1938 and in the United States the same year. The same music was used by Tudor for the Canadian National Ballet's *Orpheus in the Underworld*.

HELEN of TROY (*Arranged by Antal Dorati*)

Dorati, Minneapolis Symphony Orchestra. 12″ Victor LM-9033.

The music of various Offenbach works, arranged and re-orchestrated by Antal Dorati. Another gay piece of Offenbachiana, skillfully arranged and crisply played.

A ballet choreographed by David Lichine for Ballet Theatre in 1942, and still occasionally revived by that organization.

PISTON, Walter (1894—)

THE INCREDIBLE FLUTIST

Festival Concert Orchestra. 2 12″ Camden 145.

Fiedler, Boston Pops. 3 12″ Victor LM-6113 (with other works)

Rother, Berlin Radio Symphony. 12″ Urania C-7092.

The Fiedler recording (above) is the best of the trio of this

gay music commissioned for a Boston choreographer, Jan
Veen.

POULENC, Francis (1899—)

AUBADE-CONCERTO CHOREOGRAPHIQUE

*Jacquinot, Fistoulari, Westminster Symphony. 12" MGM
3069.*

Ballet choreographed by both Bronislava Nijinska and
George Balanchine, a work not seen these days.

LE BAL MASQUÉ

Galjour, Fender Orchestra. 12" Esoteric 518.

LES BICHES

*Désormière, Orchestre Paris Conservatoire. 12" London LL-
624.* •

Fistoulari, London Symphony. 12" MGM 3098.

Both recordings excellent, but my personal preference is for
the Désormière version.
Ballet by Bronislava Nijinska, choreographed for the
Diaghileff Ballet in 1924 and seen in the United States in
1950, in the repertory of the Marquis de Cuevas Grand
Ballet. A gay and insouciant score, well worth repeated
listening.

PROKOFIEFF, Serge (1891-1953)

CHOUT (The Buffoon)

Golschmann, St. Louis Sym. Orch. 12" Capitol P-8257.
Horenstein, Paris Phil. Orch. 12" Vox PL-9180.
Wolff, Lamoreux Orchestra. 12" Vox PL-6060.

The three LP recordings are about equal in both perform-ance and recording, but, of the three, the Horenstein is to be preferred.

Ballet on a Scythian theme, composed for, but not produced by, the Diaghileff Ballet.

CINDERELLA

Braithwaite, Royal Opera Orch. 12" Columbia ML-4229.
Stasevich, Bolshoi Symphony. 12" Concert Hall-1304.

Braithwaite's recording preferred.

In the repertory of the Sadler's Wells. The version known to the U.S. is that choreographed by Frederick Ashton for the Sadler's Wells Ballet, in 1948; a work in the grand style embellished with taste. The full work is a gem in the repertory of the Soviet Ballet.

CLASSICAL SYMPHONY IN D

Ansermet, Orch. Paris Conservatoire. 10" London LD-9114.
Ansermet, Orch. Paris Con. 12" London LI-864.
Berlin Sym. 12" Royale 1420.
Ceilbidache, Berlin Phil. 12" Victor LBC-1009.
Horenstein, Colonne Orch. 12" Vox PL-9170.
Fricsay, RIAS Sym. 12" Decca 9737.
Koussevitzky, Boston Sym. 12" Victor LM-1215.
Markevitch, Phil. Orch. 12" Angel 35008.
Martinon, Lamoureux Orch. 12" Epic 3LC-3042.
Munch, Orch. Paris Con. 12" LL-169.
Ormandy, Phila. Orch. 10" Columbia ML-2035.
Schuler Sym. 12" Camd. 215.
Stasevich, Orch. 12" Kings 251.
Steinberg, Pitts. Sym. 12" Capitol P-8290.
Toscanini, NBC Sym. 12" Victor LM-9020.
Walther, Hamburg Phil. 12" MGM 3087.

Music used by Antony Tudor for his gay and witty ballet, *Gala Performance,* originally produced for the Ballet Rambert in London, and for more than a decade in the repertory of Ballet Theatre. The work also utilizes the First Movement of Prokofieff Piano Concerto No. 3 in C. Of which the Kapell, Dorati, Dallas Orch. (12″ Victor LM-1058) is, perhaps, the best.

RUSSIAN SOLDIER (*Lieutenant Kije, Suite, Opus 60*).

Désormière French Natl. Sym. 12″ Capitol P-1849.
Horenstein, Paris Phil. 12″ Vox PL-9180.
Koussevitzky, Boston Sym. 12″ Victor LCT-1144.
Kurtz, Royal Phil. 12″ Columbia ML-4683.
Rubahn, Berlin Sym. 12″ Royale 1324.
Scherchen, Vienna Sym. 12″ Westminster 5091.

Music used by Michel Fokine for his ballet *Russian Soldier* choreographed for Ballet Theatre in 1942. A ballet no longer performed. Horenstein 12″ Vox PL-9180, preferred.

PETER AND THE WOLF

Centennial Sym. 12″ Camd. 101.
De Wilde, Swarowsky. Pro Musica Sym. 12″ Vox PL-9280.
Godfrey, Kostelanetz, Orch. 12″ Columbia CL-720.
Guiness, Fiedler, Boston Pops. 12″ Victor LM-1761.
Hale, Fiedler, Boston Pops. 12″ Victor LM-1803.
Philips, Malko, London Phil. 10″ London LS-151.
Pickles, Markevitch, Phil. Orch. 12″ Victor LBC-1015.
Rathbone, Stokowski & Orch. 12″ Columbia ML-4038.
Walker, Leopold, Orch. 12″ Royale 1246.

Hale—Fiedler (Victor LM-1803) and Pickles—Markevitch (Victor LBC-1015) preferred.
Ballet first choreographed for Ballet Theatre in 1940, by

Adolph Bolm and one of the stand-bys of that company's repertoire. Also staged in London by Frank Staff for the Ballet Rambert later the same year.

THE PRODIGAL SON

Barzin, NYC Ballet Orch. 12" Vox PL-9310.
Sebastian, Colonne Orch. 12" Urania A-7139.

One of George Balanchine's most evocative ballets, first choreographed by him in Paris, for the Diaghileff Ballet in 1929, and revived by him for the New York City Ballet in 1950. A version of the work, with the same scenery and costumes, was staged by David Lichine for the Original Ballet Russe. Sebastian-Colonne version preferred.

ROMEO AND JULIET

Only suites have been recorded:

Suite No. 2, Op. 64
Federer, Rhineland Sym. 12" Regent 5046.
Koussevitzky, Boston Sym. 12" Victor LCT-1144.
Mravinsky, Leningrad Phil. 12" Vanguard 6004.
Prokofieff, Moscow Phil. 12" Vox PL-6060.

Suite No. 3
Stasevitch, Bolshoi Sym. Concert Hall 1304.

Suites Nos. 1, 2, 3 (excerpts)
Stokowski, NBC Sym. 2-12" Victor LM-6028.

The Stokowski recording gives five excerpts from Prokofieff's magnificent ballet score, produced at the Bolshoi Theatre, Moscow in 1935. Magnificently played and contained in a most attractive album, containing *Romeo and Juliet* by Tchaikowsky and Berlioz, and spoken excerpts from the Shakespeare play. An album to be cherished.

Outstanding and moving work in the repertoire of the Soviet Ballet.

Staged by Frederick Ashton in 1955 for the Royal Danish Ballet.

SCYTHIAN SUITE, OP. 20.

Defauw, Chicago Sym. 12" Victor LBC-1057.
Kleinert, Berlin Radio Sym. 12" Urania C-7138.
Ormandy, Phila. Orch. 12" Columbia ML-4142.
Scherchen, Vienna Sym. 12" Westminster 5091.

Music composed for Sergei Diaghileff but never used by him.

THE STONE FLOWER

Kostelanetz, N. Y. Phil. Orch. 12" Columbia CL-809.

Based on a story from *The Malachite Box,* the music here recorded from this ballet consists of five different dances during the wedding scene. It is probably the last complete work written by the late composer.

It is delightfully folksy in tone, well played and excellently recorded.

RACHMANINOFF, Serge (1873-1943)

RHAPSODY ON A THEME OF PAGANINI, OP. 43.

Cherkassky, Menges, London Sym. 12" LBC-1066.
Kapell, Reiner, Robin Hood Dell Orch. 12" Victor LM-9026.
Karolyi, Rother, Berlin Sym. 12" Urania C-7149.
Katchen, Boult, London Phil. 12" London LL-1018.
Rachmaninoff, Stokowski, Phila. Orch. 12" Victor LCT-1118.
Rubinstein, Susskind, Phil. Orch. 12" Victor LM-1744.

Despite its age, the Rachmaninoff-Stokowski-Philadelphia Orch. version (Victor LCT-1118) remains the best.

Ballet choreographed by Michel Fokine for Col. de Basil Ballet Russe in London, in 1939, and one of the most popular works in the latter-day repertory of this company. It is no longer performed.

RAVEL, Maurice (1875-1937)

BOLERO

Ansermet, Orch. Paris Con. 12" London LL-1156.

Branco, Champs-Élysées Orch. 12" Westminster 5297.

Cluytens, Orch. Radiodiffusion Française. 12" Angel 35102.

Centennial Sym. 12" Camden 161.

Ferrero Sym. 12" Tempo 2042.

Keltzki, Orch. Nat'l Française. 12" Columbia RL-3058.

Kostelanetz, Robin Hood Dell Orch. 10" Columbia ML-2009.

Koussevitzky, Boston Sym. 12" Victor LM-1012.

Leibowitz, Orch. Radio-Sym. 12" Vox PL-8150.

List, Berlin Sym. 12" Royale 1313.

Munch Orch. Paris Con. 12" London LL-22.

Ormandy, Phila. Orchestra. 10" Columbia AL-51.

Paray, Detroit Sym. 12" Mercury 50020.

Rother, Berlin Sym. 12" Urania C-7151.

Ansermet (London LL-1156) preferred.

Bronislava Nijinska originally staged the ballet for Ida Rubenstein. Many others, including the American Ruth Page, who titled her ballet *Iberian Monotone,* have used it for dance.

DAPHNIS ET CHLOÉ

Ansermet, Orch. Suisse Romande. 12" London LL-693.

Dorati, Minn. Sym. 12" Mercury 50048.
Munch, Boston Sym. 12" Victor LM-1893.
Ormandy, Phil. Orch. 12" Columbia ML-4316.

Ansermet, Orch. Suisse Romande (London LL-693) preferred.

Ballet originally choreographed for the Diaghileff Ballet Russe by Michel Fokine in Paris in 1912. Also staged by Catherine Littlefield for the Philadelphia Ballet in Philadelphia in 1937, and subsequently completely restaged by Frederick Ashton for the Sadler's Wells Ballet in 1951. In the repertory of the latter company.

L'ENFANT ET LES SORTILÈGES

Bour, Soloists, Orch. 12" Columbia ML-4153.
Ansermet, Danco, Wend. 12" London XLL-LL80.

The latter recording preferred (London XLL-LL80).
Inspired by the famous French authoress, Colette, this *opéra danseé* was called by her "Ballet pour ma fille." An enchanting work it belongs in the record library of everyone who loves fantasy, charm and delicacy. First produced in Monte Carlo in 1925.

MA MÈRE L'OYE (Mother Goose Suite)

Ansermet, Orch. de la Suisse Romande. 12" London LL-388.
Centennial Sym. 12" Camden 161.
Kostelanetz, Orch. 12" Columbia ML-4355.
Koussevitzky, Boston Sym. 12" Victor LM-1012.
Previtali, London Sym. 12" Victor LBC-1009.
Schreiber, Dresden Sym. 12" Roy 1468.

Ansermet (London LL-388) preferred.
Ballet by Todd Bolender for the American Concert Ballet in New York in 1943, subsequently by the New York City Ballet in 1948.

PAVANE POUR UNE INFANTE DÉFUNTE

Ansermet, Orch. de la Suisse Romande. 12" London LL-696.
Branco, Champs-Élysées Orch. 12" Westminster 5297.
Cluytens, Orch. Nat'l. 12" Angel 35102.
Leibowitz, Orch. Radio-Sym. 12" Vox PL-8150.
Munch, Boston Sym. 12" Victor LM-1741.
Ormandy, Phila. Orch. 12" Columbia ML-4983.

Ansermet, Orch. de la Suisse Romande (London LL-696) preferred.
Ballet choreographed by, among many others, Ruth Page and Serge Lifar.

LE TOMBEAU DE COUPERIN

Ansermet, Orch. de la Suisse Romande. 12" London LL-795.
Cluytens, Orch. Nat'l. 12" Angel 35102.
Golschmann, Concert Arts. Orch. Capitol P-8244.
Mitropoulos, Minn. Orch. 10" Columbia ML-2032.
Reiner, NBC Sym. Victor 12" LM-1724.

Ansermet's recording (London LL-795) is the best.
Ballet choreographed for the *Ballet Suédois* by Jean Borlin in 1920.

LA VALSE

Ansermet, Orch. Paris Con. 12" London LL-22.
Barbirolli, New York Phil. 12" Columbia RL-3046.
Borsamsky, Leipzig Phil. 12" Urania C-7151.
Branco Champs-Élysées Orch. 12" Westminster 5297.
Leibowitz, Orch. Radio-Sym. 12" Vox PL-8150.
Markevitch, Phil. Orch. 12" Angel 35008.
Munch, Boston Sym. 10" Victor LRM-7016.
Ormandy, Phila. Orch. 10" Columbia AL-51.

Paray, Detroit Sym. 12" Mercury 50029.

Reiner, Pitts. Sym. Orch. 12" Columbia ML-4021.

Ansermet, Orch. Paris Con. (London LL-22) is the best.

In the George Balanchine ballet of the same name this was originally coupled with *Valses Nobles et Sentimentales,* of which again the Ansermet performance (London LL-795) is definitive.

Ballet choreographed by George Balanchine for the New York City Ballet in 1951. Still in the repertory of this company.

REGER, Max (1873-1916)

BALLET SUITE, OP. 130

Schrader, Dresden Phil. 12" Urania C-7050.

RESPIGHI, Ottorino (1879-1936)

THREE VIRGINS AND A DEVIL (Antiche Danze ed Arie)

EIAR Sym. Orch. Failoni. 10" Cetra 40003.
Lange, Berlin Radio Ch. Sym. 12" Urania C-7093.
Litschauer, Vienna St. Op. Orch. 12" Vanguard 433.
Munchinger, Stuttgart Ch. Orch. 12" London LL-312.

Litschauer, Vienna St. Op. Orch. (Vanguard 433) preferred. Some of the music from these "Antique Airs" was used by Agnes de Mille for her comedy ballet, *Three Virgins and the Devil,* for the Ballet Theatre in 1941. Occasionally revived by this company.

RIEGGER, Wallingford (1885—)

NEW DANCE

Hanson, Eastman-Rochester Sym. 12" Mercury 40005.

Music commissioned for a group dance by Doris Humphrey
in 1935.

RIMSKY-KORSAKOV, Nicolas (1844-1908)

ANTAR

Ansermet, Orch. Suisse Romande. 12" London LL-1060.
Leinsdorf, Cleveland Orch. 10" Columbia ML-2044.
Paray, Detroit Sym. 12" Mercury 50028.
Scherchen, London Sym. 12" Westminster 5280.

Ansermet, Orch. Suisse Romande (London LL-1060) preferred.
Ballet choreographed by Leo Staats for the Paris Opera, in
1921.

CAPRICCIO ESPAGNOL, OP. 34

Ansermet, Orch. de la Suisse Romande. 12" London LL-694.
Barbirolli, N.Y. Phil. 12" Columbia RL-3046.
Cluytens, Orch. Paris Con. 12" Vox PL-7670.
Desarzens, Winterthur Sym. 12" Concert Hall 1106.
Désormière, French Sym. 12" Capitol P-8155.
Festival Concert Orch. 12" Camden 150.
Fiedler, Boston Pops. 10" Victor LM-164.
Herman, Berlin Sym. 12" Royale 1294.
Kleinert, Leipzig Radio Sym. 12" Urania C-7133.
Kondrashin, St. Radio Orch. 12" Kingsway 271.
Kostelanetz, and his Orch. 10" Columbia ML-2161.
Mehlich, Austrian Sym. 10" Remington 149-45.
Ormandy, Phila. Orch. 12" Columbia CL-707.
Paray, Detroit Sym. 12" Mercury 50020.
Scherchen, London Sym. 12" Westminster 7002.
Schuchter, Phil. Orch. 12" MGM 3022.

Ansermet, Orch. de la Suisse Romande (London LL-694) again preferred.

Ballet by Leonide Massine and Argentinita for Ballet Russe de Monte Carlo, in 1939, which follows closely the five divertissements of the music. Also filmed in Technicolor.

COQ D'OR SUITE

Ansermet, Orch. de la Suisse Romande. 12" London LL-694.
Beecham, Royal Phil. 12" Columbia ML-4454.
Desarzens, Winterthur Sym. 12" Concert Hall 1106.
Désormière, French Sym. 12" Capitol P-8155.
Dobrowen, Phil. Orch. 12" Angel 35010.
Fekete, Vienna Tonkunstler Sym. 12" Etude 706.

The Ansermet recording preferred (London LL-694). Opera-ballet, first produced in this form by Michel Fokine for Diaghileff Ballet Russe in Paris in 1914. Was revived by Fokine, without singers, for Col. de Basil Ballet Russe in 1937.

SCHÉHÉRAZADE

Ansermet, Orch. Paris Con. 12" London LL-6.
André, Orch. Nat'l Belge. 12" Telefunken 66018.
Brown, Viennese Orch. 12" Remington 199-11.
Dobrowen, Phil. Orch. 12" Angel 35009.
Dorati, London Phil. 12" Victor LBC-1006.
Dorati, Minneapolis Sym. 12" Mercury 50009.
Federer, Rhineland Sym. 12" Regent 5044.
Ferrero, Italian Sym. 12" Tempo 2030.
Giehlen, Vienna St. Opera Orch. 12" GAR 33-302.
Golovanov, Bolshoi Theatre Orch. 12" Colosseum 135.
Ladis, Paris Phil. 12" Vox PL-9380.
List, Berlin Symp. 12" Royale 1260.
Monteux, San Fran. Sym. 12" Victor LM-1002.

Ormandy, Phila. Orch. 12" Columbia ML-4888.
Quadri, Vienna St. Opera Orch. 12" Westminster 5234.
Rodzinski, Cleveland Orch. 12" Columbia RL-3001.
Rucht, Berlin Radio Sym. 12" Urania C-7133.
Stokowski, Phil. Orch. 12" Victor LM-1732.

The choices are: Ansermet (London LL-6), Dorati (Mercury 50009), and Ormandy (Columbia ML-4888)
Michel Fokine's recreation of Oriental splendor, first staged by him for Diaghileff Ballet Russe in Paris in 1910. The third movement is omitted in ballet performances. One of the most popular ballets of all time, even in the inferior performances of today.

RODGERS, Richard (Contemporary American composer)

SLAUGHTER ON TENTH AVENUE

Fiedler, Boston Pops Orch. 12" Victor LM-1726.

A full-bodied and complete recording of the George Balanchine ballet from *On Your Toes*, played with zest and vigor and impeccably recorded.

ROSSINI, Gioacchino (1792-1868)

LA BOUTIQUE FANTASQUE

Ansermet, London Sym. 12" London LL-274.
Galliera, Phil. Orch. 10" Angel 30001.
Kurtz, Royal Phil. 12" Columbia ML-4367.
Rignold, Royal Opera Orch. 10" Decca 7518.

Ansermet, London Symphony (London LL-274) is preferred. The commissioned score, arranged and orchestrated by Ottorino Respighi, for the delicious Leonide Massine ballet. The work was first performed by the Diaghileff Ballet Russe in London in 1919. The work is now in the repertoire of the Sadler's Wells Ballet.

CON AMORE

Three Rossini overtures: *La Gazza Ladra and Il Signor Buschino,* Toscanini and NBC Orch. Victor LM-358. *La Scala di Seta,* Van Beinum, Concertgebouw Orch. London LL-358.

Ballet by Lew Christensen for the San Francisco Ballet in 1953. Now in the repertory of New York City Ballet.

ROSSINIANA

Braithwaite, Royal Opera Orch. 12" MGM 3013.
Steinkopf, Berlin State Opera Orch. 12" Urania C-7030.

When Ottorino Respighi orchestrated and rearranged the Rossini music for *The Fantastic Toy-Shop,* there was too much music. That which was not used in the ballet, was made into the above suite. It is delightful music.

WILLIAM TELL OVERTURE AND BALLET MUSIC

Braithwaite, Royal Opera Orch. 12" MGM 3028.
Previtali, London & Rome Syms. 12" Victor LBC-1092.

ROUSSEL, Albert (1869-1937)

BACCHUS ET ARIANE

Munch, Boston Sym. 12" Victor LM-1741.

Commissioned score for the ballet of the same name by Léo Staats for the Paris Opera in 1931. The music has a lovely transparency, is at the same time frankly colorful and full-bodied.

SPIDER'S FEAST

Ansermet, Orch. Suisse Romande. 12" London LL-1179.
Paray, Detroit Sym. 12" Mercury 50035.

The Ansermet recording (London LL-1179) is superlatively good.

The first of Roussel's three ballets, originally produced at the Théâtre des Arts in Paris, with choreography by Léo Staats. In 1934 Andree Howard choreographed a version of the work for the Vic Wells Ballet.

SAINT-SAËNS, Camille (1835-1921)

DANSE MACABRE, OP. 40.

Ansermet, Orch. de la Suisse Romande. 12" London LL-696.
Malko, Danish Nat'l Orch. 12" Victor LBC-1019.
Mitropoulos, N.Y. Phil. 10" Columbia AL-8.
Quadri, London Phil. 12" Westminster 7009.
Stock, Chicago Sym. 12" Columbia RL-3022.
Toscanini, NBC Sym. 12" Victor LM-1118.

HENRY VIII (Ballet suite)

Bath, Hastings Sym. 12" Allegro 3028.

INTRODUCTION & RONDO CAPRICCIOSO, OP. 28.

David Oistrakh, Munch, Boston Sym. Orch. Victor LM-1988.
Francescatti, Ormandy, Phila. Orch. 10" Columbia ML-2194.
Heifetz, Steinberg, RCA Victor Sym. 10" Victor LRM-7055.

SATIE, Erik (1866-1925)

PARADE

Kurtz, Houston Sym. 10" Columbia ML-2112.

Markevitch, Phil. Orch. 3-12" Angel 3518-C (Homage to Diaghileff)

The Markevitch recording in "Homage to Diaghileff" is more complete and more sensitively played.

Extremely interesting experimental ballet choreographed by Leonide Massine from a scenario by Jean Cocteau, for the Diaghileff Ballet Russe in Paris in 1917. A contemporary score to treasure.

SCARLATTI, Domenico (1685-1757)

THE GOOD HUMORED LADIES

Braithwaite, Royal Opera Orch. 12" MGM 3034.
Désormière, Orch. Paris Con. 12" London LL-624.
Litschauer, Vienna St. Opera Orch. 12" Vanguard 440.
Markevitch, Phil. Orch. 3-12" Angel 3518-C (Homage to Diaghileff)

Désormière (London LL-624) recording is preferred.

Delightful ballet score for a humorous ballet by Leonide Massine, choreographed for the Diaghileff Ballet Russe in Italy in 1917. Based on Goldoni's *Le Donne di Buon Umeure,* now in the repertoire of the de Cuevas Ballet.

SCHMITT, Florent (1870—)

LA TRAGÉDIE DE SALOMÉ

An LP recording is promised, but there is still available (if you hunt for it) the 78 rpm. recording of this exciting score —Columbia album 157, or English Columbia 67924/7.

Ballet by Boris Romanoff, for the Diaghileff Ballet Russe, in 1912.

SCHÖNBERG, Arnold (1874-1951)

PIERROT LUNAIRE, OP. 21

Howland, Winograd Ensemble. 12" MGM 3202.
Stiedry-Wagner, Schönberg Orch. 12" Columbia ML-4471.

One of the theater's (and music's) most controversial works. There is no middle ground, apparently, in approaching it. One is either for it wholeheartedly, or simply can't bear it. Composed in 1912, this is the language of atonality.

PILLAR OF FIRE (Verklärte Nacht)

Hollywood Quartet, Reher, Dinkin. 10" Capitol L-8118.
Kletzki, Israel Phil. 2-12" Angel 3526-B.
Ormandy, Phila. Orch. 12" Columbia ML-4316.
Schuyler Sym. 12" Camden 178.
Stokowski, Orch. 12" Victor LM-1739.

Written when the composer was twenty-five years old, it has originality and novelty in a romantic setting. The Ormandy recording (Columbia ML-4316) is excellent in all respects. *Verklärte Nacht* (Transfigured Night) served as the score for Antony Tudor's truly wonderful ballet, *Pillar of Fire*, which was given its world première by the Ballet Theatre in April, 1942, with a cast including Nora Kaye, Hugh Laing and Tudor.

SCHUBERT, Franz (1797-1828)

GERMAN DANCES

Leibowitz, Paris Phil. 12" Esoteric 512.
Litschauer, Vienna St. Opera Orch. 12" Vanguard 435.

LABYRINTH (Symphony No. 7 in G)

Barbirolli, Halle Orch. 12" Victor LBC-1085.
Boult, Phil. Prom. Orch. 12" Westminster 18026.
Furtwangler, Berlin Phil. 12" Decca 9746.
Heger, Bamberg Sym. 12" Mercury 10075.
Krips, Concertgebouw Orch. 12" London LL-619.
Rother, Berlin Sym. 12" Urania C-7152.
Stock, Chicago Sym. 12" Columbia RL-3008.
Toscanini, NBC Sym. 12" Victor LM-1040.
Von Karajan, Vienna Phil. 12" Columbia ML-4631.
Walter, N.Y. Phil. 12" Columbia ML-4093.
Woss, Austrian Sym. 12" Remington 199-48.

In the series of "symphonic" ballets created by Leonide Massine, this, the sixth, was to this symphony of the "heavenly length." It's thematic basis came from Greek mythology. Its setting and costumes were by Salvador Dali.

WANDERER FANTASIE, OP. 15.

Johannesen, Goehr, Netherlands Phil. 12" Concert Hall 1176.

There have been at least two ballets to this music. One, by George Balanchine, was seen in the Ballet Theatre repertoire for a short Metropolitan Opera House season. Balanchine created it originally for the American Ballet, and it had the inestimable boon of a magnificent setting by Pavel Tchelitcheff. The music was also used by Frederick Ashton, in 1941, for a ballet for Sadler's Wells. In each case, the theme was Proustian, an expression of the remembrance of things past.

SCHUMAN, William (1910—)

JUDITH: CHOREOGRAPHIC POEM

Whitney, Louisville Orch. 12" Mercury 10088.

Commissioned for Martha Graham by the Louisville Orchestra and first performed in 1952.

UNDERTOW

Levine, Ballet Theatre Orch. 12" Capitol P-8238.
Schuman, Louisville Orch. 12" Mercury 10088.

The Company's own version is preferred (Capitol P-8238). Ballet by Antony Tudor, after a suggestion by John van Druten, choreographed for Ballet Theatre in 1945.

SCHUMANN, Robert (1810-1856)

CARNAVAL

Irving, Phil. Orch. 12" Victor LBC-1025.
Kurtz, Royal Phil. 12" Columbia ML-4367.
Rignold, Royal Opera Orch. 12" Decca 9548.
Stratford Sym. 12" Camden 193.

The Efrem Kurtz version of this orchestration of the famous Schumann piano work is preferred (Columbia ML-4367) Ballet by Michel Fokine, a masterpiece of its kind. First staged by him in 1910.

SCHUMANN CONCERTO (*Concerto in A, Op. 54*)

Numerous recordings of which by far the best is that by the young genius, Dinu Lipatti, with the Philharmonia Orch. & Von Karajan. (Columbia ML-4525)

PERSEPHONE (*Symphony No. 1, in B Flat*)

Ansermet, Orch. Suisse Romande. 12" London LL-391.
Leinsdorf, Cleveland Orch. 12" Columbia ML-4794.
List, Berlin Symphony. 12" Royale 1334.
Munch, Boston Sym. 12" Victor LM-1190.

First staged by John Taras for San Francisco Civic Ballet in 1948, and re-staged by him for Grand Ballet de Marquis de Cuevas two years later in Paris.

SHOSTAKOVITCH, Dmitri (1906—)

BALLET RUSSE

Kurtz, Columbia Sym. 12" Columbia ML-4671.

BALLET SUITE NO. 1

Berlin Sym. 12" Urania C-7146.
Gauk, USSR Orch. 12" Vanguard 6004.
Gauk, Stassevich, USSR St. Radio Orch. 12" Classic 3012.

THE GOLDEN AGE

Fiedler, Boston Pops Orch. 12" Columbia LM-1726.
Mitchell, Nat'l Sym. 12" Westminster 5319.

Four dances from this ballet are included. Composed in 1930. The theme of this ballet in the repertory of the Soviet Ballet is political; one would never guess it from the calm lyricism and waggish humor of the music. The sound is excellently reproduced.

The Fiedler, Boston Pops recording (Columbia LM-1726) of the well-known "Polka" contains in addition well recorded excerpts from De Falla's *The Three-Cornered Hat*, Khatchaturian's *Gayne*, Menotti's *Sebastian*, and Stravinsky's *Petrouchka*.

ROUGE ET NOIR (*Symphony No. 1 in F, Op. 10*)

Kondrashin, State Orch. USSR 12" Vanguard 6014.
Pflüger, Berlin Sym. 12" Urania C-7128.
Mitchell, Nat'l Sym. 12" Westminster 5319.
Rodzinski, Cleveland Orch. 12" Columbia ML-4881.

Leonide Massine's striking "symphonic" ballet, choreographed for the Ballet Russe de Monte Carlo in 1939. Unfortunately no longer to be seen.

SIBELIUS, Jean (1865—)

KHADRA

A 78 rpm version only is available for this Sibelius music used for the ballet, *Belshazzar's Feast*, played by Robert Kajanus and the London Symphony Orchestra. HMV DB 9024-8.

SMETANA, Bedrich (1824-1884)

DANCES FROM THE BARTERED BRIDE

Czech Nat'l Theatre. 12" Symphonic 3.
Wallenstein, Los Angeles Phil. 10" Decca 4014.

BOHEMIAN DANCES

Byrns, Chamber Sym. 12" Capitol P-8174.
Rauch, Maxim, etc. 12" Mercury 10046.

STRAUSS, Johann (1825-1899)

LE BEAU DANUBE

It is, in its way, a remarkable omission that the L.P. catalogues do not list a single recording of this gaily infectious Strauss ballet, as arranged by Roger Désormière. It is an omission one hopes may soon be rectified. Meanwhile, there is an excellent 78 rpm recording by Antal Dorati and the London Philharmonic Orchestra, Victor album: DM 414. One of Leonide Massine's gayest creations, dating from 1924.

GRADUATION BALL

Dorati, Dallas Sym. 12" Victor LM-1061.
Fiedler, Boston Pops Orch. Victor.
Fistoulari, New Sym. 12" London LL-883.

Fistoulari is more complete.
Ballet created by David Lichine in 1940 for the Original Ballet Russe and now in the repertory of the Ballet Theatre and Ballet Russe de Monte Carlo.

RITTER PASMANN (Ballet suite)

Guhl, Berlin Sym. 12" Urania C-7165.

STRAUSS, Richard (1864-1949)

LE BOURGEOIS GENTILHOMME

Berendt, Phil Sym. 12" Allegro 3101.
Krauss, Vienna Phil. 12" London LL-684.
Reiner, Pittsburgh Sym. 12" Columbia ML-4800.

The Reiner version preferred (Columbia ML-4800) and, for the ballet-lover, this also contains on one record *Don Juan* and *Till Eulenspiegel*.
Ballet by George Balanchine first staged by him for the de Basil Ballet Russe in 1932, and for the Ballet Russe de Monte Carlo in 1944. Based on Molière's play of the same name.

DIM LUSTRE (*Burlesque in D for Piano & Orchestra*)

Berendt, Orch. 12" Allegro 3144.
Century Sym. 12" Camden 191.
Gulda, Collins, London Sym. 12" London LL-1158.
Jacquinot, Fistoulari, Phil. Orch. 12" MGM E-3004.
Ney, Rother, Berlin Radio Sym. 12" Urania C-7101.

The Fistoulari version (MGM E-3004) is well played and recorded and has the advantage of Dohnanyi ballet music as a coupling.

Dim Lustre, a ballet to this music by Antony Tudor for the Ballet Theatre in 1943, has a Proustlike theme.

TILL EULENSPIEGEL (*Op. 28*)

Centennial Sym. 12" Camden 101.
Fricsay, Berlin Phil. 12" Decca 9529.
Furtwangler, Berlin Phil. 12" Period 716.
Furtwangler, Vienna Phil. 12" Victor LHMV-19.
Gui, Florentine Music Festival Orch. 12" Tempo 2032.
Horenstein, Bamberg Sym. 12" Vox PL-9060.
Jochum, Concertgebouw Orch. 12" Epic 3LC-3032.
Krauss, Vienna Phil. 12" London LL-233.
Ormandy, Phila. Orch. 10" Col. AL-46.
Reiner, RCA Sym. 12" Victor LM-1180.
Rodzinski, Cleveland Orch. 12" Columbia ML-4884.
Szell, Cleveland Orch. 12" Columbia 3ML-4800.
Steinberg, Pittsburgh Sym. 12" Capitol P-8291.

The Reiner version is my choice out of numerous records (Victor LM-1180).

Ballet produced in America by Vaslav Nijinsky with the Diaghileff Ballet Russe in 1916, and a later version by Jean Babileè in 1949 in Paris, and for a season in the repertory of Ballet Theatre. A version has been staged for the New York City Ballet by Jerome Robbins and George Balanchine.

STRAVINSKY, Igor (1882—)

APOLLON MUSAGÈTE

Hollreiser, Vienna Ch. Orch. 12" Vox PL-8270.
Stravinsky, RCA Victor Orch. 12" Victor LM-1096.

Stravinsky, in this case, preferred, and also contains as a coupling the music used for the ballet, *The Cage.* Moving ballet, first staged in Washington by Adolph Bolm in 1928, subsequently by George Balanchine for the Diaghileff Ballet Russe in Paris, later the same year; in New York for the American Ballet, in 1937; and for the Ballet Theatre in 1945. It may be once again re-staged for the New York City Ballet.

LE BAISER DE LA FÉE (*The Fairy's Kiss*)

Ansermet, Orch. Suisse Romande. 12" London LL-390.
Markevitch, Orch. Radiodiffusion Francaise. 12" Angel 35143.

Ansermet preferred (London LL-390).
Nijinska for Ida Rubinstein in 1928. George Balanchine for American Ballet in 1937; for Ballet Russe de Monte Carlo in 1940; and New York City Ballet in 1950.

THE CAGE (*Concerto Grosso in D for String Orchestra*)

Page, Orch. Soc. of Boston. 10" Cook 1062.
Stravinsky, RCA Victor Sym. 12" Victor LM-1096.

Stravinsky, preferred (Victor LM-1096).
Ballet by Jerome Robbins, choreographed for the New York City Ballet in 1951.

DANSES CONCERTANTES

Hull, Rochester Ch. Orch. 12" Concert Hall 1229.

Classic ballet by George Balanchine for the Ballet Russe de Monte Carlo, 1944. No longer in the repertoire.

FIREBIRD

Ansermet, Orch. de la Suisse Romande. 12" London LL-889.
Berlin Sym. 12" Royale 1462.
Dorati, Minn. 12" Mercury 50004.
Ormandy, Phila. Orch. 12" Columbia ML-4700.
Scherchen, London Phil. 12" Westminster 7032.
Stokowski, Orch. 12" Victor LM-9029.
Stravinsky, N.Y. Phil. 12" Columbia ML-4882.

The choice lies between Ansermet (London LL-889) and Dorati (Mercury 50004) out of the above list.
A Michel Fokine masterpiece for Diaghileff Ballet Russe in 1910; a shortened version by Adolph Bolm, in 1945 for Ballet Theatre; a revised version by George Balanchine for New York City Ballet in 1949; a restored version of the work by Tamara Karsavina for the Sadler's Wells Ballet in 1954, with the collaboration of Serge Grigoriev and Lubov Tchernicheva.

L'HISTOIRE DU SOLDAT

Bernstein, Boston Sym. Orch. 12" Victor LM-1078.
Oubradous, Instrumental Ens. 12" Vox PL-7960.
Mario Rossi. 12" Vanguard 452.
Weaver, Harkins, Warriner Vardi. 12" Vox PL-8990.
Stravinsky, NW German Radio Orch. 12" Columbia ML-4964.

Stravinsky, unfortunately without text (Columbia ML-

4964). Vox with Text (Vox PL-8990) preferred.
Narrative ballet with speaker first presented in Switzerland in 1918, in the U.S. in 1928. (Eight instruments.)

JEU DES CARTES (Card Game or Poker Game)

Rubahn, Berlin Sym. 12" Royale 1489.
Stravinsky, Berlin Phil. 12" Mercury 10014.

Stravinsky (Mercury 10014) preferred.
Ballet by George Balanchine for the American Ballet in 1937, for Ballet Russe de Monte Carlo in 1940, and for the New York City Ballet, in 1951.

ORPHEUS

Stravinsky, RCA Sym. 12" Victor LM-1033.

Evocative and moving ballet to a score possessing the same qualities by George Balanchine for the Ballet Society in 1948. In the repertoire of the New York City Ballet.

PETROUCHKA

Ansermet, Orch. Suisse Romande. 12" London LL-130.
Berlin Sym. 12" Royale 1342.
Brendei. 12" Vox PL-9140.
Dorati, Minn. Sym. 12" Mercury 50058.
Mitropoulos, N.Y. Phil. 12" Columbia ML-4438.
Ormandy, Phila. Orch. 12" Columbia ML-5030.
Scherchen, London Phil. 12" Westminster 7011.
Stokowski & Orch. 12" Victor LM-1175.
Stravinsky, N.Y. Phil. 12" Columbia ML-4047.
Warwick, Sym. 12" Camden 203.

Ansermet far and away the best (London LL-130).
In a sense, Michel Fokine's masterpiece, created for the Diaghileff Ballet Russe in 1911. Today's versions, at the

hands of Ballet Theatre and others, show how foolhardy it is to reproduce it without knowledge or taste. There is said to be an excellent Fokine version with the Royal Danish Ballet.

LES NOCES

Hillis, N.Y. Concert Choir & Orch. 12″ Vox PL-8630.
Lux, Moosen, Schreiber, Dresden St. Op. Orch. 10″ Allegro 4010.
Mario Rossi, 12″ Vanguard 452.

Hillis preferred (Vox PL-8630).
Ballet created by Bronislava Nijinska for the Diaghileff Ballet Russe in 1923. Seen in America with the de Basil Ballet Russe de Monte Carlo. A stimulating, provocative score.

PULCINELLA

Hoillreiser, Vienna Ch. Orch. 12″ Vox PL-8270.
Markevitch, Orch. Radiodiffusion Francaise. 12″ Angel 35143.
Rother, Berlin Radio Sym. 12″ Urania C-7093.
Stravinsky, Cleveland Orch. 12″ Columbia ML-4830.

Stravinsky (Columbia ML-4830) preferred.
Ballet, based on music by Giovanni Pergolesi, created by Leonide Massine for the Diaghileff Ballet Russe in 1920, with voices. Staged by Todd Bolender for the Ballet Russe de Monte Carlo under the title *Musical Chairs.*

RENARD (The Fox)

Craft, Chamber Art. Soc. 12″ Dial 10.

Ballet created by Bronislava Nijinska for the Diaghileff Ballet Russe in 1922, re-staged by Serge Lifar in 1929, and for the Ballet Society by George Balanchine in 1947. Ballet utilizing both singer and dancers.

LE SACRE DU PRINTEMPS

Ansermet, Orch. Suisse Romande. 12" London LL-303.
Dorati, Minn. Sym. 12" Mercury 50030.
Fricsay, RIAS Sym. 12" Decca 9781.
List, Berlin Sym. 12" Royale 1465.
Markevitch, Phil. Orch. 12" Victor LHMV-1.
Monteux, Boston Sym. 12" Victor LM-1149.
Ormandy, Phila. Orch. 12" Columbia ML-5030.
Steinberg, Pittsburgh Sym. 12" Capitol P-8254.
Stravinsky, N.Y. Phil. 12" Columbia ML-4882.

Choice lies between Ansermet (London LL-303) and Dorati (Mercury 50030).
Epoch-making ballet, originally staged by Vaslav Nijinsky, for the Diaghileff Ballet Russe in 1913; re-staged by Leonide Massine, in 1920; and staged by Massine in the U.S. in 1930.

SCÈNES DE BALLET

Stravinsky, N.Y. Phil. 12" Columbia ML-4047.

First presented by Billy Rose with choreography by Anton Dolin in 1944. An entirely new version by Frederick Ashton for the Sadler's Wells Ballet in 1948, and now in the repertoire of that company.

SONG OF THE NIGHTINGALE

Cromwell Sym. 12" Camden 189.

Ballet created by Leonide Massine for the Diaghileff Ballet Russe in 1920. Re-staged by George Balanchine for the same company in 1925.

TCHAIKOWSKY, Peter Ilitch (1840-1893)

AURORA'S WEDDING

Braithwaite, Royal Opera Orch. 12" MGM 3052.
Stokowski, Orch. 12" Victor LM-1774.
Stratford Sym. 12" Camden 211.

Braithwaite (MGM 3052) preferred.
A one-act divertissement out of the last act of *The Sleeping Beauty*. Given in various versions known under following titles: *Aurora's Wedding, Princess Aurora,* and *Divertissement,* depending on the company.

BALLET IMPERIAL (*Concerto No. 2 in G for Piano & Orch. Op. 44*)

Farnadi, Scherchen, Vienna St. Op. Orch. 12" Westminster 5309.
Mewton-Wood, Goehr, Orch. 12" Concert Hall 1125.
Moiseiwitsch, Weldon, Liverpool Phil. 12" Victor LCT-1127.
Nikolayeva, Anosov Orch. 12" Classic 3008.
Pinter, Rother, Radio Berlin Sym. 12" Urania C-7081.
Wührer, Swarowsky, Pro Musica Sym. 12" Vox PL-9200.

That by Benno Moiseiwitsch (Victor LCT-1127) is preferred.
Classic ballet by George Balanchine, first staged for the New Opera Co. in 1941. Also in repertory of the Ballet Russe de Monte Carlo, Sadler's Wells Ballet, and Royal Danish Ballet.

FRANCESCA DA RIMINI

Centennial Sym. 12" Camden 159.
Dobrowen, Phil. Orch. 12" Victor LBC-1010.

Golschmann, St. Louis Sym. Capitol P-8225.
Jorda, Orch. Paris Con. 12" London LL-376.
Stokowski, N.Y. Phil. 12" Columbia ML-4381.

That of Stokowski (Columbia ML-4381) is preferred.
Ballet by David Lichine for the de Basil Ballet Russe in
1937. No longer to be seen.

HAMLET

Boult, London Phil. 12" London LL-582.
Fistoulari, Phil. Orch. 12" MGM 3002.
Irving, Phil. Orch. 12" Victor LBC-1090.
Rachmilovich, Stockholm Radio Sym. 12" Mercury 10112.

Boult (London LL-582) preferred.
Ballet choreographed by Robert Helpmann for the Sadler's
Wells Ballet in 1942. A version also has been choreographed
by Bronislava Nijinska.

MOZARTIANA

Fistoulari, Phil. Orch. 12" MGM 3026.
Rodzinski, N.Y. Phil. 12" Columbia ML-4048.

Fistoulari (MGM 3026) is preferred.
Ballet by George Balanchine for his Les Ballets 1933, and
later for the Ballet Russe de Monte Carlo in 1945. No longer
in the repertoire.

THE NUTCRACKER (Op. 71)

Dobrindt, Berlin Radio Sym. 2-12" Urania C-237.
Dorati, Minn. Sym. 2-12" Mercury OL-2-101.

Numerous recordings of Suite.
Ballet by Lev Ivanov for the Imperial Russian Ballet in 1892.
Re-staged for Sadler's Wells Ballet in 1937. Again revived
by Fedorrova for Ballet Russe de Monte Carlo in a shorter

version in 1942. A bowdlerized but substantially complete version by George Balanchine for the New York City Ballet in 1954. The Dorati version is magnificently played and recorded, and contains music never used outside Russia.

SERENADE (*Serenade for Strings in C, Op. 48*)

Again a dozen LP recordings of this singing work for strings by Tchaikowsky are ready for choice. From these I prefer the

Koussevitzky, Boston Sym. 12" Victor LM-1056.
Mengelberg, Amsterdam Orch. 12" Capitol P-8060.

Ballet without story by George Balanchine created for the American Ballet in 1934, and later in the repertoire of the Ballet Russe de Monte Carlo and the New York City Ballet.

THE SLEEPING BEAUTY

Dorati, Minn. Sym. 3-12" Mercury OL-3-103.
Fistoulari, Orch. Paris Con. 2-12" London LL-636/7.
Irving, Royal Opera Orch. 2-12" Victor LM-6034.

And eleven recordings of various excerpts.
The apotheosis of classic full-length ballet by Marius Petipa in St. Petersburg in 1890. There have been distinguished revivals: by Diaghileff Ballet Russe and Sadler's Wells Ballet, in whose repertoire this masterpiece remains.

SWAN LAKE (*Le Lac des Cygnes*)

Dorati, Minn. Sym. 3-12" Mercury OL-3-102.
Fistoulari, London Sym. 2-12" London LL-565/6.

There are numerous recordings of excerpts. An excellent recording of Acts II and III by Stokowski (Victor 12" LM-1894), has recently been issued, with an attractive album, with notes and decorations, the former by John Martin.

One of the most admired dramatic ballets of all time, originally mounted by Julius Reisinger; re-staged by Lev Ivanov
and Marius Petipa in St. Petersburg, in 1895. The most distinguished contemporary production is that of the Sadler's
Wells Ballet. The Dorati version is superlative.

LES PRÉSAGES (Symphony No. 5 in E. Op. 64)

There are over twenty recordings of this popular symphony
and the choice lies between Von Karajan, Phil. Orch. (12"
Angel 35055); and Dorati, Minn. Sym. (12" Mercury
50008). One of Massine's first symphonic ballets. First staged
for de Basil Ballet Russe in London, 1934. No longer in any
repertoire.

THEME AND VARIATIONS (from Suite No. 3 in G)

Barbirolli, N.Y. Phil. 12" Columbia ML-4121.
Goehr, Concert Hall Orch. 12" Concert Hall CHS-1144.
Malko, Phil. Orch. 12" Victor LBC-1024.
Schuricht, Orch. Paris Con. 12" London LL-640.

Schuricht (London LL-640) preferred.
Ballet by George Balanchine, to the third movement of
Tchaikowsky's *Suite No. 3 in G.* for the Ballet Theatre.

ALEKO (Trio in A, Op. 50)

Gilels, Kogan, Rastropovich. 12" A440 AC-1202.
Rubinstein, Heifetz, Piatigorsky. 12" Victor LM-1120.

Ballet by Leonide Massine, choreographed by him for the
Ballet Theatre in 1942. Based on Pushkin's famous poem of
the same name, it utilizes an unrecorded orchestration by
Erno Rapée of the Tchaikowsky *Trio in A, Op. 50*. The
work, a highly dramatic one, is occasionally revived by Ballet
Theatre. The Trio was also used as such by John Taras

when he choreographed *Design for Strings,* for the Metropolitan Ballet, London, 1948. Later he recreated it for Ballet Theatre in the U.S. in 1950; for de Cuevas Ballet, Paris, 1952; and Royal Danish Ballet, Copenhagen, 1954.

THOMSON, Virgil (1896—)

BAYOU (*Louisiana Story, Acadian Songs and Dances*)
Scherman, Little Orch. Soc. 12" DL-Decca 9616.

Music from the documentàry film, *Louisiana Story,* utilized by George Balanchine for his ballet, choreographed for the New York City Ballet.

FILLING STATION
Barzin, N.Y.C. Ballet Orch. 12" Vox PL-9050.

Excellent recording of the music for the ballet by Lew Christensen, first staged for the American Ballet Caravan in 1938, and now in the repertoire of the New York City Ballet.

THE HARVEST ACCORDING

Ballet by Agnes de Mille for Ballet Theatre in 1952, utilizing various works by Virgil Thomson, including his *Violoncello Concerto: Janssen Sym. 12" Columbia ML-4468*

VAUGHAN WILLIAMS, Ralph (1872—)

JOB (*Masque for Dancing*)
Boult, London Phil. 12" London LL-1003.

A truly magnificent recording of an equally magnificent score.
A masque for dancing, with choreography by Ninette de

Valois originally staged for the Camargo Society, London, in 1931, and now in repertoire of the Sadler's Wells Ballet.

OLD KING COLE

Boult, Phil. Promenade Orch. Westminster 12" WL 5228.

The composer's first experiment for dance, written in 1923. Splendidly played and excellently recorded.

WAGNER, Richard (1813-1883)

BACCHANALE

Kletzki, Phil. Orch. 12" Angel 35059.
Ormandy, Phila. Orch. 12" Columbia ML-4865.
Stokowski & Orch. 12" Victor LM-1066.

The first "surrealist" ballet, choreographed by Leonide Massine, to the *Overture to Act I* and the *Venusburg Music* from *Tannhäuser*, for the Ballet Russe de Monte Carlo in 1939. The Ormandy (Columbia ML-4865) recording is preferred.

MAD TRISTAN

Ormandy, Phil. Orch. 12" Columbia ML-4742.

Second "surrealist" ballet by Leonide Massine choreographed for de Cuevas International Ballet, to the *Prelude, Liebestod* and *Liebesnacht* from *Tristan & Isolde* in New York, 1944.

WALTON, Sir William (1902—)

FAÇADE

Hillsberg, Phila. Pops. 10" Columbia AL-17.
Irving, London Sym. 12" London LL-771.

Lambert, Phil. Orch. 12" Columbia ML-4793.
Edith Sitwell, Ch. Orch. 10" Columbia ML-2047.
Sitwell, Pears, Collins. 12" London LL-1133.

Lambert (Columbia ML-4793) is preferred.
Perhaps the most popular of the gay and inconsequential ballets of Frederick Ashton, originally choreographed for the Camargo Society in London in 1931, and still one of the most popular works in the repertoire of the Sadler's Wells Ballet.

WARLOCK, Peter (1894-1930)

CAPRIOL SUITE

Boyd Neel String Orch. 12" London LL-801.

A genuinely beautiful classic, exquisitely played.
The earliest choreographic work of Frederick Ashton in current ballet repertory, originally staged in 1930, now performed by the Sadler's Wells Theatre Ballet.

WEBER, Carl Maria Von (1786-1826)

LE SPECTRE DE LA ROSE (*Invitation to the Dance*)

Kostelanetz, N.Y. Phil. 12" Columbia CL-809.
Fistoulari, New Sym. Orch. 10" London LD-9108.
Ormandy, Phila. Orch. 10" Columbia ML-2043.
Rignold, Royal Opera Orch. 12" Decca 9549.

Fistoulari (London LD-9108) is preferred for both musical and balletic versions.
A romantic *pas de deux* by Michel Fokine that brought Vaslav Nijinsky his first international fame; choreographed in 1911, and revived periodically by numerous ballet companies.

COLLECTIONS AND ANTHOLOGIES

BALLET MUSIC PROGRAM—Colosseum 12"—CRLP 102.

CONTAINS: *Christmas Eve,* Rimsky-Korsakoff, Golovnoff and Bolshoi Theatre Orch; *Raymonda,* Glazounov, Fach and Bolshoi Orch; *Cinderella, Waltz No. 19,* Prokofieff, Fach and Bolshoi Orch; *Absalom and Elius,* Paliashvilli: (Same artists); *Waltz from Masquerade,* Katchaturian, Yurev and Orch; *Scene from Gayne,* Golovnoff and Orch.

FRENCH BALLET MUSIC—Sebastian and French National Opera Orch., Urania URLP-7058.

CONTAINS: *Faust Ballet Music,* Gounod; *Thais Ballet Music,* Massanet; *L'Arlesienne Suites No. 2 and 3,* Bizet.

AT THE BALLET—12" Columbia RL-3056.

BALLET FROM VIENNA—12" Epic 3LC-3102.

Beethoven, Mozart, Lully—12" Urania C-7111.

EVENINGS AT THE BALLET—6-12" Camden CFL-102.

Fournet, Orch. 12" Epic 3LC-3030.

Toscanini, Monteux, Munch, Stokowski, Fiedler—3-12" Victor LM-6113.

HOMAGE TO DIAGHILEFF—Markevitch, Philharmonia Orch. —3-12" Angel 3548C.

PORTRAIT OF THE WALTZ—Markevitch, Philharmonia Orch., 12" Angel 35154.

MASTERPIECES OF THE DANCE—Willis Page, Boston Festival Orch., Cook 10646.

CONTAINS: *Dance of the Buffoons,* Rimsky-Korsakoff; *Emperor Waltz,* Strauss; *Danse Macabre,* Saint-Saëns; *Hungarian Dance No. 2,* Brahms.

Magnificently recorded by Cook Laboratories, this provides sparkling music for the dance for every listener.

Index

A

Academy of Music, St. Petersburg, 41
Adam, Adolph, 103, 138
Adam Zero, 123, 124
Afternoon of a Faun, The, 39
Age of Anxiety, The, 108
AGMA (American Guild of Musical Artists), 53, 54, 59
Allers, Franz, 22
American Ballet, 92, 192
Andersen, Hans Christian, 85
Annie Get Your Gun, 82, 134
Ansermet, Ernest, 22
Apollon Musagéte (Apollo), 97, 101, 102, 109
Appia, 90
Armistead, Horace, 91
Armitage, Merle, 109
Armstrong, John, 92
Arnell, Richard, 124
Arno, Peter, 111
Arnold, Matthew, 176
Aronson, Boris, 91
ASCAP, 141
Ashton, Frederick, 78, 82, 84, 87, 119, 120, 121, 148

Astaire, Fred, 83
Astuzi Femminili, Le, 113
Auden, W. H., 108
Avery Memorial Theatre, Hartford, Conn., 192
Ayrton, Michael, 93

B

Babes in Arms, 127
Babillé, Jean, 14
Bach, Johann Sebastian, 14, 175
Bakst, Léon, 38, 90, 91, 104, 105, 200
Balanchine, George, 40, 83, 101, 106, 115, 116, 117, 118, 120, 127, 154, 192
Ballard, Lucinda, 92
Ballet Caravan, 92, 192
Ballet Comique de la Reine, 32
Ballet Imperial, 116
Ballet Russe de Monte Carlo, 4, 40, 41, 53, 83, 102, 109, 118, 185, 189, 190, 191, 193, 194, 199
Ballet Society, 92, 192
Ballet Theatre, 13, 35, 40, 53, 82, 92, 107, 191, 195

303

Furse, Roger, 93
Furtwängler, Wilhelm, 18

G

Gaité Parisienne, 83
Gardel, Maximilian, 33
Gardel, Pierre, 33
Gardens of Aranjuez, 113
Gautier, Théophile, 34, 96, 116, 117
Gershwin, George, 111, 161
Gheltzer, Ekaterina, 40
Ghost Town, 126
Gilbert & Sullivan, 124, 125
Giselle, 29, 34, 68, 87, 95, 103, 104, 118, 138, 164, 207, 211
Gluck, Christoph Willibald, von, 83
Goethe, 176
Good-Humored Ladies, The, 96, 113
Goosens, Eugene, 22
Gontcharova, Nathalie, 91
Gordon, Gavin, 13
Gottschalk, Louis Moreau, 13
Gould, Morton, 13
Grahn, Lucille, 35
Grant, Duncan, 92
Green Grow the Lilacs, 130
Grigorieff, Serge, 102, 103, 104
Grisi, Carlotta, 34
Guns & Castanets, 119

H

Hamlet, 122
Harlequin in April, 124
Haskell, Arnold, 207
Haydn, Franz Joseph, 176
Heimel, Mlle., 33
Heine, Heinrich, 96
Helburn, Theresa, 130
Helpmann, Robert, 13, 82, 84, 122, 123, 124

Henry of Navarre, 32
Hewitt, James, 188
High Button Shoes, 82, 134
Hightower, Rosella, 197
Hindemith, Paul, 13, 162
His Majesty's Theatre, London, 33, 35
Hokinson, Helen E., 111
Holm, Hanya, 199
Homage to the Queen, 87
Houston Symphony Orchestra, 22
Hugo, Victor, 96
Hunchbacked Horse, The, 96
Hunchback of Notre Dame, 96
Hurok, S., 84, 190, 191
Hurry, Leslie, 93
Hutchinson, Ann, 211

I

Illuminations, Les, 121
I Married an Angel, 127
Invitation to the Dance, 84
Ireland, John, 163
Irnebizolle, 115
Irvin, Rea, 111

J

Jerome, Jerome K., 123
Job, 121
Johnson, Albert, 110
Junyer, Joan, 91

K

Kahn, Otto H., 56
Kansas City Symphony Orchestra, 22
Karinska, Barbara, 92
Karsavina, Tamara, 38, 47
Kauffer, E. McKnight, 93
Kay, Hershy, 13
Kaye, Danny, 85
Kaye, Nora, 197
Kchessinska, Mathilde, 40